A SEMANTIC AND STRUCTURAL ANALYSIS OF THE JOHANNINE EPISTLES

Grace E. Sherman and John C. Tuggy

Summer Institute of Linguistics
1994

All rights reserved.
No part of this book may be produced in any manner without prior written permission from the copyright owner.

© Copyright 1994 by the Summer Institute of Linguistics, Inc.
ISBN: 1-55671-008-9
Library of Congress Catalog Card Number: 94-69312
Printed in the United States of America

Copies may be obtained from:

International Academic Bookstore
Summer Institute of Linguistics
7500 W. Camp Wisdom Road
Dallas, TX 75236

CONTENTS

PREFACE v
ABBREVIATIONS vi

GENERAL INTRODUCTION 1

INTRODUCTION TO THE SEMANTIC STRUCTURE OF FIRST JOHN 5
   OVERVIEW 9
THE SEMANTIC UNITS OF 1 JOHN 13
   1 JOHN 1:1–5:21 (EPISTLE) 13
   1 JOHN 1:1–4 (PROLOGUE) 15
   1 JOHN 1:5–5:12 (BODY) 18
   1 JOHN 1:5–2:27 (SECTION 1) 20
   1 JOHN 2:28–4:6 (SECTION 2) 53
   1 JOHN 4:7–5:12 (SECTION 3) 79
   1 JOHN 5:13–21 (CLOSING) 98

INTRODUCTION TO THE SEMANTIC STRUCTURE OF SECOND JOHN 103
   OVERVIEW 104
THE SEMANTIC UNITS OF 2 JOHN 105
   2 JOHN 1–13 (EPISTLE) 105
   2 JOHN 1–3 (OPENING) 106
   2 JOHN 4–11 (BODY) 108
   2 JOHN 12–13 (CLOSING) 119

INTRODUCTION TO THE SEMANTIC STRUCTURE OF THIRD JOHN 121
   OVERVIEW 123
THE SEMANTIC UNITS OF 3 JOHN 124
   3 JOHN 1–15 (EPISTLE) 124
   3 JOHN 1–4 (OPENING) 125
   3 JOHN 5–12 (BODY) 127
   3 JOHN 13–15 (CLOSING) 137

GLOSSARY 139
BIBLIOGRAPHY 143

PREFACE

The initial work on this commentary on the Epistles of John was done by Grace Sherman. In September 1983 John Tuggy was assigned the task of readying the work for publication. In view of the many new developments in the theory of semantic discourse structure, we decided to collaborate to complete the work using more rigorous criteria and defenses of the decisions presented.

Working together on this project has been a special privilege. Most beneficial to both of us has been to experience to some extent the reactions of the original readers by understanding the total significance of each letter. We have learned to react by having our knowledge, emotions, and behavior challenged and changed.

We owe a debt of gratitude to John and Kathleen Callow for developing a sound semantic theory which we could apply to the text. They provided advice on many details of analysis and exegesis. We also want to thank our colleagues Ellis Deibler and John Banker for their valuable suggestions. Roy Ledgerwood and James E. Mignard contributed by their expertise in Greek. Special thanks go to Elizabeth Eastman for her careful attention to detail in the copyediting. Sheila Tuggy, John's wife, has given encouragement over the years to complete this task. All these have improved the presentation and content of the book.

Our intensive efforts in preparing this commentary will be completely repaid as translators, Bible scholars, and others use it to better communicate the true message that the Apostle John intended: that Christians must be pure as God is pure and that Christ is the only true God and anything that takes the place of God robs us of eternal life.

ABBREVIATIONS IN THE DISPLAYS

Relational-structure labels that are in uppercase letters indicate that the unit is prominent.

A°	unmitigated appeal	gen	generic
alt	alternation/alternate	grd	grounds
amp	amplification	hd	head
B°	slightly mitigated appeal	hort	in hortatory discourse
C°	more mitigated appeal	idn	identification
ccl	conclusion	[MET]	metaphor
cir	circumstance	mns	means
cnd	condition	mot	motivational
cns	concession	[MTY]	metonymy
cnq	consequence	neg	negative
ctr	contrast	ori	orienter
ctx	contraexpectation	pos	positive
D°	highly mitigated appeal	pur	purpose
[DOU]	doublet	rea	reason
dsc	description	res	result
equ	equivalent	[RHQ]	rhetorical question
[EUP]	euphemism	spf	specific
(exc)	exclusive	[SYN]	synecdoche

ABBREVIATIONS IN TEXT

BAGD	Arndt and Gingrich	NT	New Testament
NIV	New International Version	OT	Old Testament
NRSV	New Revised Standard Version	UBS	United Bible Societies

BAGD is cited in text with a page number followed by the letter *a*, *b*, *c*, or *d*. The letter refers to one of the page's four quadrants, *b* being the upper right portion of the page, and *c* the lower left.

GENERAL INTRODUCTION

Purpose of this book

The Semantic and Structural Analysis (SSA) commentaries are specifically designed to assist translators, especially those translating into non-European languages. Due to the careful attention to meaning at all levels of the discourse, they should also be useful for Bible scholars, teachers, preachers, and anyone interested in a thorough understanding of the biblical text. The analysis is firmly based on discourse linguistics and assumes that each New Testament book is an integrated whole. Although the analytical process required careful attention to Greek grammar and lexicon, this work is especially concerned with presenting the meaning of the text and the linguistic evidence for the decisions.

Theoretical basis

Our theoretical basis is Beekman and Callow's theory of discourse analysis, presented in *The Semantic Structure of Written Communication* (1981) and further developed by Kathleen Callow in *Meaning and the Analysis of Texts* (1989). This is not to say that other theoretical approaches have been ignored. A large body of biblical scholarship has been considered.

This commentary is called *A Semantic and Structural Analysis* because its primary interest is the organized meaning of the text. The aim is to present, to the extent possible, the organization and meaning that the biblical author intended his audience to understand. We approach the text with several underlying assumptions about language as a communicative medium:

1. The writer used written language signals in his attempt to communicate meaning, emotion, and social relations to his readers.
2. The writer assumed a vast body of shared information with his audience, such as language, culture, world view, social relations, sociopolitical circumstance, specific circumstances, and time of the writing. Beekman, Callow, and Kopesec (1981) call this the "communication situation."
3. The writer's own intended purpose and communication meaning were prior to and have priority over the written surface forms. Yet, our main access today to the biblical writer's purpose and meaning is through the written text. (For further discussion of a writer's intent to affect his audience in hortatory discourse, see "Longacre's Contribution" on pp. 6–7.)
4. Communicated meaning consists of units of meaning logically related to other units of meaning.
5. Some meaning units are nuclear or central; others are satellitic or supportive to the nuclear units. These bundles of meaning are also bundled together with other, larger, units of meaning. In other words, meaning units are organized hierarchically in a discourse, giving rise to the "natural prominence" of the units (so Beekman, Callow, and Kopesec).
6. The ways in which units are related to each other (their "communication relations") are relatively few. These relationships are basic to human intelligence and makeup and are used in all languages whether or not there is a corresponding surface form expressing them. It should also be kept in mind that even in the same language a particular surface form is not necessarily the one that will be used to express a specific relation, and conversely any surface form may be used to express *more* than one semantic relation.
7. When two meaning units are related to each other, each unit in this relationship carries out a "communication role."
8. Every language has certain grammatical and lexical devices that an author may use to mark specific meaning units as prominent. This is called "marked prominence."
9. There are limited ways in which communication relations can be arranged so that a whole arrangement is a purposive and complete unit. Such an arrangement forms a communication paragraph, or "paragraph pattern."
10. Each communication unit has a "theme," that is, a central topic and an argument about that topic, understand-

able from the prominence structure of the unit. (This is not to be confused with "motif," which is a prosodic and coherence feature that runs through units of various sizes.)

In order to present the meaning and structure of any written communication, the writers of the SSA series have developed their own metalanguage using various diagramming devices and certain recurrent terms and basic English grammatical structures. This is both a strength and a weakness in the presentation of the text. The main weakness is that the uninitiated reader may find the information difficult to grasp and so miss much of what is signaled. The strength lies in the preciseness with which the meaning is presented.

Semantic relations and paragraph patterns

Semantic relations (i.e., communication relations) between propositions are the basic joining elements at all levels of a discourse. Paragraph patterns are made up of these relations with the additional elements of purposiveness and completeness. (An explanation of the total array of semantic relations between propositions is available in Beekman, Callow, and Kopesec's work.)

Of the two charts that follow, the first shows the paragraph patterns used in this analysis, and the second shows the communication relations and unit roles. Most of the terms in the charts are self-explanatory; those that are not, are accessible elsewhere (in Tuggy 1992 and Beekman, Callow, and Kopesec 1981). A small volume to serve as a manual for SSAs will be published before long.

In the chart of communication relations, the relations are given in the usual order in which they are found in the Greek of the New Testament. Where no natural prominence has been established (i.e., where there is only *contextual* prominence), both relations are shown in lowercase letters, for example, generic-specific.

Mitigation in hortatory discourse

A feature of hortatory discourse that needs special attention is that an appeal may be presented with varying degrees of forcefulness. This universal feature of hortatory discourse is well illustrated in the Epistles of John, where an imperative and at least three degrees of mitigation are used:

1. An entirely unmitigated appeal is expressed by a second person imperative. This is the most direct and forceful form of appeal. We label it *A° APPEAL*. But an appeal can be made less bluntly. This universal feature of hortatory discourse is well illustrated in the Epistles of John.
2. The least degree of mitigation is expressed by the reference to a command or proclamation with the obvious implication that it must be obeyed. In the SSA displays this is labeled *B° APPEAL*.
3. The next degree is expressed by ἵνα with the subjunctive or by ὀφείλω 'ought to'. In displays this is labeled *C° APPEAL*.
4. The greatest degree of mitigation is expressed by a conditional clause attached to an independent clause whose meaning content is of positive value to the reader. In displays this is labeled *D° APPEAL*.

It must always be remembered that John writes out of a father's love for the encouragement of his spiritual children, appealing to them rather than demanding a change.

Conventions used in displays of the semantic units

Each semantic unit is presented first as a display, followed by discussion of the unit's structure and exegesis. The vertical and horizontal lines used in the displays show structural relationships (as in Beekman, Callow, and Kopesec 1981). A dotted vertical line signifies a relation to all the units that follow at that level, not just to the immediately following proposition.

Italics in the propositions indicate implicit material. Bold type indicates prominence when prominence cannot be conveyed lexically or by any other means such as a cleft construction.

The English first person plural pronouns are to be taken in the inclusive sense unless otherwise noted.

An asterisk marks certain key words in the displays, an indication to the reader that the word is discussed in the Glossary.

		SOLUTIONALITY	CAUSALITY	VOLITIONALITY
I D E A S	EXPOSITORY −sequence	+problem(expo)+SOLUTION ±evidence^n ±(complication+SOLUTION)	+cause^n+EFFECT or +major+minor+INFERENCE or +evidence^n+INFERENCE^n or +application^n+PRINCIPLE	+justification^n+CLAIM
	NARRATIVE +sequence	+problem+RESOLUTION ±resolving incident^n ±(complication+RESOLUTION)	+occasion+OUTCOME	+step^n+GOAL
E M O T I O N	EXPRESSIVE −sequence	+problem(emot)+SOLUTION ±seeking ±(complication+SOLUTION)	+situation^n+REACTION ±belief	+belief^n+CONTROL ±belief
	DESCRIPTIVE +sequence	+problem(desc)+SOLUTION ±experience^n ±(complication+SOLUTION)	+situation^n+REACTION	+description^n+DECLARATION
B E H A V I O R	HORTATORY −sequence	+problem(hort)+APPEAL ±evidence^n ±(complication+SOLUTION)	+basis^n+APPEAL or +APPEAL+application^n	+motivation+ENABLEMENT^n or +motivation^n+APPEAL
	PROCEDURAL +sequence	+problem(proc)+SOLUTION ±step^n ±(complication+SOLUTION)	+APPEAL+outcome^n	+STEP^n+accomplishment

Paragraph Pattern Subtypes in Various Discourse Genres

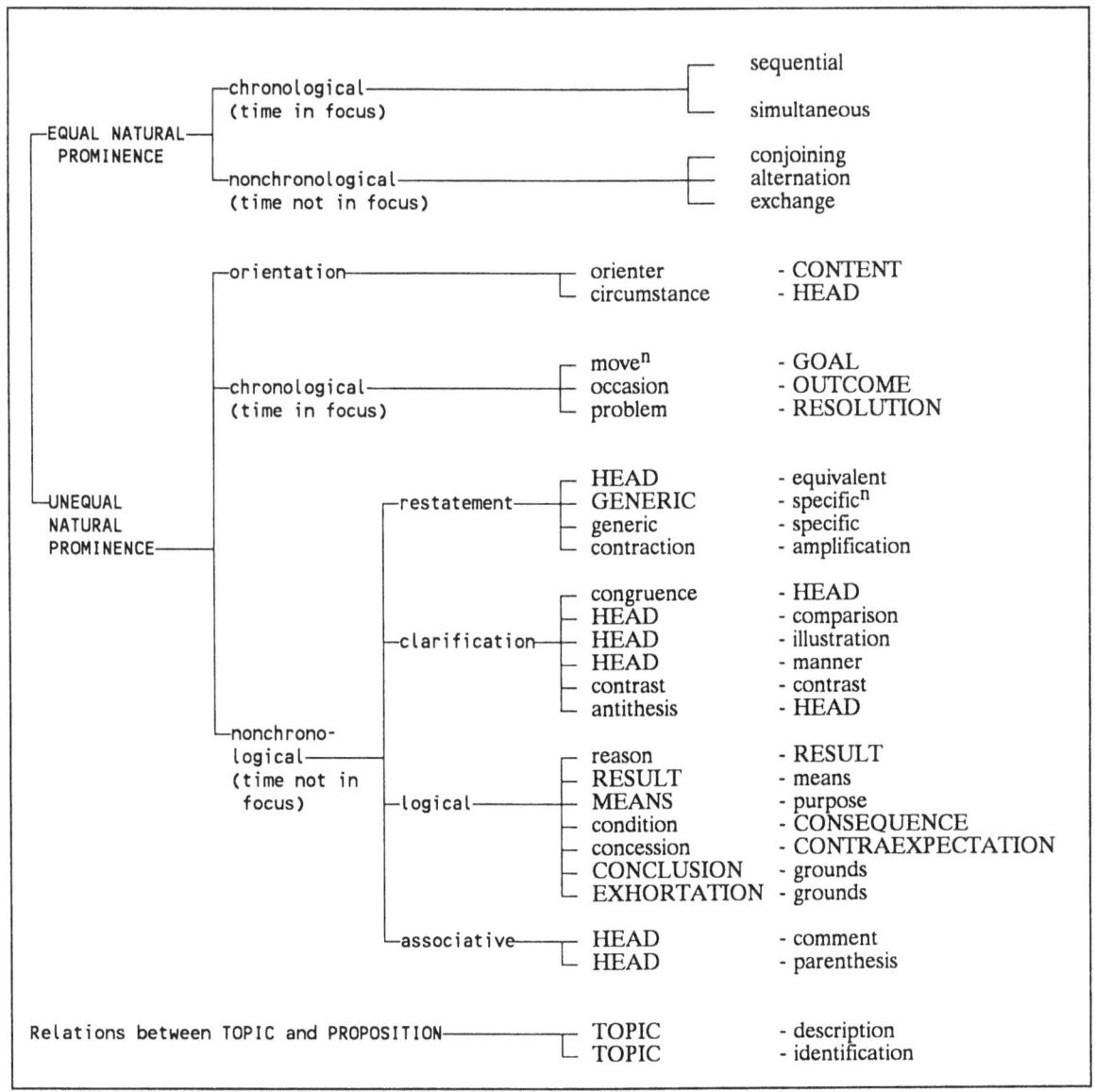

Communication Relations

INTRODUCTION TO THE SEMANTIC STRUCTURE OF FIRST JOHN

The importance of recognizing the communication situation

A written document reflects the situation in which it was written—the general historical situation and the particular situation of the writer and recipient(s). (This fact is an integral part of Beekman and Callow's theory.) Any document reflects the personality, beliefs, and circumstances of the writer and the knowledge and assumptions that the writer brings to the document concerning the circumstances of the readers. Further, the overall purpose of the document is closely related to the particular situation that gave rise to it.

These features of the communication situation are least obvious in a third person narrative and most obvious in such materials as an autobiography or a personal letter. Since the Johannine Epistles are in this last category, it is of value to the translator to be familiar with its communication situation, since it provides the background against which various exegetical decisions are made.

Authorship of the Johannine Epistles

Though early tradition attributes the three Epistles of the New Testament which bear the name of John to the apostle of that name, the question of authorship has long been debated. The writer did not affix his name to 1 John. Even in 2 John and 3 John he uses only the title 'the Elder'. So there have been questions about his identity and whether or not the same person wrote all three discourses.

There is little doubt that 2 John and 3 John were written by the same person because of the form of writing. As to whether 1 John was written by the same author, comparison of their lexical and theological expressions leads to the conclusion that the three writings were indeed from the same source.

The growing trend at present is to attribute the writings to members of a "Johannine Community" held together by a tradition established by the Apostle John. As to whether such a community could produce coherent canonical writings, those who hold this view consider the problem solved by the assumed solidarity of the group, whose members would have considered themselves participants in the experience of eyewitness and direct hearing through their fellowship. But the existence of such a fellowship is only an assumption (based to some degree on the use of the first person plural pronoun in 1 John).

Other scholars hold that the author of the three Epistles was the Apostle John, who also wrote the Gospel which bears his name. Their position is based, not on "assumptions" made to fill in historical gaps, but on internal evidence as well as early tradition.

The principal arguments for the Johannine authorship are as follows:

1. Of the NT writings which bear the name of an author there are no two by the same author that show as great a degree of similarity in message and language as the Johannine Epistles and the Gospel of John show to each other.

2. Differences between these Epistles and the Gospel of John are easily accounted for by the lapse of time and different purposes, addressees, and circumstance.

3. The variations that occur in the Johannine Epistles show a freedom in style indicative of a single author rather than imitators.

4. The prologue of 1 John, which is a testimony of personal experience, stresses the author's being an eyewitness of Christ. This crucial fact is emphasized by the references to 'our own eyes' and 'our hands' and repetition of important verbs.

5. The pronoun 'we' represents the writer and his fellow apostles who accompanied Jesus during his earthly ministry so that they might become his witnesses. The occurrence of the word μαρτυροῦμεν 'we witness' after 'revealed' and 'we have seen' in 1 John 1:2 supports this interpretation.

Based on this evidence and early tradition, the position taken in this study is that the three Johannine Epistles were written by a specific person, namely the Apostle John, who had specific purposes for writing, who addressed specific situations, and who wrote to specific people. He used rhetorical devices intended to carry out his purposes for writing. This does not deny, but rather strengthens the assumption that he wrote, under the control and guidance of God's Spirit, in natural language to communicate a vital message.

The occasion for writing

The corrections and warnings in 1 John lead us to look to contemporaneous history to identify the occasion for writing. We cannot specifically identify the foes the Apostle warned against, but the strong influence of certain Docetic philosophies toward the end of the first century was a major threat that menaced the pure faith of the young church. Thus John found it necessary to fortify his "children," as he called his parishioners, against the dangers surrounding them.

Well-attested tradition indicates that the Apostle John spent his later years in Ephesus. At that time a philosopher named Cerinthus was resident in Ephesus. He was both contemporary with and in opposition to John (Stott, p. 46). He taught that Jesus was human at birth but endowed as the Christ, probably at his baptism, and he supposed the Christ to have departed from Jesus before his passion. This false teaching had both theological and ethical implications and may have been the heresy that John was denouncing in this letter, which upholds the Person of Christ and the significance of his mission. Another widespread false teaching that may have been in John's thinking was the incipient Gnostic belief that the body is inherently evil and therefore the divine Christ could not have been a true human being—he only appeared to be. It was probably to counteract this that John emphasized Christ's having come in human form.

John also addressed ethical problems in this letter, such as the erroneous concept of sin held by some and a lack of love among the members of the congregation. In 1 John 2:19 we learn that some whose views were in opposition to John's teaching had seceded. They were probably trying to draw others away with them, and this threat too motivated John to write to the faithful.

Genre

Since neither address nor farewell is found in 1 John, there is some conjecture concerning its genre. Some think that the author could have intended it as a tract or published sermon for the general edification of the church. It is clearly different in form from 2 and 3 John, which are in the common form for a letter during this period. But the constant use of first and second person pronouns do suggest a letter, and the fact that the recipients are not named suggest that it might have been a circular letter. In any case, all three of the Johannine Epistles are hortatory as seen by the use of imperatives and other mitigated forms of exhortation.

From the tone of intimacy and authority throughout the discourse, 1 John has been judged to be a truly personal message addressed to a particular congregation by a teacher anxious about the spiritual welfare of his charge. The writer seems to be well acquainted with the needs of the congregation and deeply concerned for its members. Thus du Rand (1979:3) says: "It is a pastoral document in a homiletic form." John moves into his subject gradually, dwelling with emphasis on a key word, introducing an idea, and then leaving it for elaboration at a later point.

That the discourse was written rather than delivered orally is evident from the frequent reference to writing. It is a pastoral letter with strong emotion, demonstrating keen insight into the situation of the readers and requiring a change of action by the readers.

Longacre's contribution

Work on the present study was already in progress at the time Longacre's 1983 article "Exhortation and Mitigation in First John" was published. Without reference to Longacre, we had already concluded that 1 John is a hortatory discourse, based on the occurrence of imperative verbs and other command forms. (Longacre's conclusion was the same.) But other insights of his did prove very helpful in developing this analysis:

(1) *Re mitigated exhortations* (see our own summary on p. 2). It is commonly understood that such forms as "Would you like to do the dishes?" means "I would like you to wash the dishes; please wash them." This is a gentle way of suggesting that someone do something. Greek, English, Spanish, and probably many other European languages use this (and other devices) for gentle suggestions. For instance, we all react to the sentence "If we confess our

sins, he will cleanse us" as meaning "We should confess our sins, since he will cleanse us." Notice the mismatching between the surface grammar and the meaning which it expresses. Grammatically, the sentence is made up of a dependent conditional clause attached to an independent clause. Semantically, however, the relationship is reversed; that is, the *central* appeal unit is expressed by the dependent clause, and the *supporting* motivational unit is expressed by the independent clause. This mismatching between the grammar and the meaning is a device for making the exhortation or command a gentle one. Longacre's article not only made this observation, but gave a theoretical base to it. Referring to 1 John 1:5–10, he says (p. 7):

> I consider this paragraph to be Expository.... But this is not the whole story. Looking at the component sentences in more detail, we note that not only every sentence except that which is found in v. 5 is conditional, but that certain further features occur as well: (a) the main clauses inculcate a value system to which (b) the conditional clauses are related so that (c) correlations are set up between alternative behavioral choices and those values.... The main clauses express both the *problem* (a universe that is morally and spiritually polarized) and the *motivation*—which holds provided that one accepts the indicated positive values. What, then, of the preposed "if" clauses? They now emerge as *covert commands*. Thus, to say (6) "if we say that we have fellowship with him and walk in darkness, we lie and do not the truth" becomes equivalent to "don't say that you have fellowship with Him and walk in darkness—because you don't want to be on the side of the lie rather than on the side of truth."... I believe, then, that this paragraph (1 John 1:5–10) is expository in surface structure but hortatory in its underlying or notional structure.

In other words, one kind of mitigated exhortation in 1 John is a conditional clause attached to an independent clause whose meaning content is of positive value to the reader. If the meaning content of the conditional clause is true, then the meaning content of the (motivational/positive value) independent clause will be a reality. Such a conditional clause is introduced by ἐάν 'if' or by ὁ followed by the participle. This form expresses exhortations with the *greatest degree of mitigation* (see 1:7, 9; 2:1, 3, 10, 17; 5:1).

Another mitigated-exhortation device is the present subjunctive mood. Another is the word ὀφείλω 'ought to do' (in 2:6; 3:16; 4:11). These convey a *lesser degree of mitigation*.

Still another form of mitigation in 1 John is a reference to a command of Jesus, implying that one must do what Jesus commands. This has the *least degree of mitigation* (3:11, 23).

Imperatives are the *strongest* exhortations: they are not mitigated at all (2:15, 24, 27, 28; 3:7, 13; 4:1; 5:21).

(2) *Re semantic paragraph pattern in hortatory discourse,* Longacre made an important observation: "The basic schema in a hortatory discourse is: problem, command, motivation" (p. 3). Our view is similar: The hortatory paragraph pattern presents a "problem" (which we call "intended change") and a "command" (which we call an "appeal") and a "basis" for the appeal. The basis can be axiomatic, motivational, trusting, and warning.

(3) *Re sentence structure,* Longacre says (p. 3.),

> the individual sentences have a general surface structure ± preposed + main ± postposed —where preposed elements are conditional adverbial clauses ("if" clauses) or articular participial phrases; and where postposed elements are adverbial cause clauses (*hoti*) or purpose clauses (*hina*) ...

In our view, this general surface structure together with the basic hortatory paragraph pattern is a deliberate choice by the author. Other sentence-initial forms also occur such as ὁ 'the one who' and πᾶς ὁ 'all who' repeated to set off these sentences. Compared to nonhortatory prose in the New Testament, conjunctions in hortatory prose are scarce. The surface form of 1 John is similar to modern English free poetry. This deliberate patterning of the surface structure makes it difficult to know what the relations are between the various parts because a particular device may be used two or three ways so that the surface structure is the same but the *meaning* of the device quite different in each case.

Du Rand (1979:1) expresses the difficulty of analysis well:

> Initially a structural analysis of 1 John does not seem such an impossible undertaking at all. This is the first impression. It is after all written in the so-called "easier" Greek of the New Testament. However, when one begins to make syntactical combinations from the given surface structure to result in a definition of its semantic function, it

must be admitted that such an undertaking is not easy at all.

(4) *Re discourse peak.* A peak with demonstrable lexical, grammatical, and notional (semantic) turbulence is, according to Longacre, an important feature in any discourse. He says about 1 John (p. 5),

> I consider that the Introduction, itself an embedded discourse, contains three pre-peak points, a double peak (ethical and doctrinal) and a closure. In gross structure it resembles the body of the epistle, which has four pre-peak points, a double peak (doctrinal and ethical) and a post-peak point.

We agree that *peak* is a surface manifestation of the author's intentional emphasis on the total meaning of the discourse, which he expresses at certain points. The author, intending to bring his subject to a *climax,* uses many prominence devices involving the lexicon and grammar. He starts the discourse low key, builds up in excitement until he presents the main issues most forcibly, then drops off to conclude. We are also in accord with Longacre's judgment as to *where* the peaks of 1 John occur (2:12–27 and 4:1–11) and with his concept of each peak being a double climax. This amounts to having four climaxes in the Epistle: the first and second (2:12–25 and 2:26–27) occur contiguously, and the third and fourth (4:1–6 and 4:7–11) also occur contiguously. Each of them is thereby doubly forceful.

Differences with Longacre's view

In a few matters our analysis is different from Longacre's. Longacre says, "Vocatives serve mainly to delineate paragraphs" (p. 3). In our opinion, the vocatives serve either to tone down the upcoming exhortation or underline the author's confidence in his readers. The word γράφω 'I write' is used for the same purpose and not as a landmark of structural coherence or juncture. It is semantic coherence intersecting with grammatical cohesion that marks units and borders.

Due to our different criteria for determining units and borders, we view the overall structure of the Epistle differently than Longacre. Generally, we agree regarding the specific smaller units (except for some transitional paragraphs), but we see the macrostructure differently.

According to Longacre (p. 3), "The surface structure of the book is that of a long, somewhat overbalanced, and meandering Introduction (1:1–2:29), Body (3:1–5:12), and Closure (5:13–21)." But in our view, although we see the macrostructure as consisting of the same three parts, we segment them differently, the Introduction being 1:1–4, the Body 1:5–5:12, and the Closure 5:13–21. We consider Longacre's long Introduction to be a generic statement and generic appeal attached to the Body. (Our defense of this is presented under the discussion of the respective units.)

Some statements in 1 John that we regard as reiterations of statements set forth by the false teachers are taken as mitigated exhortations by Longacre. We do not accept these as mitigated exhortations. Our position is based on the threatening situation in which we deem the letter to have been written and on certain lexical choices made by the author (e.g., ἐὰν εἴπωμεν, literally 'if we say', which can well mean 'if someone says').

Contribution of other analysts

Du Rand's (1979) study is another that takes a discourse-analysis approach to 1 John. Unfortunately, du Rand does not state his theoretical linguistic basis, nor does he define what he means by his term *cola.* He seems to ignore the fact that the genre of the discourse is hortatory; his evidence for relations and junctures is based on expositional genre premises. His bases for unity are lexical items within semantic domains. Thus he joins some units to others because of lexical similarities instead of viewing them as fulfilling what according to our view is a transitional function. However, his analysis supports the vast majority of the decisions we made regarding the discourse units and confirms some of the theme statements. His review of scholarship on 1 John may be of interest to the reader with regard to the macrostructure of the Epistle.

THE CONSTITUENT ORGANIZATION OF 1 JOHN

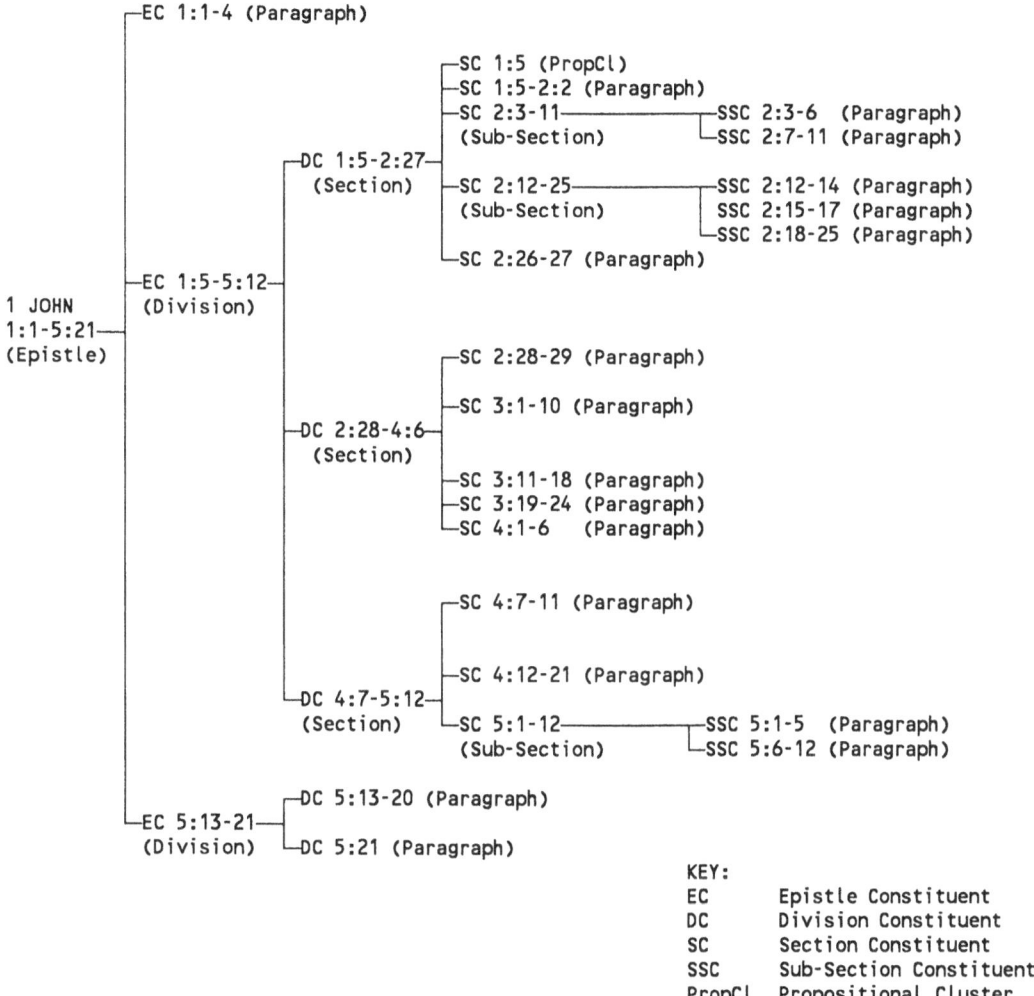

KEY:
EC   Epistle Constituent
DC   Division Constituent
SC   Section Constituent
SSC   Sub-Section Constituent
PropCl Propositional Cluster

OVERVIEW: MAJOR THEMATIC UNITS AND THEIR THEME STATEMENTS

FIRST JOHN 1:1-5:21 (Epistle)
Theme: Continue to live united to Christ and to love your Christian brothers in accordance with what you were originally taught.

    EPISTLE CONSTITUENT 1:1-4 (Descriptive Paragraph: Prologue of the Epistle)
    Theme: We proclaim to you the message about the One who always lives so that you may be joined together with us and be completely happy.

    EPISTLE CONSTITUENT 1:5-5:12 (Hortatory Division: Body of the Epistle)
    Theme: You must continue to live united to Christ and love your Christian brothers in accordance with what you were originally taught, in order that you may be confident that you associate properly with God. You also must be pure, truly love each other, believe in Christ, and test whether teachers teach the truth or not, since God has caused us to live spiritually forever.

        DIVISION CONSTITUENT 1:5-2:27 (Hortatory Section: Generic appeal of 1:5-5:12)
        Theme: Do not love the evil manner in which other people live in the world, but continue to behave according to what you were originally taught by God's Spirit, since God is completely morally pure.

SECTION CONSTITUENT 1:5 (Expository Propositional Cluster: Axiomatic basis of 1:6–2:27)
Theme: God is absolutely morally pure and in no way morally impure.
SECTION CONSTITUENT 1:5–2:2 (Hortatory Paragraph: Specific appeal$_1$ of 1:5–2:27)
Theme: We should continue to be morally pure, since God is morally pure and is able to forgive our sins on the basis that Jesus died to acquit us of the guilt of all our sins.
SECTION CONSTITUENT 2:3–11 (Hortatory Sub-Section: Specific appeal$_2$ of 1:5–2:27)
Theme: Since God is morally pure, we ought to behave just as Christ behaved, especially to love our Christian brothers, in order that we can be assured that we know God experientially.
SECTION CONSTITUENT 2:12–25 (Hortatory Sub-Section: Specific appeal$_3$ of 1:5–2:27)
Theme: Do not love the evil manner in which other people live in the world, but continue to behave according to God's true message, since you have come to know God.
SECTION CONSTITUENT 2:26–27 (Hortatory Paragraph: Generic appeal of 1:5–2:27)
Theme: Continue to behave according to what you were originally taught by God's Spirit.
DIVISION CONSTITUENT 2:28–4:6 (Hortatory Section: Specific appeal$_1$ of 1:5–5:12)
Theme: In order that we may be confident before Christ at his return, let us be pure, truly love one another, believe in Christ, and be very careful to test whether teachers teach people the truth or not.
SECTION CONSTITUENT 2:28–29 (Hortatory Paragraph: Generic appeal of 2:28–4:6)
Theme: In order that you may be confident that you associate properly with Christ when he manifests himself, continue to live united to Christ, doing what is right, since you want to show that God has caused you to live spiritually.
SECTION CONSTITUENT 3:1–10 (Hortatory Paragraph: Specific appeal$_1$ of 2:28–4:6)
Theme: Do not allow anyone to seduce you to sin, because we are God's children and his children maintain themselves free from evil behavior by not continuing to sin as the devil's children do.
SECTION CONSTITUENT 3:11–18 (Hortatory Paragraph: Specific appeal$_2$ of 2:28–4:6)
Theme: Since we have been changed from being spiritually dead people to being spiritually living people, we should love each other genuinely by helping our Christian brothers who are in need.
SECTION CONSTITUENT 3:19–24 (Hortatory Paragraph: Specific appeal$_3$ of 2:28–4:6)
Theme: We must believe in God's Son and love each other in order to be confident that we associate properly with God and receive what we ask from him.
SECTION CONSTITUENT 4:1–6 (Hortatory Paragraph: Specific appeal$_4$ of 2:28–4:6)
Theme: Since I know you have prevailed over false teachers, I say to you, Continue to test the teaching you hear to know whether or not it is from God. You should test it by whether or not it acknowledges that Jesus Christ came in human form and by who it is that listens to the teaching.
DIVISION CONSTITUENT 4:7–5:12 (Hortatory Section: Specific appeal$_2$ for 1:5–5:12)
Theme: In order to be assured that we behave according to God's character, we must love each other. We must do so since, as God's Spirit testifies, Jesus came to cause us to live spiritually forever.
SECTION CONSTITUENT 4:7–11 (Hortatory Paragraph: Appeal$_1$ of 4:7–5:12)
Theme: My dear friends, let us love each other, since God shows us how to love.

SECTION CONSTITUENT 4:12-21 (Hortatory Paragraph: Appeal$_2$ of 4:7-5:12)
Theme: In order to be assured that we behave according to God's character and that we love God and our Christian brothers just as he intended us to, we must love our Christian brothers, because God loved us first.
SECTION CONSTITUENT 5:1-12 (Expository Sub-Section: Basis of 4:7-5:12)
Theme: If a person believes that Jesus is God's Anointed One, he is one whom God has caused to live spiritually and he loves his Christian brothers. He also overcomes the evil of human society. We know this is true because God's Spirit testifies that Jesus came to save humankind.

EPISTLE CONSTITUENT 5:13-21 (Hortatory Division: Closing of 1:5-5:21)
Theme: Since we are united to both God and his Son, and since he causes his people to live spiritually forever, and since Jesus Christ is the real God, guard yourselves from worshiping unreal gods.

DIVISION CONSTITUENT 5:13-20 (Descriptive Paragraph: Closing description of 5:13-21)
Theme: Jesus Christ is the real God, and we are united to both God and his Son, and he causes his people to live spiritually forever.
DIVISION CONSTITUENT 5:21 (Hortatory Paragraph: Final appeal of 5:13-21)
Theme: Since Jesus is the real God, guard yourselves from worshiping unreal gods.

THE SEMANTIC UNITS OF FIRST JOHN

FIRST JOHN 1:1–5:21 (Epistle)
Theme: Continue to live united to Christ and to love your Christian brothers in accordance with what you were originally taught.

MACROSTRUCTURE	CONTENTS
prologue	1:1–4 We proclaim to you the message about the One who always lives so that you may be joined together with us and be completely happy.
BODY	1:5–5:12 You must continue to live united to Christ and love your Christian brothers in accordance with what you were originally taught, in order that you may be confident that you associate properly with God. You also must be pure, truly love each other, believe in Christ, and test whether teachers teach the truth or not, since God has caused us to live spiritually forever.
closing	5:13–21 Since we are united to both God and his Son, and since he causes his people to live spiritually forever, and since Jesus Christ is the real God, guard yourselves from worshiping unreal gods.

INTENT AND MACROSTRUCTURE

The First Epistle of John is composed of a marked *prologue* (1:1–4), BODY (1:5–5:12), and *closing* (5:13–21). Its intent is expressed primarily through purpose statements, promises of future events, warnings about some false assertions made by false teachers, and exhortations to change behavior or belief. There is no question as to the letter's hortatory character.

Some of John's purposes in writing are overtly stated (e.g., 1 John 5:13), and others covertly (e.g., 1 John 2:28). Thus they are presented to the reader in a hierarchical generic-specific relation. The purposes most overtly stated are in 1:3 and 5:13. In 1:3 the purpose for writing is stated in terms of κοινωνία 'joining together', that is, joining together with the apostles and with God the Father and his Son Jesus Christ. The author then moves from κοινωνία to ζωὴν ... αἰώνιον 'eternal life' (5:13). In other words, his overt purposes are 'that you also may join together with us according to the moral character of the Father' (1:3) and 'that you may know that you are living spiritually forever' (5:13). These two purposes are essentially the one purpose of participating in God's character. John keeps to this purpose throughout, giving exhortations that are the means for attaining that life and exposing what is inconsistent with it. Many of his appeals are mitigated, but are summed up in an imperative, 'continue to live united to Christ' (2:27–28).

John's more covertly stated specific purposes can be summarized as 'to give life' (4:9; 5:13, 16); 'to have confidence before God' (2:28; 4:17); 'to know the truth' (5:20); and 'to be pure (forgiven of sin)' (1:9; 2:1; 3:5, 8). The overt purpose of participating in God's character could be called the generic purpose whereas the covert purposes are specifics.

Very closely tied to the author's intent are the future-event promises. These expressions of purpose are prominent since they are as yet unfulfilled. There are four of them: 'you will continue to live united to both the Son and God the Father' (2:24); 'we will be like him in moral purity' (3:2); 'we will set our conscience at ease' (3:19); and 'God will restore our Christian brother to living spiritually' (5:16). They clearly relate to the semantic area of the author's stated intent (that the audience might participate in God's character).

John also intends to warn the audience regarding wrong conduct and false assertions by false religious teachers as seen in such statements as 'if we say that we have not sinned'. He has a keen concern for adherence to the truth of the original message presented by him and others who had firsthand experience with Christ (see the 1:1–4 *prologue*, especially v. 3). This concern is explicit in 2:26 ('I have written to you to warn you about those who want to deceive you') and 3:7 ('let no one deceive you, but obey the true teachings').

A summary of the false assertions John warns against can be made by noting the words with the meaning component of 'speaking' (εἶπον or λέγω 'say', ὁμολογέω 'confess', ἀρνέομαι 'deny', πλανάω 'deceive', ψεύδομαι 'lie', μαρτυρέω 'testify', and λόγος 'word' with various verbs). Sometimes such a word is followed by a description of conduct that denies the affirmation: 'if we/someone should say . . .' (in 1:6, 8, 10; 2:4, 9; 4:20); 'to deny (or not confess) that Jesus is from God' (in 2:22, 23; 4:3, 20; 5:10); and the true doctrine as contrasted to the false (in 4:2, 15; 5:1, 5).

That the author intends to change the conduct of the addressees is most clearly seen in the mitigated exhortations throughout the Epistle. The form of these exhortations is that if the reader obeys the exhortation then he will participate in God's character and eternal life.

BOUNDARIES AND COHERENCE

Semantic coherence in 1 John is achieved by the author's consistently adhering to the effect he intends on his audience. The most generic appeal is 'continue to live united to Christ' (2:27–28). The frequently reiterated specific appeals are: 'be morally pure' (1:7, 9; gfd2:1, 15); 'do God's will' (2:3, 7, 17; 3:22; 5:2); 'truly love each other' (2:10; 3:11, 18, 23; 4:12, 19, 21); 'believe in God's Son' (3:23; 5:21); and 'hold to the true message' (2:24; 4:1, 15; 5:21). The purposive clauses, promises, warnings, and exhortations all support John's intended effect on his audience.

Semantic coherence is also seen in the 159 references to its main motifs: 28 to false or deceptive teaching, 33 to loving relationships, 18 to believing or having confidence in God, 30 to purity of life, and 50 to the believer's relationship to God which constitutes eternal life.

For such a short Epistle key words are very frequent. There are 70 words in the semantic domain of 'evil', 45 in the semantic domain of 'righteousness', 57 in the domain of 'love/hate', 43 in the domain of 'know', 40 in the domain of 'message', 35 in the domain of 'remain', and 20 in the domain of 'conduct'. This list gives a fair idea of the letter's major motifs and exhortations. They bring coherence to it.

The Epistle is also structurally coherent, having a marked *prologue* (1:1–4), BODY (1:5–5:12), and *closing* (5:13–21). (The structural coherence within the BODY of the Epistle will be discussed under that unit.)

In spite of these evidences of semantic, lexical, and structural coherence there are those who do not recognize them, but rather see the message as coming from various sources and handled by one or more redactors. R. E. Brown's 1982 work gives a full discussion of that subject (pp. 36–46).

PROMINENCE AND THEME

The prominent units of 1 John are difficult to see because most of the exhortations or appeals are mitigated and presented as subordinate grammatical constructions rather than as independent imperative constructions. Also, the author uses vocatives and 'I write' orienters in a way that is rather unusual: to mitigate or soften appeals and certain subjects. They are not used to set off major junctures in the discourse (see the discussion of this on p. 8 under "Differences with Longacre").

For these reasons there is a diversity of opinion about what the author is emphasizing. Some see the exposure of heretical doctrine with its source in the spirit of antichrist (4:3) as prominent. Others take the Epistle as an appeal for love within the Christian family (4:7). Indeed there is such an appeal, but it is not the only one. It is interesting that in the *closing* (5:13–21) no form of the word ἀγάπη 'love' is found. Faith in the Son of God is strongly emphasized, but again it is only one of many other exhortations. There is also constant reference to purity of life (2:6). Sometimes it is difficult to separate these motifs. For instance, a warning against hatred as a way of life is tied in to the appeal for love of the brethren (2:9). Faith and love are united in a single command in 3:23. In view of all this, it is clearly not easy to describe the prominence structure of the book. Nevertheless, even though we must not latch on to one particular concept and proceed to demonstrate that the book is structured around that single idea, as text analysts we do need to observe the text and the prominence structure of its parts to ascertain the structure of the total discourse.

There are two climaxes in the book, each of which is a double climax. The first is in 2:12–27; the second, in 4:1–11. (The characteristics of these climaxes will be discussed later under the respective units.)

The Epistle is clearly hortatory, and the prominence structure is carried primarily by the mitigated appeals that occur throughout in a hierarchical arrangement. There are no appeals in the *prologue* (1:1–4) and only a summary appeal 'guard yourselves from false gods' in the *closing* (5:13–21). So, it is the BODY (1:5–5:12) that is prominent. This is the discourse's natural, or structural, prominence. The theme of the book is therefore derived from the BODY's most prominent statement.

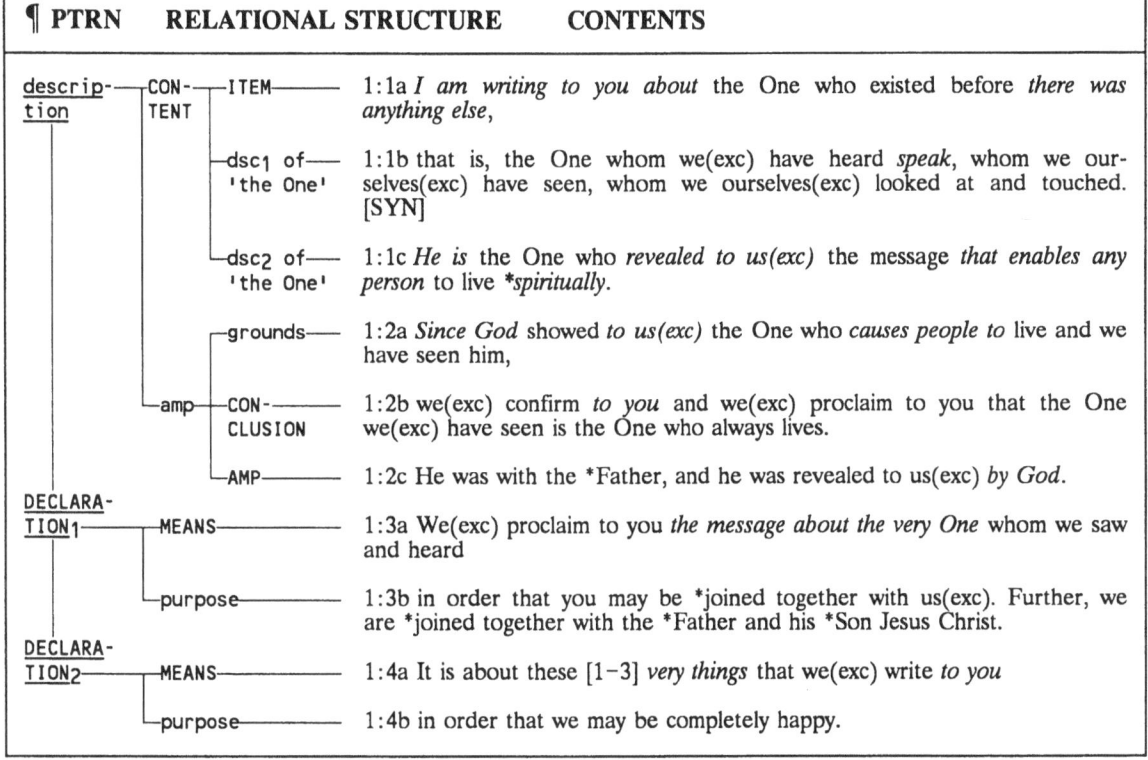

EPISTLE CONSTITUENT 1:1–4 (Descriptive Paragraph: Prologue of the Epistle)
Theme: We proclaim to you the message about the One who always lives so that you may be joined together with us and be completely happy.

INTENT AND PARAGRAPH PATTERN

The author's primary purpose in the 1:1–4 paragraph is to establish rapport with the recipients of the letter and to identify his own authority and that of his message. Rapport is normally established with an audience through the emotions so that they will be willing to listen to what the author or speaker has to say.

The paragraph is composed of three propositional clusters (vv. 1–2, 3, and 4): a circumstance followed by two conjoined heads. Thus it could be considered a simple volitional paragraph, either descriptive or expository. Since the primary intent is to affect the emotions, we consider it volitional descriptive, the principal constituents being + *description* + DECLARATION.

NOTES

1:1a *I am writing to you about* This proposition presents the person John intends to write about. Since there is no finite verb in the Greek, the verb from 1:4a is supplied. In many languages (including English) such information is required at the beginning for proper orientation to the whole letter.

Throughout the letter 'you' is plural both in the Greek grammatical form and the semantic referent of the second person.

the One who The intrinsic meaning of the verb 'proclaim' in 2b is to tell a message about some happening or person. Here the Greek grammar presents a person as the content of the proclamation. The message is the person. In the display this person is introduced in the 1:1–2 *description*, even though by doing it this way the artistic effect of the text is lessened.

before *there was anything else* The phrase ἀπ' ἀρχῆς 'from the beginning', which expresses the eternity of God, must be rendered in a way that goes further back than creation. A 'beginning' has an implicit referent to a temporal event, hence 'before there was anything else'.

1:1b we(exc) have heard *speak* Semantically, ἀκούω 'hear' requires what is experienced to be supplied.

whom we ourselves have seen, whom we ourselves ... touched The use of synecdoche here (τοῖς ὀφθαλμοῖς ἡμῶν 'our eyes' and αἱ χεῖρες ἡμῶν 'our hands' stand for the whole person) emphasizes the fact that they themselves, and not someone else, saw and felt him.

1:1c *revealed to us(exc)* The personification of λόγος 'message' to refer to Christ is a figure that is also used in the Gospel of John. He is not only the messenger from God but the One who reveals God; that is, he is the message about God. Since 'to reveal' is a basic meaning component of λόγος 'message', it is supplied here.

the One who *revealed to us(exc) the message that enables any person* **to live** Christ is said to be τοῦ λόγου τῆς ζωῆς 'the word of life' in the sense that the message he spoke enabled them to live spiritually.

spiritually An asterisk in the display refers the reader to an entry in the Glossary.

1:2a the One who *causes people to* **live** The reference of ἡ ζωή 'the life' is to Christ, who created and sustains living beings and causes those who believe to live eternally.

1:2b we(exc) confirm *to you* **and ... proclaim to you that the One we(exc) have seen is the One who always lives** Both μαρτυρέω 'testify' and ἀπαγγέλλω 'announce' are speech acts, and as such they require an addressee and communiqué.

1:2c the Father In the displays, here and in those that follow, the capitalized term 'Father' refers to God. In many languages 'father' is never used with an extended or figurative meaning. Rather, the meaning is limited to male biological progenitor, connoting family tie, high status, and certain social privileges and responsibilities. In such a language it may be possible to use something like 'God, everyone's Father'.

1:3a We(exc) proclaim to you *the message about the very One* The verb ἀπαγγέλλομεν 'we announce/proclaim' requires a communiqué to be supplied, here 'the message about the very One'.

1:3b joined together In 3b κοινωνία 'close relationship' occurs twice, and is implicit in 1b in the intimate experience of hearing, seeing, and touching the One revealed by God (2a, c). It is also implicit in its source, that is, in the intimacy of the Father and Son before the incarnation (2c), as signaled by πρός 'with' (see the discussion in the Glossary under 'joined together').

with the Father and his Son The purpose in writing is said to be that the readers may share a common character and relationship with the author and those who were eyewitnesses with him of the revelation of Christ. But lest it be limited to a relationship between believers, he immediately specifies it as also with the Father and his Son. Repeatedly throughout the Epistle he shows that the vertical aspect must include the horizontal and vice versa.

1:4a these [1–3] *very things* The pronoun ταῦτα 'these' is neuter plural. Its referent can be (1) what precedes, (2) what follows, or (3) the whole letter. The first possibility has been chosen for the display because of the conjunction καί 'and' and the tight coherence with what precedes. Here the author makes explicit reference to the message and redirects the topic from the One the message is about to the implications of the message itself.

we(exc) Some manuscripts have the nominative form ἡμεῖς 'we' following ταῦτα γράφομεν 'these things we write'; others have the dative ὑμῖν 'you' in that same position. The 'we' is signaled in the verb, and the 'you' is semantically required with the action and understood from the context. So the meaning is clear regardless of the pronoun accepted. The question remains whether 'we' is an epistolary plural or a real plural. If epistolary, then the meaning is 'I', but for the display we have taken it to be a real plural referring to the writer and those who saw Jesus.

1:4b we ... happy The pronoun ἡμῶν 'our' follows χαρά 'joy', and as in 4a it has a textual variant, ὑμῶν 'your'. This can be attributed to an attraction from John 16:24; also, the substitution of ὑμῶν seems more probable as a scribal error than a change to ἡμῶν would be. Thus in our analysis we accept χαρὰ ἡμῶν 'our joy'. Here 'our' is taken to be inclusive. (All first person plural pronouns in the displays are inclusive unless marked by 'exc'.)

BOUNDARIES AND COHERENCE

The closing boundary is marked by ἔστιν αὕτη ἡ ἀγγελία 'this is (indeed) the message' (1:5), which begins the next unit and corresponds to ταῦτα γράφομεν 'these things we write' in 1:4, making a tail-head construction. Topic focus switches from the author's authority in vv. 1-4 to the content and implications of the message in 5ff. Also, most of the information presented in the 1-4 unit is in the aorist or perfect tense, but in v. 5 it is in the present tense. Finally, the genre changes from proclamation in the prologue to exhortation and argument in 5ff. as evidenced by the first use of the formula ἐὰν εἴπωμεν 'if we say' in v. 6.

The coherence of the 1-4 unit lies in its announcing a message to be presented and the writer's authority to present the message. It is introduced by four object clauses, each beginning with ὅ 'that which' in v. 1. The subject of the message (1c) is said to be 'the word of life'. After this comes the verb, though the sentence is interrupted by a parenthesis in v. 2 and resumed in v. 3. There is a strong contrast between 'we(exc)' and 'you(pl)' in this unit.

Repetition of lexical items adds to the coherence: ἀκηκόαμεν 'we heard' (1b, 3a); ἑωράκαμεν 'we saw' (1b, 2a, 3a); ἐφανερώθη 'he was shown' (2a, c); ἀπαγγέλλομεν 'we proclaim' (2b, 3a); and ζωῆς 'life' (1c, 2a, b).

The 1-4 unit also shows coherence in its relational structure. There are two central *DECLARATIONS* of the writer's purpose in writing, namely that those who accept the message may be participants of God's character and that their happiness may be complete (3-4). These are supported by a *description* of the message to the effect that it has eyewitness and personal-contact authority (1-2).

PROMINENCE AND THEME

The prominence structure of the 1-4 paragraph is complicated by the fact that the structurally nonprominent *description* of the message is marked by several prominence devices. For one, it is highlighted, as it is introduced, by the four object clauses in v. 1, which precede and are widely separated from the verb in v. 3. Another highlighter is the pronoun ὅ 'that which' (pointing to the One who is the message); it stands out by its repetition at the beginning of each of these clauses. A third highlighting device is the use of contrast in the assertion that the author and his group were eyewitnesses, not speaking secondhand.

Structurally, the *DECLARATION* units are the prominent parts of the paragraph. (They contain a generalized reference to what is proclaimed.) But the *DECLARATIONS* alone are not sufficient for the theme statement because of the prominence features of the *description*. Thus the theme is derived from the most prominent generic elements of the *DECLARATIONS* (vv. 3-4) and the prominent elements of the *description* (vv. 1-2) not mentioned in v. 3.

> **EPISTLE CONSTITUENT 1:5–5:12 (Hortatory Division: Body of the Epistle)**
> *Theme: You must continue to live united to Christ and love your Christian brothers in accordance with what you were originally taught, in order that you may be confident that you associate properly with God. You also must be pure, truly love each other, believe in Christ, and test whether teachers teach the truth or not, since God has caused us to live spiritually forever.*

MACROSTRUCTURE	CONTENTS
GENERIC APPEAL	1:5–2:27 Do not love the evil manner in which other people live in the world, but continue to behave according to what you were originally taught by God's Spirit, since God is completely morally pure.
SPECIFIC APPEAL₁	2:28–4:6 In order that we may be confident before Christ at his return, let us be pure, truly love one another, believe in Christ, and be very careful to test whether teachers teach people the truth or not.
SPECIFIC APPEAL₂	4:7–5:12 In order to be assured that we behave according to God's character, we must love each other. We must do so since, as God's Spirit testifies, Jesus came to cause us to live spiritually forever.

INTENT AND MACROSTRUCTURE

The intent of the BODY of the letter has already been stated under the discussion of 1 John 1:1–5:21.

The author's intent to affect the behavior of the recipients of the letter is carried out by a GENERIC and two SPECIFIC APPEALS. This all results from his expressed concern that the recipients live in a way that is consistent with God's character, be confident before God, and be assured that they will live forever.

The overall structure (macrostructure) of the BODY of the letter is three units in which the first (1:5—2:27) is a GENERIC APPEAL and the other two (2:28—4:6 and 4:7—5:12) are SPECIFIC APPEALS.

The GENERIC APPEAL is that the readers 'continue to behave according to what you were originally taught'. The SPECIFIC APPEALS are (1) that they 'be pure, truly love one another, believe in Christ, and test the teachings they hear' and (2) that they 'must love each other and continue to live united to God's Son'.

BOUNDARIES AND COHERENCE

The opening boundary of the 1:5–5:12 unit is not disputed by many commentators, but there are those who consider all of the first chapter as introductory. They usually base this on the surface-structure vocative addressed to the readers at 2:1. However, the vocatives that occur throughout the BODY and even in the *closing* are used for focusing on the head constituent and for reassuring the addressees of the author's confidence in them, not for marking a boundary. In our analysis 1:5 is accepted as the initial boundary of the BODY (the other factors indicating this have already been mentioned in the discussion under the 1:1–4 unit).

As for the closing boundary, we take it to be marked by the summary of 5:12, even though some commentators include 5:13 in the body of the Epistle due to its continuation of the reference to eternal life, the immediately preceding topic. In their view, v. 13 is considered to refer only to 5:1–12. However, many other commentators consider 5:12 to be the final statement of the body. They see ταῦτα ἔγραψα ὑμῖν 'I have written these things to you' as referring to the whole letter and corresponding to ταῦτα γράφομεν (ἡμεῖς or ὑμῖν) 'we write these things to you' in 1:4. (These two references to the writing of the Epistle constitute a sandwich construction.) The similarity to the close of the John's Gospel (John 20:31) is another good reason for regarding 5:12 as referring to the whole discourse. Moreover, the pattern of summaries at the end of units throughout the discourse seems to justify calling 5:12 a summary marking the close of the body. It also seems to justify calling 5:13 a transition in the discourse: it takes up the topic of eternal life mentioned in 5:12, forming a tail-head construction. In 5:13 the independent verbs switch from the present to the perfect tense;

this marks the summary character of the book's *closing*.

Coherence in the BODY of the Epistle is essentially the same as that demonstrated for the whole letter: Adherence to the purpose expressed in the *prologue* (to promote the participation of the believer in the character of God the Father and of his Son Jesus Christ) produces coherence in the BODY.

Motifs—concepts repeated throughout the text—also give it coherence. Even though they do not necessarily provide the relational structure for the discourse, they do have a prosodic function, giving coherence and unity in 1 John. Three motifs can be seen in the first section: (1) God's forgiveness of confessed sin (1:5–2:2); (2) assurance of knowing God (2:3–11); and (3) God's provision for the believer to overcome evil (2:12–25). These motifs are the grounds for living united to Christ (2:26–27).

The same motifs are present in 2:28–4:6 and 4:7–5:12. In 2:28–4:6 they are: (1) Jesus revealed to take away sin and destroy the works of the devil (3:5–8); (2) assurance rooted in love (3:19–24); and (3) overcoming that depends on the mutual indwelling of the believer in God and he in the believer (3:24; 4:4). In 4:7–5:12 they are: (1) Christ's love in providing forgiveness as the motivation for believers to love each other (4:9–10); (2) assurance based on faith and love (4:16); (3) faith that springs from love as the resource provided for overcoming the world spirit (5:4–5). (For 'world spirit' see the Glossary.)

Three times, then, the same motifs of forgiveness, assurance, and overcoming evil are treated, distinct, however, as to intent, means, goal, or grounds. (Since motif is a cohesive and not a structural feature, we do not consider this to have a bearing on the structure.)

In the 1:5–2:27 unit the grounds that God is morally pure and the concern that believers participate in God's character and keep to the original message are central. In 2:28–4:6 the concern that we have confidence before God and keep to the original message is central. In 4:7–5:12 the grounds that God loved us and the concern that we live forever are central.

The BODY of the Epistle (1:5–5:12) is composed of GENERIC APPEALS about living united to Christ (1:5–2:27); SPECIFIC APPEALS to be pure, love each other, believe in Christ, and test the teachers (2:28–4:6); and SPECIFIC APPEALS to love each other and continue to live united to God's Son (4:7–5:12).

PROMINENCE AND THEME

The two SPECIFIC APPEALS, 2:28–4:6 and 4:7–5:12, are the naturally and structurally prominent units in the BODY. The theme statement is derived from the prominent elements of the GENERIC APPEAL as well as of these two SPECIFIC APPEALS, especially the second one.

> **DIVISION CONSTITUENT 1:5–2:27 (Hortatory Section: Generic appeal of 1:5–5:12)**
> *Theme: Do not love the evil manner in which other people live in the world, but continue to behave according to what you were originally taught by God's Spirit, since God is completely morally pure.*

MACROSTRUCTURE	CONTENTS
axiomatic basis	1:5 God is absolutely morally pure and in no way morally impure.
specific appeal₁	1:5–2:2 We should continue to be morally pure, since God is morally pure and is able to forgive our sins on the basis that Jesus died to acquit us from the guilt of all our sins.
specific appeal₂	2:3–11 Since God is morally pure, we ought to behave just as Christ behaved, especially to love our Christian brothers, in order that we can be assured that we know God experientially.
SPECIFIC APPEAL₃	2:12–25 Do not love the evil manner in which other people live in the world, but continue to behave according to God's true message, since you have come to know God.
GENERIC APPEAL	2:26–27 Continue to behave according to what you were originally taught by God's Spirit.

INTENT AND MACROSTRUCTURE

The 1:5–2:27 unit is hortatory and is composed of a *basis* and *APPEALS*. The author's concern in this unit, as expressed by intent statements, is that the believer be free from sin through the forgiveness provided in Christ (1:9; 2:1); that he be separate from false religious teachers (2:19); and that he be assured that he will remain united to Christ (2:24). Several topics discussed in this unit are taken up again for elaboration in subsequent units, but the appeals to fulfill the author's purpose that the readers be joined together according to God's character (1:3) are most clearly presented in this one.

As to the unit's paragraph patterns, v. 5 is obviously the *basis*. But the question is, Which of the four *APPEALS* is generic or are they simply a series of specific appeals? Is the generic appeal the one that is contiguous to the basis, or the one that is the final appeal in the section (to continue living united to Christ)?

Since one of the author's main rhetorical devices is to move into his subject matter slowly and gently, and since the first *APPEAL* is primarily a reiteration of principles of Christian living upon which he and the readers agree, we conclude that the *GENERIC APPEAL* is later in the section (if, in fact, there is one at all). The *APPEALS* are: (1) be morally pure (1:5–2:2); (2) love your Christian brothers (2:3–11); (3) do not love the evil manner in which other people live (2:12–25); and (4) continue to behave according to what God's Spirit taught you (2:26–27). The grammatical forms of the *APPEALS* in 1:5–2:2 and 2:3–11 are mitigated, not imperative. However, the form of each of the *APPEALS* in 2:12–25 and 2:26–27 is imperative; thus we see that the author intended these as a double climax. These last two *APPEALS* are bound by the motif that they should be observed 'in accordance with God's true message'. The final *APPEAL* (2:26–27) is by far the shortest of the four and can be considered a summary; in that sense it is a *GENERIC APPEAL*.

It could be questioned whether 2:26–27 is a summary because of the limiting phrase περὶ τῶν πλανώντων ὑμᾶς 'concerning those who would deceive you', which could be taken as referring only to 2:18–25. However, the deception that is in view is the deception of the world spirit (see Glossary), and this is the generic topic of the whole section. Moreover, there are many subsequent references to deceptive doctrines that seem like quotations from the false teachers. (They are introduced by ἐὰν εἴπωμεν 'if we say'.) These might be overlooked by present-day readers, but would be evident to the readers of John's day.

BOUNDARIES AND COHERENCE

The initial boundary of the 1:5–2:27 unit is co-terminous with the juncture of units 1:1–4 and 1:5–5:12, and has been discussed under those units.

The closing boundary is marked by a chiasm at the end of 1:5–2:27. Also there is a tail-head construction: the exhortation μένετε ἐν αὐτῷ 'remain in him' is repeated in 2:28. For this reason some view 2:28–29 as the conclusion of the section, but since 2:28–29 introduces the topics for discussion in the following section it is better taken as transitional. The next unit (2:28–4:6) opens with a vocative and καὶ νῦν 'and now' and an imperative verb (one of the few in the whole Epistle, even though the letter's general character is hortatory).

Though many ways of dividing the BODY have been proposed, there is a definite structural coherence in 1:5–2:27. It is a semantic inclusio: 1:5 declares the 'message announced' and 2:27 refers to the 'message as originally taught'; and within these boundaries, the entire discussion centers on the need to keep morally pure because God is morally pure. As might be expected, key terms having to do with this semantic domain occur: sin versus righteousness (1:5, 6, 7, 8, 9, 10; 2:1, 2, 8, 9, 11, 12, 13, 14, 15, 16, 17); joining together according to God's character (1:7, 10; 2:5, 10, 13, 14, 16, 17, 25); and remaining united to God (1:10; 2:3, 4, 5, 14, 20, 21, 22, 23, 24, 27).

In 2:27 there is a chiastic structure:

A ἀλλ' ὡς τὸ αὐτοῦ χρῖσμα διδάσκει ὑμᾶς 'but as that same anointing teaches you'
  B καὶ ἀληθές ἐστιν 'and is true'
  B' καὶ οὐκ ἔστιν ψεῦδος 'and is not a lie'
A' καὶ καθὼς ἐδίδαξεν ὑμᾶς 'and as it taught you'

This chiasm is followed by an APPEAL, 'continue behaving according to God's Spirit', thus forming an appropriate and coherent closure to the subject of participating in God's character introduced in 1:6–7.

An alternate internal structure could be posited as follows.

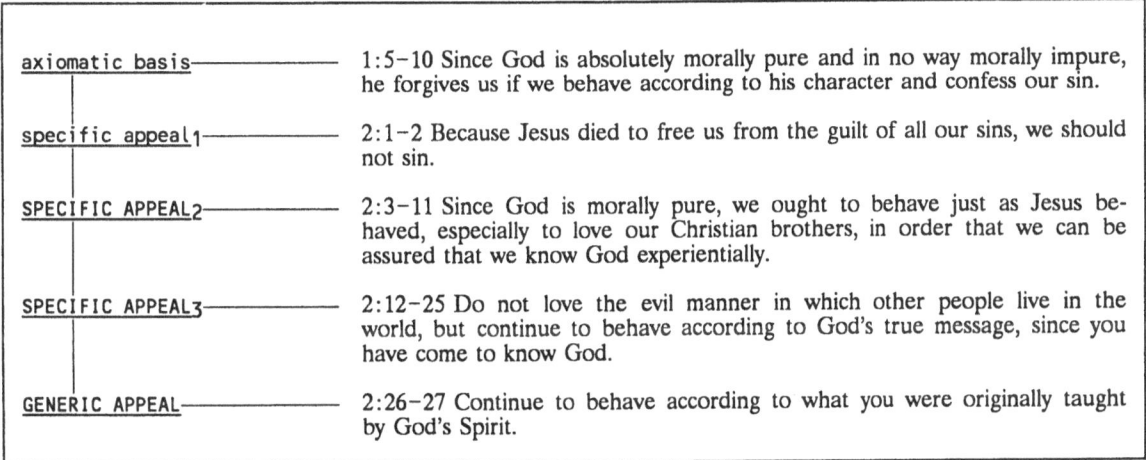

In this alternative analysis the opening and closing boundaries are the same as in the main display, and the same function of the vocative and the words 'I write' in 2:28 is recognized. The difference is that 1:5–10 is interpreted as one paragraph functioning as the *basis* for the *APPEALS* in 2:1–27. But this analysis is weak. Placing a boundary between 1:10 and 2:1 rejects the textual evidence of degrees of mitigated exhortation in 1:5–10, and it causes 1:10 to dangle and not fill out the structural parallel modeled in 1:6–7 and 8–9. It also rejects the vocative as a gentle moving into the stronger exhortations of 2:12–14 and 3:7, 13.

PROMINENCE AND THEME

The features of marked prominence in 1:5–2:27 are as follows:

1. Multiple vocatives in 2:12–14 (a device that focuses prominence on the APPEAL), making the SPECIFIC APPEAL in 2:12–25 especially prominent.
2. The overt negative command in 2:15, μὴ ἀγαπᾶτε τὸν κόσμον 'do not love the world'.
3. The chiastic structure in the 2:26–27 GENERIC APPEAL.
4. The overt command μένετε ἐν αὐτῷ 'remain in him' in the 2:26–27 APPEAL.

Here again there is some difference of opinion because the verb form μένετε 'remain' could be either indicative or imperative. Almost all versions take it to be imperative. Commentators, however, are divided. Brooke (p. 63) mentions a doubt concerning the imperative because of the indicative μένει ἐν ὑμῖν 'abides in you' occurring in the same sentence (it refers to the anointing). But many agree with Bultmann, who says (p. 41), "The indicative μένει includes the imperative μένετε ἐν αὐτῷ ('you abide in it'). . . . in v. 27 [it] can only refer to Jesus Christ." The analysis in the display is based on its being an imperative because of the specific appeals which lead up to it as a generic exhortation.

As mentioned earlier in the discussion under the entire letter, the span 2:12–27 is the climax in this part of the letter. (The climax is discussed further under units 2:12–25 and 2:26–27.) Therefore, we are convinced that the GENERIC APPEAL (to continue to behave according to God's Spirit) is the main exhortation of the section, hence naturally prominent in the section. The theme statement is derived from the HEAD propositions of the third SPECIFIC APPEAL (2:12–25) and the GENERIC APPEAL (2:26–27).

SECTION CONSTITUENT 1:5 (Expository Propositional Cluster: Axiomatic basis of 1:5–2:27)
Theme: God is absolutely morally pure and in no way morally impure.

RELATIONAL STRUCTURE	CONTENTS
┌orienter───────	1:5a This [5b] **is** *truly* the message we(exc) heard from Christ and announce to you:
└CONTENT───────	1:5b God is *absolutely morally pure like* light and has no *impurity like* darkness at all. [MET]

INTENT AND PARAGRAPH PATTERN

Verse 5 functions at two levels simultaneously: It constitutes the grounds of the three exhortation units that follow it (see the display of 1:5–2:2 below); on the higher level, it is the *axiomatic basis* for the whole of 1:5–2:27. For this reason v. 5 is shown in two displays.

NOTES

1:5a This In 1 John every occurrence of οὗτος 'this' followed by ὅτι 'that' or ἵνα 'that' points forward to the content introduced by these particles. All other occurrences of οὗτος also refer to the following information, except the second one in 5:11.

is *truly* The verse begins with a forefronted ἔστιν 'is'. This forefronting gives it unusual prominence and points emphatically to what the message is: it is true in contrast to the falsity of the heretics. The verb is not merely copulative but also predicative (Westcott).

Christ The Greek has a pronoun here; we have specified it as 'Christ'.

1:5b God is *absolutely morally pure like* light and has no *impurity like* darkness The symbolism of light and darkness is used to reveal the moral nature of God and man respectively. This is a frequent figure in John's writings. Commentators do not bring out the point of similarity in the metaphor; they unknowingly make a semantic leap from 'purity' to 'holiness'.

In the metaphor φῶς 'light' the topic is God's character, the image is light, and the point of similarity is purity or holiness. In the metaphor σκοτία 'darkness' the topic is bad character, the image is darkness, (i.e., lack of light), and the point of similarity is the lack of purity. These figures connote moral purity and moral impurity, sinfulness.

Some commentators variously attribute to φῶς 'light' the meanings of 'glory', 'revelation', 'truth', and 'holiness'. But since σκοτία 'darkness' is generally considered to mean 'moral evil', 'error', 'sin', and 'enmity with God' (all in the semantic domain of 'sinfulness'), we prefer to maintain a contrast with this. Hence, we take 'light' primarily to mean 'holiness'.

The word καί 'and', meaning 'that is' in this context, reinforces the prominent contrast between 'light' and 'darkness'. This is expressed in the display by 'absolutely morally pure'.

Translators frequently desire to preserve the contrasting metaphors in 'God is light and has no darkness'. But a metaphor can be interpreted correctly only if in the receptor language the image conveys a common point of similarity with the topic. In many languages the words 'light' and 'darkness' have the semantic components of visibility and invisibility, or understanding and not understanding. Even if the meaning of moral purity and moral impurity be *taught* to the readers, it will not necessarily become part of the linguistic community. In preserving any metaphor, the translator must, above all, be certain that it will not result in a *wrong* meaning.

BOUNDARIES AND COHERENCE

The 1:5 unit is a propositional cluster, not a paragraph; it does not have the pattern characteristics of a semantic paragraph. It could be considered a paragraph only if taken as a descriptive paragraph composed of a *description* and DECLARATION, which is a doubtful position.

Verse 5 serves as the *basis* for the APPEALS in the 1:5–2:27 section. But it is more closely tied to the 1:6–2:2 APPEALS than to the rest of the section. Therefore v. 5 is shown as the *basis* of the APPEALS in both units.

The opening boundary has been discussed under 1:1–4. Since 1:5 is not a paragraph, we cannot of course speak of a closing boundary.

The semantic coherence of 1:5 derives from its being a definition of the message in terms of a figurative description of God's character. The figures of light and darkness speak of the stark contrast between the righteousness of God and the alienating sin of man. They continue in 1:6–7 and 2:8–11, but here in 1:5 are presented in a generic sense that includes the sense of the two later occurrences. These repetitions cohere within the larger 1:5–2:27 unit and remind the reader that the author is still dealing with the believer's need to conform to God's character. But these repetitions do not form a 1:5–7 or 1:5–2:11 structural unit.

PROMINENCE AND THEME

The 1:5 unit consists of an *orienter* and a CONTENT unit, the latter being naturally prominent. It has marked prominence as well: the sharp contrast between 'light' and 'darkness' is further heightened by the double negation of οὐκ ἔστιν οὐδεμία 'there is none at all' and the nominative complements φῶς 'light' and ἐν αὐτῷ 'in him' are fronted in each part of the contrast.

The theme statement is derived from the CONTENT unit since it is the most prominent.

SECTION CONSTITUENT 1:5–2:2 (Hortatory Paragraph: Specific appeal₁ of 1:5–2:27)

Theme: We should continue to be morally pure, since God is morally pure and is able to forgive our sins on the basis that Jesus died to acquit us of the guilt of all our sins.

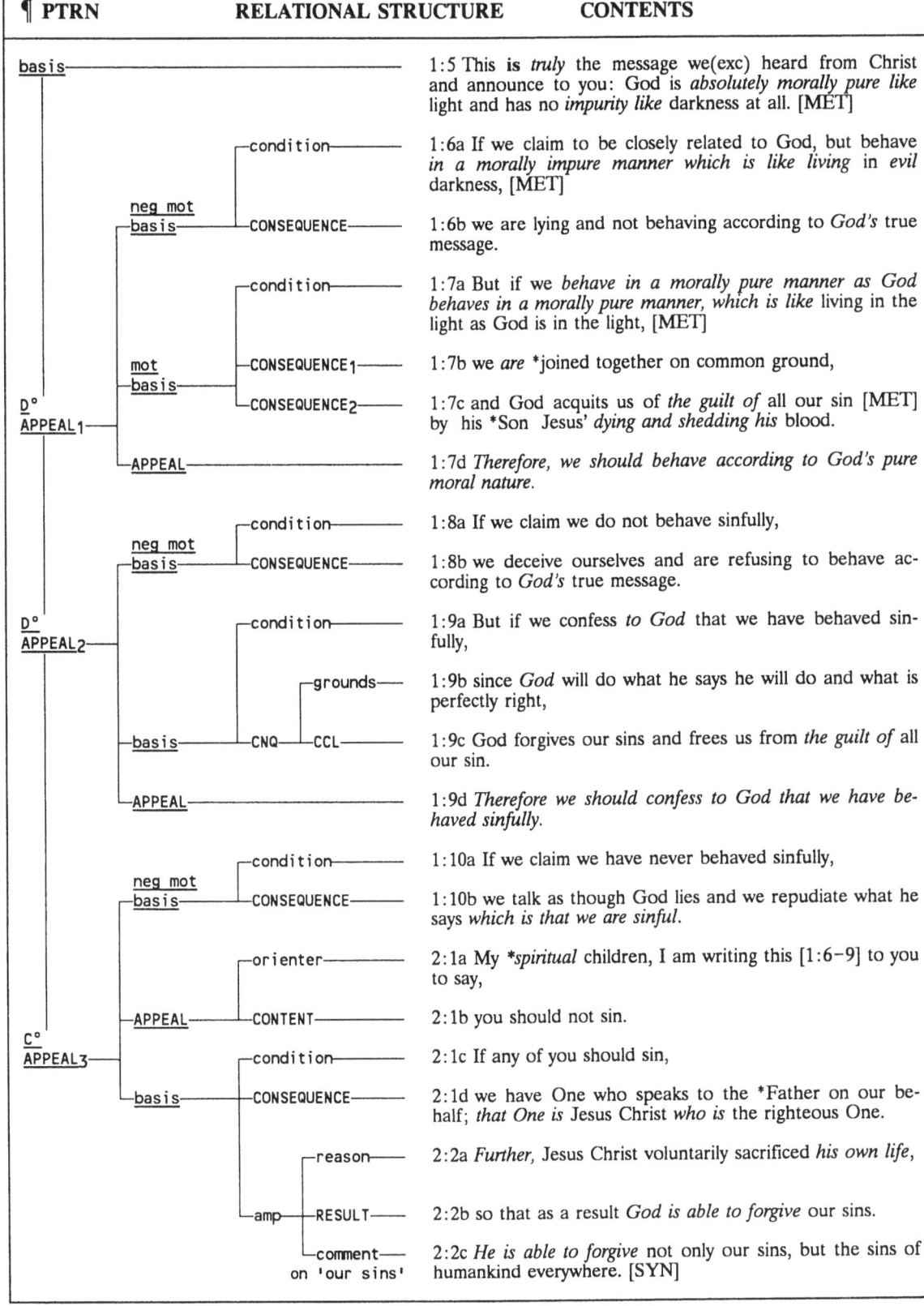

¶ PTRN	RELATIONAL STRUCTURE	CONTENTS
basis		1:5 This *is truly* the message we(exc) heard from Christ and announce to you: God is *absolutely morally pure like* light and has no *impurity like* darkness at all. [MET]
	condition	1:6a If we claim to be closely related to God, but behave *in a morally impure manner which is like living* in *evil* darkness, [MET]
neg mot basis — CONSEQUENCE		1:6b we are lying and not behaving according to *God's* true message.
	condition	1:7a But if we *behave in a morally pure manner as God behaves in a morally pure manner, which is like* living in the light as God is in the light, [MET]
mot basis — CONSEQUENCE₁		1:7b we *are* *joined together on common ground,
— CONSEQUENCE₂		1:7c and God acquits us of *the guilt of* all our sin [MET] by his *Son Jesus' *dying and shedding his* blood.
D° APPEAL₁ — APPEAL		1:7d *Therefore, we should behave according to God's pure moral nature.*
	condition	1:8a If we claim we do not behave sinfully,
neg mot basis — CONSEQUENCE		1:8b we deceive ourselves and are refusing to behave according to *God's* true message.
	condition	1:9a But if we confess *to God* that we have behaved sinfully,
	grounds	1:9b since *God will do what he says he will do and what is perfectly right,*
D° APPEAL₂ basis — CNQ — CCL		1:9c God forgives our sins and frees us from *the guilt of* all our sin.
— APPEAL		1:9d *Therefore we should confess to God that we have behaved sinfully.*
	condition	1:10a If we claim we have never behaved sinfully,
neg mot basis — CONSEQUENCE		1:10b we talk as though God lies and we repudiate what he says *which is that we are sinful.*
	orienter	2:1a My *spiritual children, I am writing this [1:6–9] to you to say,
— APPEAL — CONTENT		2:1b you should not sin.
	condition	2:1c If any of you should sin,
C° APPEAL₃ basis — CONSEQUENCE		2:1d we have One who speaks to the *Father on our behalf; *that One is* Jesus Christ *who is* the righteous One.
	reason	2:2a *Further,* Jesus Christ voluntarily sacrificed *his own life,*
amp — RESULT		2:2b so that as a result *God is able to forgive* our sins.
— comment on 'our sins'		2:2c *He is able to forgive* not only our sins, but the sins of humankind everywhere. [SYN]

INTENT AND PARAGRAPH PATTERN

As John gets to the main message of the letter here in 1:5-2:2, his intent is to affect the actions of the reader using a low-key admonition: he wants to make certain that all the readers will continue behaving according to God's character. This paragraph is composed of a propositional cluster (1:5) and three embedded paragraphs (1:6-7, 1:8-9, and 1:10-2:2) each of which is exhortative.

The 1:5-2:2 paragraph could be considered either causal hortatory or expository. Since the primary intent is to affect the readers' behavior, we consider it causal hortatory.

Commentators generally do not say that this paragraph is hortatory. (Their own presentation method, being expository, perhaps influences them to see it as expository.) However, they unconsciously slip into using such words as 'choose', 'submission', 'subjection', 'confession'. Kistamaker (p. 248) unwittingly says when summarizing this paragraph,

John *encourages* the reader. He says that if we walk in the light, and confess our sins, God will forgive us our sins and purify us through the blood of Jesus, his Son. *Therefore, we must walk in God's light* [italics added].

This certainly is an admission of the mitigated hortatory intent and force of the paragraph.

Decisions regarding the structure and boundaries of this paragraph are complex and difficult. The preceding display presents what we think best accounts for the text and the larger context. Particularly difficult is how to demonstrate the dual function of v. 5. We have included it as part of this paragraph and also as part of the higher-level 1:5-2:27.

If Longacre's view that the conditional clauses are used to express mitigated exhortations is rejected, one is left with various options, posing still further problems. They are variously handled, as shown by the alternative analyses that follow.

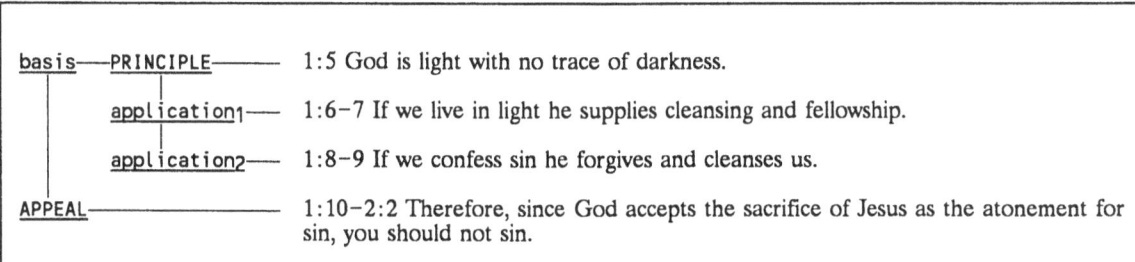

The preceding analysis is the most acceptable one if the theoretical basis that accounts for degrees of exhortation is considered untenable. However, this analysis does not have structural coherence; that is, it does not make sense to say, 'Since God is absolutely pure and supplies fellowship, cleansing, and forgiveness, you should therefore not sin'. It is also difficult and clumsy to extract a theme statement for this analysis without including such words as 'should' or 'would' in the *applications*.

Another way of analyzing this paragraph is as follows, in which it is taken to be a solutionality type (problem-solution).

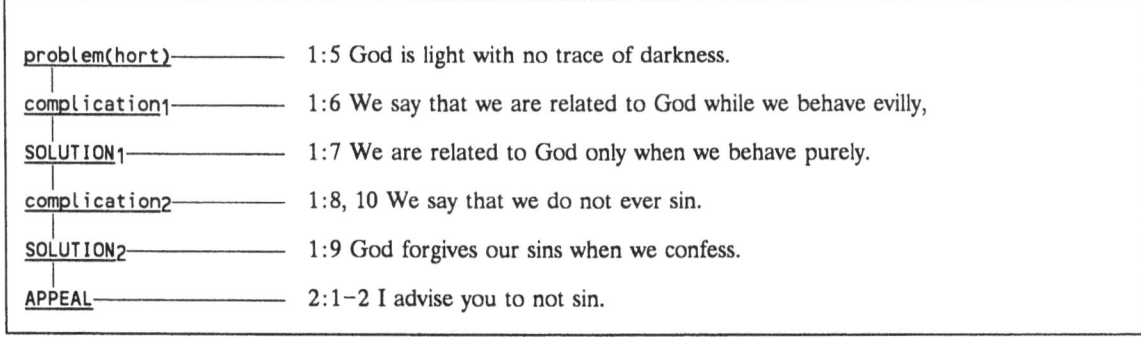

The difficulty with the above analysis is that it views v. 5 as stating a problem, which clearly it does not. Rather, it is a *principle* or *basis*.

The following is yet another way of showing the relationships within the paragraph:

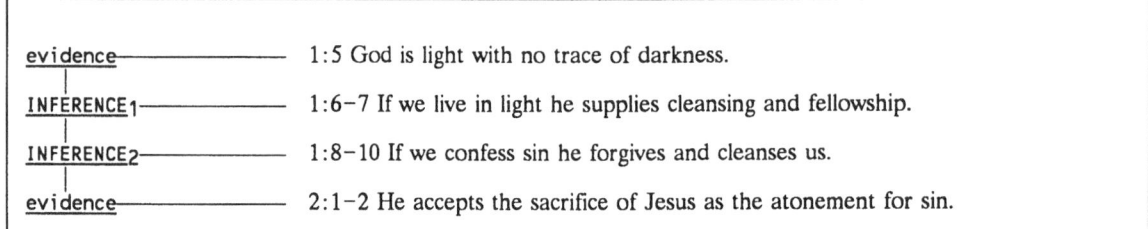

In the above analysis the *INFERENCES* show what God is prepared to do to restore man's relationship to himself. The *evidence* in 1:5 is further elaborated in 2:2 showing the basis for God's forgiveness in the sacrifice of Jesus Christ. The paragraph is presented as expository, as if the author intends to inform the readers and not necessarily change their actions. (This is different from our analysis in the main display, which presents it as hortatory.) But the structure here does not account for the prominent C° APPEAL of 2:1, nor for the fact that the author is encouraging the audience to continue behaving according to God's moral character.

In the following analysis the practical consequences of the basic message that God is morally pure are highlighted, and the paragraph is viewed as expository. The request in 2:1 not to sin is taken as being of hortatory import and prominent in the propositional cluster and therefore inconsistent with the paragraph pattern.

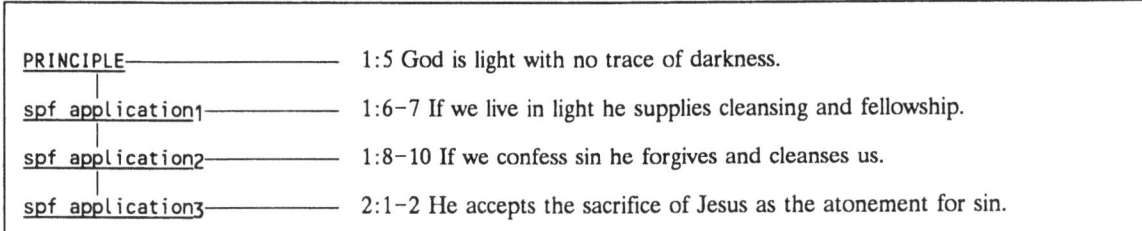

The relational structure shown in our own display of 1:5-2:2 is the preferred one. It should be noted again that 1:5 is the *basis* of all of 1:5-2:27, though it is closely tied with 1:6-2:2 as well. The "Boundaries and Coherence" section under 1:5-2:27 shows that the unit is dealing with the matter of sin being contrary to God's nature.

NOTES

1:5 The notes on v. 5 are under the display on p. 22.

1:6a we claim The meaning is not 'we collectively claim', but rather 'any one of us hypothetically claims'.

behave *in a morally impure manner which is like living* **in** *evil* **darkness** The author continues to use the 'darkness' metaphor introduced in 1:5b and with the same significance, namely sinfulness. The figurative use of 'walk' here refers to every aspect of behavior.

1:6b according to *God's* **true message** The noun τὴν ἀλήθειαν 'the truth' is, semantically, an abstraction. Since it is a noun, commentators tend to assign it a "thing" referent, such as Christ himself, principles of thought and action, and virtues. Throughout John's Epistles it is used with two primary senses: (1) the true Christian teaching, that is, the true message, or (2) actions consonant with the true message. In the context (cf. 1:5a), the first of these senses is appropriate.

1:7a *behave in a morally pure manner as God behaves in a morally pure manner, which is like* **living in the light as God is in the light** The 'light' metaphor introduced in 1:5b is continued here, with the same significance, namely pure moral character. The 'walk' metaphor, signifying behavior, is also continued.

1:7b joined together on common ground There is an ambiguity here as to whether the communality is between one believer and another or between a believer and God. Most commentators take it to be the latter. By not specifying the referent and by focusing on 'common ground', which better expresses the meaning here, we have left it ambiguous.

1:7c acquits us of *the guilt of* all our sin More literally this is 'cleanses us from all unrighteousness'. There are problems in expressing this since almost any possible rendering is metaphorical ('cleanse', 'free', 'acquit'). The image is 'to clean something that is dirty', while the referent is 'evil behavior'; the point of similarity is 'to rid a person of consequences'. In English this seems to be most adequately expressed by 'acquit'. In the Jewish view of sinning, when a person sinned he became unfit for religious events and society and needed to be made fit by ceremonial cleansing. The unfitness was viewed as dirtiness, filthiness, which had to be cleansed. In modern Western society we understand this better with a court-of-justice metaphor: When a person violates another person's rights, he is guilty of doing what is wrong and must be acquitted to be restored to a good social position. The act of acquittal frees the alleged offender from guilt. This judicial expression has been chosen for the display since it is easily understood. However, not all commentators see this cleansing as only canceling guilt; rather, some say, it includes changing the person's character and relieving the conscience so that the person may be prepared for God's service. Further, they primarily understand 'sin' as a *principle* (e.g., 'fallen nature') or *power*, not a reference to specific acts of sinning. By personifying 'sin' and using it as a noun, sinning can be viewed in this way. But 'sin' in semantic theory is an event and, as such, if taken as a principle, would be rendered 'all humans sin according to their nature'. If taken as a power, it would be rendered 'all humans sin because they are unable to resist'. But 'cleansing' with its many extended meanings does not collocate with either of these. The rendering in the display accounts for the text better than these other alternatives (see Louw and Nida 88.310).

dying and shedding his **blood** BAGD (p. 23*a*:2.b) gives the meaning of 'blood' here as "Blood and life as an expiatory sacrifice ... Esp. of the blood of Jesus as a means of expiation."

1:7d *Therefore, we should behave according to God's pure moral nature* Here is what we consider the first occurrence of a mitigated exhortation in this Epistle (see the discussion about mitigation in the Introduction under "Longacre's Contribution"). It is expressed by a conditional clause that presents a choice of actions (1:7a), followed by an independent clause that states the desired value (1:7b–c) achievable only by making the correct choice (Longacre, p. 7). (Although 1:6a could be taken as this kind of exhortation based on the same criterion, we prefer not to take it this way. The clause 'if we claim ...' probably harks back to what false teachers were claiming, and the choice presented in the 6b independent clause would be a negative value.) Here in 1:7a John is suggesting to his readers that they do something that is definitely of value to them. He gives them a positive choice. The import is: I advise that we behave according to God's moral nature, since if we do so, we will then be joined together on that shared basis, and when we fail to do so, the blood of his Son, Jesus, frees us from all guilt.

1:8a do not behave sinfully More literally this is 'not have sin'. There is some division of opinion as to whether this refers to the act of sinning or to the characteristic principle of sinning, though it is difficult to know what the commentators mean by the latter, which is very abstract. (It could be referring to the natural human tendency to do evil.) A rendering based on this second interpretation would be 'If we claim that we do not tend to do evil'.

1:8b we ... are refusing to behave according to *God's* true message Here ἡ ἀλήθεια οὐκ ἔστιν ἐν ἡμῖν 'the truth is not in us' continues the concept of participating in a common characteristic, that is, not sharing the divine characteristic of truthfulness as expressed in the message given by the apostles.

1:9a if we confess The question arises, To whom are we to confess? Commentators all agree that we must confess to God, but some say that we must confess to men as well.

1:9b since Here ἵνα 'as a result' might seem to suggest a reason-RESULT relationship. However, 9b does not give the reason why 9c is true, but rather it substantiates the claim of 9c. Therefore, the relationship is labeled grounds-CONCLUSION.

***God* will do what he says he will do and what is perfectly right** More literally this is 'God is faithful (πιστός) and just (δίκαιος)'. Semantically, the first adjective expresses the attribute of an event, 'to act faithfully' and requires an actor, 'someone', and an effect, 'that God will do what he says he will do'. The abstraction focuses on the effect, and this is supplied in the proposition. The second adjective, 'just', is an abstraction of an event, which is supplied in the proposition as 'do what is perfectly right'.

1:9c frees us from *the guilt of* all our sins See the note on 1:7c.

1:9d *Therefore we should confess to God that we have behaved sinfully* We consider this the second occurrence of a mitigated exhortation in the Epistle. See the note on 1:7d.

1:10 There is a question whether v. 10 goes with what precedes it or what follows. If there is a paragraph break between 2:2 and 2:3, as we hold, then the 1:5–2:2 unit consists of three *APPEALS* each introduced by a contrasting *negative motivational basis* beginning with the words ἐὰν εἴπωμεν 'if we say'. Then in each case the statement of the wrong assumption is followed by the corrective mitigated *APPEAL*. In keeping with this pattern, 1:10 clearly goes with what follows.

If, however, the paragraph break were taken to be between 1:10 and 2:1, then v. 10 would dangle. It has no real function with what precedes except as suggested by some commentaries that it is a restatement of 1:8 (even though it is a very different statement).

1:10b we talk as though God lies This is a strong assertion that God does not lie. In many languages there is a great difference between 'we say that God lies' (implying that God could lie) and 'we talk as though God lies' (contrary to fact, implying that God does not lie and that we are in the wrong if we say he does).

repudiate The literal gloss is 'is not in us', meaning that God's message has been allowed no influence or control over the people who make this claim of sinlessness.

what he says *which is that we are sinful* The Greek is ὁ λόγος αὐτοῦ 'his word', which grammatically is a noun phrase, but semantically is an event that requires a communiqué: hence 'that we are sinful'. It is interesting to note the close lexical and grammatical parallel between ἡ ἀλήθεια οὐκ ἔστιν ἐν ἡμῖν 'the truth is not in us' in 1:8b and ὁ λόγος αὐτοῦ οὐκ ἔστιν ἐν ἡμῖν 'his word is not in us' in 1:10b. However, the former means to refuse to behave according to God's true message; the latter means to refuse to accept that he says that we are sinful. The difference arises from what is being refused—the message about the true way of living or the message that people do sin.

2:1–2 The 2:1c–2c unit is joined to the 2:1a–b main clause by καί 'and'. This conjunction simply means that there is a close semantic relationship with what precedes without specifying what the relationship is. The relationship of the 1c–2c unit to what precedes seems to be that of a positive value *basis* for the 1b *APPEAL*. This explanation seems satisfactory enough, since neither the conjoining 'and' nor the contrast-HEAD 'but' seems logical here, nor is it an amplification. (Having someone who speaks on our behalf does not amplify 'you should not sin'.)

The καί 'and' at the beginning of v. 2, however, joins v. 2 to 1c–d in an amplification relationship—it is giving further information as to how Christ can speak on our behalf.

2:1a this Commentators are divided as to whether ταῦτα 'this' refers to the preceding or the following context. However, in accord with the decision made in 1:4a and the discussion there, we take it to refer to the preceding context, that is, 1:6–9.

to say We take ἵνα 'that, in order that' as introducing the prominent and nuclear CONTENT in an orienter-CONTENT relationship. The primary function of ἵνα here is not to introduce a purpose clause; rather, it is an implied request, equivalent to an imperative. (Similar constructions occur in 1:4 and 5:13, but in 5:13 ἵνα 'in order that' *does* introduce a purposive clause.)

2:1b you should not sin The aorist prohibition ἵνα μὴ ἁμάρτητε 'that you not sin' suggests a definite act of sin indicating the possibility of a behavioral lapse because of human frailty rather than a set attitude of disobedience.

2:1d One who speaks to the Father on our behalf The word παράκλητος 'advocate' means a person who intercedes, pleads, gives evidence, or defends a friend in court. Although this is a noun, its main reference is to an event, requiring that a benefactor on our behalf be supplied.

For 'Father', see the note on 1:2c.

Christ Most commentaries take 'Christ' here to mean 'the Messiah'. It is not just a personal name.

2:2a-b *Further,* **Jesus Christ voluntarily sacrificed** *his own life,* **so that as a result** *God is able to forgive* **our sins** The primary reference of the noun ἱλασμός 'propitiation/expiation' is an event. It refers to someone's doing something (usually involving a sacrifice) that makes it possible for the offended party to forgive the offender: 'to propitiate' is to appease the anger of the offended person by doing or giving something (possibly a sacrifice), and 'to expiate' is to remove by some means (usually a sacrifice) the cause for the offense.

Whether 'propitiate' or 'expiate' is chosen, the central concept is that *something is done (usually the offering of a sacrifice) making it possible to forgive.*

The word περί 'concerning' occurs three times in v. 2: the 'propitiation is *concerning* sin'. That the goal of the propitiating action is forgiving sin is indicated by 'concerning'.

2:2c *He is able to forgive* **not only our sins, but the sins of humankind everywhere** The word κόσμος 'world' here is a synecdoche for people who live in the world. It should be noted that throughout the Epistle 'world' is used with one or another of five distinct meanings: (1) 'humankind' or 'people as a whole'; (2) 'godless people' or 'unbelievers'; (3) 'the evil of human society living in opposition to God' ('world spirit' in the Glossary); (4) 'evil human desires'; and (5) 'the goods that support human physical life'. (The second, third, and fourth meanings have the concept of evil in common.) In the immediate context of 2:2 the reference is to the first of these meanings, humankind everywhere, specifically all who believe in Christ Jesus.

A theological argument continues as to whether the 'propitiation concerning the whole world' *actually* occurred or *potentially* occurred. Commentaries are divided on this matter. Whichever position is taken, the text means that Christ's dying is *adequate* for everyone's sins.

BOUNDARIES AND COHERENCE

The opening boundary is marked by the first of a series of wrong assumptions or teachings introduced by ἐὰν εἴπωμεν 'if we say'. See the discussion of unit 1:5 for further evidence.

The final boundary is marked by a change of subject from 'cleansing from sin' in 1:5-2:2 to 'keeping his commands' in 2:3. From this point there are no more ἐὰν εἴπωμεν 'if we say' orienters but rather a series of ἐν τούτῳ γινώσκομεν ὅτι 'by this we know that'. The topic switches from resolving the sin problem to the need for confidence.

The whole 1:5-2:2 unit deals with the problem of how to rid ourselves of the guilt of sin in order to participate in God's nature. The false assumptions are shown to be lies because they do not really deal with the issues, whereas the exhortations give true answers to the problems of sin and guilt.

The 2:1-2 unit serves as a tie between 1:5-2:2 and 2:3-11. It could be viewed as belonging with either what precedes or what follows. We take it to belong with what precedes for several reasons:

1. The vocative τεκνία μου 'my children' in 2:1 serves to introduce a reassurance after a strong denunciation (1:10) rather than to indicate a boundary. Such use of vocatives to introduce encouragement is a characteristic feature of the letter (e.g., 2:12-13; 4:4).
2. The occurrence of καὶ ἐάν 'and if' (2:1b) introduces the last of a series of six conditional clauses, supporting the idea of a unit.
3. The general statement in 2:2 of God's provision for dealing with sin functions to close off this discussion of sin.

The central concept of this unit is sin, how it affects man and how God deals with it. Five times the word ἁμαρτία 'sin' occurs explicitly; twice the idea is referred to under the figure of darkness; and once it is referred to as lying. God has given the message (1:5a); he provides a pure character like his own and he provides cleansing (1:7b); he forgives and cleanses (1:9c); and in Christ he gives an advocate (2:1) and the atonement (2:2). He is pure light (1:5b), faithful and just (1:9b). Jesus Christ is the righteous advocate (2:1) and the sufficient sacrifice (2:2). All these statements present the positive elements of God's provision for sin.

The unit is also held together by three *APPEALS* each introduced by a contrasting wrong assumption. Each *APPEAL* is introduced by the form ἐὰν εἴπωμεν 'if we say', and then the statement of the wrong assumption is followed by the corrective mitigated *APPEAL*.

An alternate final boundary would be between 1:10 and 2:1. The majority of commentators and versions place it there. The pros and cons of this are discussed under the 1:5-2:27 unit (see "Boundaries and Coherence" there).

PROMINENCE AND THEME

The three coordinate *APPEALS* in this unit are naturally prominent. The third one ἵνα μὴ ἁμάρτητε 'that you not sin' is the most prominent of the three because of the orienter, which contains a vocative and γράφω 'I write'. All three *APPEALS* are mitigated. The first two are mitigated by the conditional construction that precedes them. The third is mitigated by its being a CONTENT construction introduced by ἵνα 'that'. (The third one is slightly less mitigated than the first two.)

The theme statement is taken from the three *APPEALS* (summarized as 'let us be morally pure') together with the *basis* for each of them (summarized as 'God is able to forgive our sins because Jesus died to free us from the guilt of all our sins').

> **SECTION CONSTITUENT 2:3-11** (Hortatory Sub-Section: Specific appeal₂ of 1:5-2:27)
> *Theme: Since God is morally pure, we ought to behave just as Christ behaved, especially to love our Christian brothers, in order that we can be assured that we know God experientially.*

MACROSTRUCTURE	CONTENTS
GENERIC APPEAL	2:3-6 We ought to behave as Christ behaved, obeying what God commands us to do, since we would then love God in the manner in which he loves us.
SPECIFIC APPEAL	2:7-11 One ought to love his Christian brother in order to continue behaving according to God's morally pure nature.

INTENT AND MACROSTRUCTURE

In the 2:3-11 unit John uses two mitigated appeals with the intent of affecting the readers' actions. The internal structure of the unit is generic-specific: a *GENERIC APPEAL* (2:3-6) and a *SPECIFIC APPEAL* (2:7-11).

BOUNDARIES AND COHERENCE

The initial boundary has been discussed under unit 1:5-2:2. The final boundary is clearly marked by a series of performatives, γράφω ὑμῖν 'I am writing to you' (2:12), and vocatives initiating a new unit.

The 2:3-11 unit shows lexical coherence in the frequent use of ἐντολή 'command', which occurs six times (2:3-4, 7-8)—the discussion centers on the importance of obeying God's command. In the first appeal (2:3-6) the plural form is used because the admonition is general, but in the second the subject is narrowed to the specific command to love. Thus, to obey is seen as a general test of experiential knowledge of God (2:3-6), which is then specified as love of the Christian brother (2:7-11).

Other recurrent lexical items are:

1. The antonyms σκοτία 'darkness' (five times, in 2:8, 9, 11) and φῶς 'light' (three times, in 2:8, 9, 10).
2. The verb γινώσκω 'know' (four times, in 2:3, 4, 5).
3. The noun ἀλήθεια 'truth' (four times, in 2:4, 5, 8).
4. The verb ἀγαπάω 'love' (three times, in 2:5, 7, 10).
5. The verbs μένω 'remain' (twice, in 2:6 and 10) and περιπατέω 'behave' (twice, in 2:6 and 11), both being in the semantic domain of behavior.

PROMINENCE AND THEME

The following prominence features are seen in the first paragraph of this unit (2:3-6):

1. Repetition of the word γινώσκω 'know' (four times).
2. Forefronting of the deictic ἐν τούτῳ 'by this' (four times).
3. The emphasis word ἀληθῶς 'really' in v. 5.

These features give prominence to the assurance of knowing God experientially.

In the second paragraph (2:7-11) the relationship of love between fellow believers ('loving our Christian brothers') is specifically called 'obeying his commands' (2:3). The emphatic ending (2:11) points out the negative results of failure to obey God's command. In the surface structure of this paragraph the negative aspect occurs more frequently than the positive, and the final dark picture is strongly contrastive.

Generally, wherever there is one generic and one specific role in a relation, the specific unit is the prominent one. Here, however, since there is much marked prominence in the generic unit, we consider the *GENERIC APPEAL* (2:3-6) equally prominent with the naturally prominent *SPECIFIC APPEAL* (2:7-11). The theme statement therefore includes both *APPEALS* (from 2:6 and 2:10) as well as the HEAD proposition of the 1:5 higher-level *basis* ('God is morally pure') and the 2:3a purpose clause 'that we can be assured that we know God experientially' (a motif throughout this unit).

> **SUB-SECTION CONSTITUENT 2:3-6 (Hortatory Paragraph: Generic appeal of 2:3-11)**
> *Theme: We ought to behave as Christ behaved, obeying what God commands us to do, since we would then love God in the manner in which he loves us.*

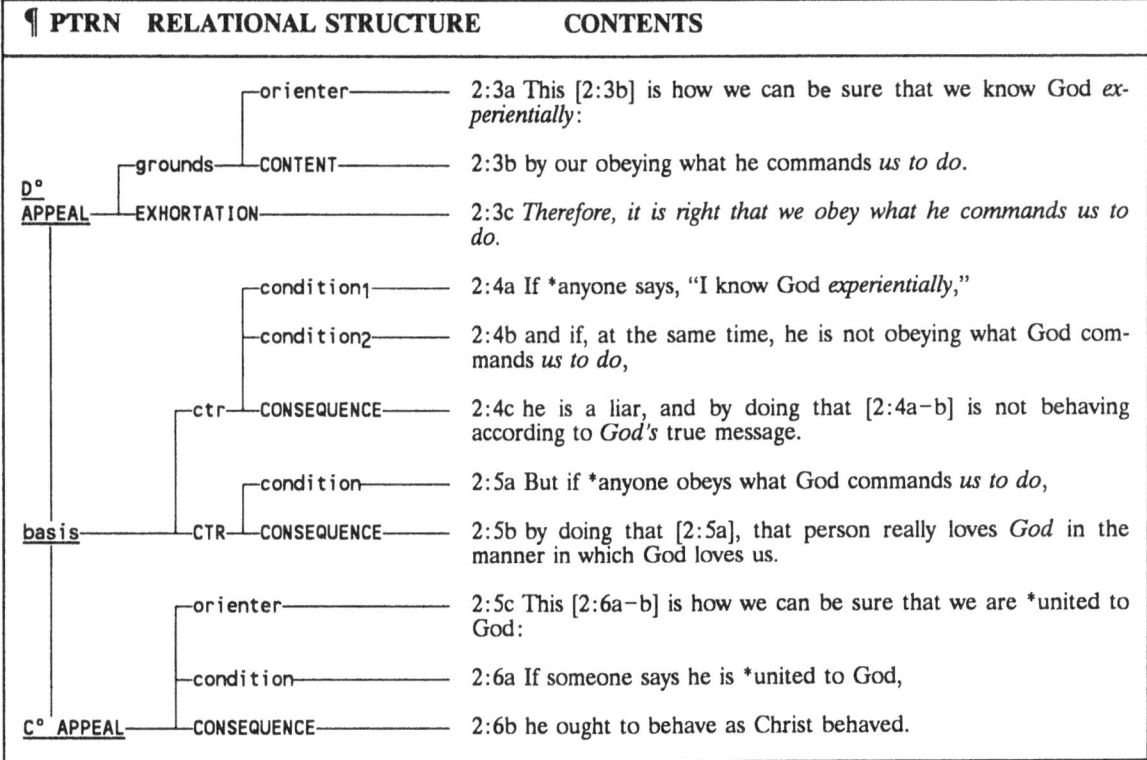

INTENT AND PARAGRAPH PATTERN

John's intent here is to affect the actions of the readers, admonishing them to behave just as Jesus behaved by obeying what God commanded. He wants to make certain that all the readers will continue behaving correctly.

The 2:3-6 paragraph consists of three propositional clusters: two nuclear (2:3 and 2:5c-6) and one satellitic (2:4a-5b). The communication relationship between these units is two hortatory units supported by an intervening grounds unit. Since the primary intent is to affect the behavior, this has been analyzed as a causal hortatory paragraph with the principal constituents being + APPEAL + basis + APPEAL. The first of the appeals is a D° APPEAL and the second a C° APPEAL; both are mitigated in form (see the discussion of mitigated appeals on p. 4). It is interesting that in the 2:3-6 paragraph both second- and third-degree mitigations are used, the most mitigated in v. 3 and a lesser degree in v. 6.

The paragraph consists of a D° APPEAL, a *basis*, and a C° APPEAL similar to the first. The difference in the prominence or forcefulness between the first and second appeal is that the first is more mitigated, therefore less prominent.

If one were to reject the analysis that v. 3 is a mitigated appeal, then the alternative is that 2:3-5b is an embedded expository *basis* supporting the APPEAL of 2:5c-6. The structure of the embedded expository paragraph would be: *evidence* (2:3), the first INFERENCE (2:4), and the second INFERENCE (2:5a-b).

NOTES

2:3a This The question here is whether ἐν τούτῳ 'by this' refers to the preceding or following linguistic context. The phrase occurs fourteen times in 1 John (2:3, 4, 5, 5; 3:10, 16, 19, 24; 4:2, 9, 10, 13, 17; 5:2), and in ten of these occurrences (all except 2:4, 2:5, 4:10 and 4:17) it is immediately followed by a cognitive-type verb ('know' or 'be manifest') with the content indicated by a noun phrase or a verb phrase preceded by ὅτι. In 2:4, 2:5, 4:10, and 4:17 ἐν τούτῳ is immediately followed by a verb that expresses a state or phase, as in all fourteen occurrences. BAGD (p. 597a) says that the construction refers "to what follows, esp. before clauses that express a statement, purpose, result, or condition." Among the critical commentators there is near unanimity that the referent *is* cataphoric in all except 2:4, 2:5, 3:19 and 4:17 (i.e., in ten of the fourteen occurrences). We, therefore, take the position that here in 2:3a ἐν τούτῳ has its referent in the following context. (But why is there such division of opinion regarding 3:19, 4:17, and 5:2, when grammatically there does not seem to be any justification? Each of these exceptional cases will be discussed where they occur.)

we can be sure Verse 3 is a mitigated exhortation that grammatically is expressed by a conditional clause (2:3b) attached to an independent clause that states something of value to both the author and the hearer (2:3a): it is of great value that believers can be certain of their relationship with God. Therefore, the words 'by this we know' are not simply to understand or acknowledge but to be certain or assured.

we know God *experientially* The verb γινώσκω 'know' is used with two different meanings in this Epistle. The first indicates having evidence of a fact or situation. The second, which is of special significance in the development of the theme of 1 John, refers to knowing experientially (as in 2:5c where it expresses union with God). Louw and Nida (27.18) define this meaning as "to learn to know a person through direct personal experience, implying a continuity of relationship."

This is the first occurrence in the Epistle of the verb 'know'. A polemic significance is noted by commentators in the choice of this word, because those whose views we assume are being refuted boasted of their "special knowledge." Here the expression for assurance (3:19-24, 4:13) is in opposition to supposed special knowledge.

2:3b by our obeying The relationship between 3b and 3a is orienter-CONTENT. This relationship is normally shown in the Greek by ὅτι 'that is' when preceded by ἐν τούτῳ 'by this means'. Why then did John use ἐάν 'if'? It is our view that he purposely used ἐάν in order to signal a mitigated appeal. According to Blass and Debrunner (202.394) ἐάν 'if' is used here rather than ἵνα 'in order that' or ὅτι 'that is' because the truth of the clause is only assumed, but this still does not justify its use after ἐν τούτῳ 'by this'. Hence a strong case can be made for interpreting this conditional construction as a mitigated exhortation.

he It is difficult to determine the referent of αὐτός 'he', which occurs twice in v. 3. There are three possibilities: God, Christ, or both without distinction. The commentaries are equally divided between the first two options, but the versions seem to favor 'God' as the referent. Apparently, in John's thinking there is no sharp distinction between God and Christ, because he frequently slips from one to the other referent in the use of pronouns. Possibly, this could be attributed to the Jewish tendency to use pronouns and passive constructions to avoid making direct reference to God. Any of the options mentioned here are adequate, but we have chosen 'God' as the referent of 'he'.

2:3c *Therefore, it is right that you obey what he commands us to do* This is another instance of John's use of a mitigated exhortation. John is again suggesting that the readers do something to achieve something of positive value. In 1:7d a similar mismatching of the grammar and semantics exists, a result of the effect of the author's intent (see the note on 1:7d).

2:4c by doing that Here the phrase ἐν τούτῳ 'by that' refers back to the preceding context, since it is not followed by ὅτι introducing a noun or verb phrase. See the note on 2:3a.

God's true message See the note on 1:6b.

2:5a what God commands *us to do* Although λόγον 'message' is a noun, it presupposes a communication event semantically. When expressed as an event, it requires the speaker 'he/God', an addressee 'us', and the communiqué 'we should do' (here expressed indirectly as the complement of 'command').

2:5b by doing that [2:5a] See the notes on 2:3a and 2:4c.

that person really loves *God* in the manner in which God loves us The meaning of this Greek clause is complex because of the mismatching between the parts of speech and the semantic functions of the concepts involved. The verb τελειόω 'be fully developed' is a process-type event. A process-type event normally involves a thing or an event that becomes something different. Here the event that becomes different depends entirely on how the genitive 'love of God' is interpreted. If it is a subjective genitive, then the meaning is 'God loves someone completely (when he keeps God's Word)'. If it is an objective genitive, then the meaning is 'we love God perfectly (when . . .)'. If the inceptive genitive (source or model) is chosen, then the meaning is either (1) 'we love other people in the manner that God loves us' or (2) 'we love God in the manner that he loves us when . . . '. Any of these could fit the context, but not with equal appropriateness. If it were to be taken as a subjective genitive, God's love for us would seem to have a conditional nature. The first of these meanings ('we love other people in the manner that God loves us') would be forced since there is no mention up to this point of our loving others (but this is not inappropriate since 'our loving others' is introduced in the following paragraph). The most acceptable interpretation is that this is an objective genitive or an inceptive genitive of the second type. We have chosen the latter: 'we love God in the manner that he loves us'.

It is *God's* manner of loving, perfect love, that is referred to here. The difference between divine love and natural human love must be shown. Behavior governed by that manner of loving should be characteristic of the believer. Even though it cannot be perfect, it can be of the same manner. In 4:12, as here, it is linked with the concept of union with God, indicating that God is the source of the loving behavior.

2:5c This [2:6a–b] The phrase ἐν τούτῳ 'by this' is taken to mean 'this is how'. It looks forward to v. 6 and serves as the orienter for the *APPEAL* (see the note on 2:3a.)

we can be sure See the note on 2:3b.

God Commentators are equally divided as to whether the pronoun refers to God or to Christ.

2:6b Christ Throughout this Epistle ἐκεῖνος 'that one (masc)' refers specifically to Jesus Christ.

BOUNDARIES AND COHERENCE

The initial boundary of 2:3–6 has already been discussed under 1:5–2:2. The final boundary of 2:3–6 is defined by (1) the inclusio structure of ἐν τούτῳ γινώσκομεν 'by this we know' in 2:3a and in 2:5c; (2) a change of topic from obedience as the test by which the believer may be assured of the experience of being united to God, which is the topic of 2:3–6, to the contents of what is to be obeyed, the topic of the next paragraph; (3) the vocative ἀγαπητοί 'dear friends' and the performative γράφω ὑμῖν 'I am writing you' (v. 7), which initiate the next unit.

The semantic coherence of this unit comes from the discussion of the subject of obeying God in order to know God. Here 'know' means experiential knowledge of God. In 2:6 we see that knowing God is ἐν αὐτῷ μένειν 'live in him', that is, in spiritual union with him.

Lexical coherence is seen in the use of terms related to the experience of knowing God: γινώσκω 'know' (various forms); τηρέω (ἐντολάς or λόγον) 'obey'; ἐν αὐτῷ εἶναι or μένειν 'live in him'; and ἐντολή 'command'.

The false assertion in 2:4 and its contrastive unit in 2:5 seem very similar to some of the contrasts found in 1:5–2:2. The grammatical structure is somewhat different, and we judge this to function more as a *basis* for the main *APPEAL* in 2:6b rather than as a mitigated *APPEAL* on its own. Certainly, 2:6b is not as highly mitigated as 1:9a because ὀφείλει 'he ought to' is stronger than a subordinate conditional grammatical construction.

Structural coherence in this paragraph is seen in that 2:3 is a highly mitigated *APPEAL*, followed by a *basis* in 2:4a–5b for the less mitigated *APPEAL* in 2:5c–6b. It could be stated this way: we should obey what he commands (*GENERIC APPEAL*), and since it is good to love God in the manner in which he loves us (*basis*), we ought to behave just as Christ behaved (*SPECIFIC APPEAL*).

PROMINENCE AND THEME

The C° *APPEAL* (2:5c–6) is the most prominent unit in 2:3–6 due to its natural prominence and the lesser mitigation of ὀφείλει 'he ought to'. Although the D° *APPEAL* (v. 3) also is prominent, it is less prominent than the C° *APPEAL* because of its greater mitigation. The theme statement is derived from the HEAD of the C° *APPEAL*, the HEAD of the D° *APPEAL*, and the *basis*.

SUB-SECTION CONSTITUENT 2:7-11 (Hortatory Paragraph: Specific appeal of 2:3-11)

Theme: One ought to love his Christian brother in order to continue behaving according to God's morally pure nature.

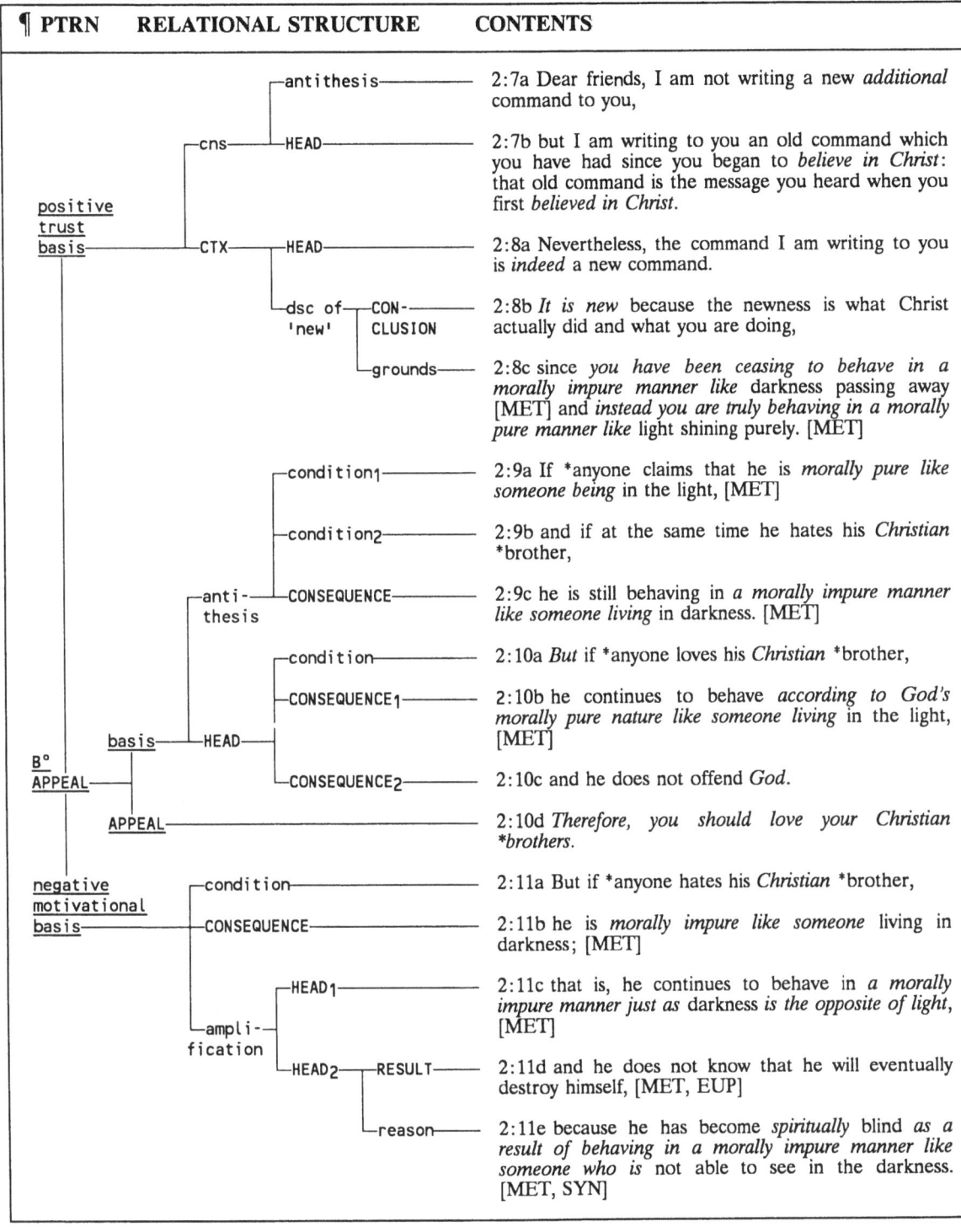

INTENT AND PARAGRAPH PATTERN

In this highly mitigated exhortation John's intent is to affect the actions of the readers so that they love their Christian brothers. The paragraph consists of three propositional clusters: a supportive unit (2:7-8) preceding the principal unit (2:9-10) and then another supportive unit (2:11). The relationship between these units is that of a single exhortational unit supported by two grounds units. Since the primary intent is to affect behavior, this is considered a causal hortatory paragraph, the constituents being + *basis* + APPEAL + *basis*.

Other analyses raise several problems. The author explicitly refers to a command that one must fulfill in order to live within the scope of Christian values. Besides, to take this unit as strictly expository would not lead the reader to any knowledge other than what he already knows, thus causing a nearly meaningless communication. If it were an expository paragraph, its structure would be: *evidence* (2:7-8), NEGATIVE INFERENCE$_1$ (2:9), POSITIVE INFERENCE (2:10), and NEGATIVE INFERENCE$_2$ (2:11). (Notice that the positive inference demands a hortatory implication.)

NOTES

2:7-8 command The word ἐντολή 'command' occurs four times in the first two verses of the 2:7-11 unit. This repetition makes 2:10d, which is the HEAD of the unit, prominent—it is the content of the command. Repeating a key word is a prominence device that John frequently uses. In introducing a subject he likes to repeat a key word where a pronoun might be expected. Other examples of this are found in 3:4-5 and 4:7-8.

2:7a I am not writing a new *additional* command The disclaimer here is probably a reference to the position of those who oppose John's doctrine. In 2 John 9 he warns against those who go too far and do not remain in the teaching of Christ. So he makes it very clear here that though the command is new in one sense, it is what his readers heard when they first believed. The word 'additional' is supplied to bring out this concept.

2:7b when you began to *believe in Christ* The implicit referent of ἀπ' ἀρχῆς 'from the beginning' is a temporal event. In 1:1a the referent was 'eternity past', in relation to God himself. Here the referent is the time that the readers first heard the message and believed in Christ, since the topic is the 'command that you had'.

2:8a Nevertheless The majority of commentators say that πάλιν 'yet/again' refers to the command in v. 7; only a few say that it refers to some other command. The minority position seems to be based on taking the 'new command' to be the new command that Jesus gave the disciples. However, our main concern with πάλιν 'yet/again' is not the referent but the relationship which it suggests between the propositions.

The relationships of 8a, b, and c are difficult, and the commentaries do not shed much light. First, the relative neuter pronoun ὅ 'which' ('newness' in 2:8b) can refer to the newness, the command, or the writing in 8a. (It cannot refer to the feminine 'love', which is not mentioned until v. 10.) If the Greek pronoun refers to the newness of the command, its function is to describe how it is new. (This is the interpretation chosen in this analysis.) If it refers to the command, its function is to identify which command. This is not possible since it does not agree with the feminine 'command', nor is the statement specific enough to identify it as the v. 10 command to love. If the pronoun refers to the writing, its function would be to justify why John is writing a new command. This would be a very unusual relative pronoun function.

***indeed* a new command** The command to love each other is new in that its source is Jesus' own demonstration to his disciples of how to love other people the way God intended. This is what the recipients of John's letter were also doing. (Speculation apart from the context here concerning any other sense in which the command might be new should be held with some skepticism.) The command to love each other is so contrary to human nature and cultures that when Jesus said this to the disciples, he did so with a new authority even though it is built on OT principles. The purpose of this love is that those who do not believe might know that we are his followers. The command is also new (i.e., renewed) whenever the Christian practices loving his Christian brother continually.

2:8b *It is new* **because the newness** See the note on 2:8a regarding the referent of the relative pronoun ὅ 'that'. We have chosen 'new' as the referent, since this best accounts for the usual function of the relative pronoun.

what Christ actually did and what you are doing This rendering of ὅ ἐστιν ἀληθὲς ἐν αὐτῷ καὶ ἐν ὑμῖν 'which is true in him and in you(pl)' is determined by the preceding context. The discussion is about the 'new command' together with the implication that a command coming from Christ must be obeyed. The command becomes 'true' in a person when he obeys or does what has been commanded. Therefore, the command is new because it has become true in both Christ and the believer; in other words, Christ obeyed the command and the believers are presently obeying it.

2:8c-9a *ceasing to behave in a morally impure manner like* **darkness ... and** *instead ... behaving in a morally pure manner like* **light shining purely** The Docetists of the period claimed "light," enlightenment. John's use of the term here may be polemic. John returns to the light and darkness metaphors with the same implicature introduced in 1:5b.

Particularly difficult to unravel and understand is 'the darkness is passing and the true light is already shining', since it involves two metaphors with their extensions. (The metaphors of 'light' and 'darkness' have already been discussed in the note on 1:5b.) If we were to render it 'evil conduct is passing and moral purity is already shining', it would not be much help. Literal light is not in view, of course: the reference is to consistent Christian conduct, moral purity, or the body of Christian teaching. Since a contrast between light and darkness (i.e., evil) is intended, and since the latter refers to an event ('a person does evil'), we interpret 'true light' as referring to Christian conduct.

In 2:8b it has already been affirmed that consistent Christian conduct is exemplified both in Jesus and the believers. Thus, the contrast between 'passing' and 'already shining' refers to the contrast in conduct between those who do not believe and those who do: 'already shining' refers to the conduct of Jesus and believers which replaces evil conduct in those who are now believers just as light dispels darkness.

2:9b *Christian* **brother** Some commentators have confused the term ἀδελφός 'brother' with πλησίον 'neighbor' in Luke 10:36, but they are not synonymous. In this Epistle John puts much stress on the family relationship with God as Father and the fellow believers as brothers and sisters in the family. Since the author says that God is love (4:8), as well as light, it is natural for him to speak of the relationship of brotherhood, which has reference to the subject of the family of God, which is discussed next.

2:10a-d *But if anyone ... Therefore, you should love your Christian brothers* Verse 10 is another instance of John's use of a mitigated exhortation (see "Intent and Paragraph Pattern" under 2:3-6). Here John is again suggesting that the readers do something to achieve something of positive value. Verse 9, on the other hand, which seems to echo what false teachers do (stated in 1:6), is not considered to be a mitigated exhortation. In 1:7d the grammar and semantics have a similar mismatching, a result of the effect of the author's intent (see the note on 1:7d).

There is a chiastic structure here, which would further suggest that the above analysis is correct:

A ὁ ... τὸν ἀδελφὸν αὐτοῦ μισῶν 'the one who hates his brother' (v. 9)
   B ὁ ἀγαπῶν τὸν ἀδελφὸν αὐτοῦ 'the one who loves his brother' (v. 10)
A' ὁ δὲ μισῶν τὸν ἀδελφὸν αὐτοῦ 'but the one who hates his brother' (v. 11)

Frequently, the middle member of a chiastic structure is prominent. Here the B member also entails the positive element. This focus indicates that 'loving one's brother' is certainly the behavior that John desires of his readers.

2:10b continues to behave Here μένω 'remain' means to continue behaving according to a stated characteristic (see 'joined together' in the Glossary).

2:10c does not offend *God* The Greek is σκάνδαλον 'cause of offense'. Commentators differ as to who it is that would not be offended. Behaving with brotherly love seems to imply that it is a *brother* who would not be offended, that is, caused to stumble. However, Marshall points out the following reasons for understanding *God* as the one who would not be offended (it is the man who walks in the light who does not stumble and cause offense against God):

1. In this context the author is focusing on the Christian's right relationship with God through proper conduct made possible by God.
2. The subject matter is the assurance of the believer, and the contrast (2:11) is the personal fate of the one who hates his brother and is lost in darkness.
3. There is a similar passage in John 11:9 in which the one who walks in the light does not stumble.
4. Stählin (in Kittel and Friedrich, vol. 7, p. 345) says, "In the N.T. as in the O.T. what is at issue in σκάνδαλον [offense] is the relation to God ... an obstacle in coming to faith and a cause of going astray in it." Further on (pp. 356–57), he says: "The Christian who does not love is in darkness ... and susceptible to σκάνδαλον. ... Love and faith are closely related here, for the man who abides in love there is no obstacle on the way of faith."

Therefore, our interpretation is: the man who walks in the light does not stumble and cause offense against God.

2:11b *morally impure like someone* **living in darkness** Darkness must be interpreted as moral darkness, sin. The 1:5–2:2 unit, which deals primarily with sin, has shown sin to be the barrier to fellowship with God and his people. It morally blinds the eyes (John 9:41, 2 Cor. 4:4). Metaphorically speaking, sin is the state of being in darkness.

2:11c *a morally impure manner just as* **darkness** Once again the metaphor introduced in 1:5b is used: 'darkness' signifies impure moral character.

2:11d will eventually destroy himself This is an extension of the walking in darkness metaphor. It could mean 'he does not know what he is doing'. However, from the Greek (καὶ οὐκ οἶδεν ποῦ ὑπάγει 'he does not know to where he is going away') it seems clear that it is his final destination that he does not know. It is not a matter of aimlessly groping about or not knowing what he is doing. The euphemism ποῦ ὑπάγει 'to where he is going away' is similar to euphemisms used elsewhere in the NT referring to eternal destruction as in Acts 1:25, which speaks of Judas going to his own place. We have spelled it out as 'destruction'. Very few commentators point out the idea of destination. Westcott comments that the verb does not refer so much to the destination as to leaving the present scene. But BAGD (837a:3) calls attention to its use concerning Jesus' going to the Father and to another occurrence of it concerning a person going to his death. Hoon (2:11) is one who sees the idea of destiny: "He does not know the inevitable disaster to which his walk leads." Bloomfield (p. 539) says the one who hated his brother was "habitually and continually in darkness, not knowing whither he went (i.e. not aware of the danger that beset his path), and was, therefore, likely ... to stumble often and grievously." Brown (1982) says: "The author shifts from stumbling to not knowing one's direction in order to hint at the loss." Even though most commentators leave the destination indefinite, ποῦ in an indirect question does indicate direction. Therefore, to make the proposition concrete we have spelled out the destination. (Destruction may be equated with spiritual death, which is separation from God.)

2:11e he has become *spiritually* **blind** *as a result of behaving in a morally impure manner like someone who is* **not able to see in the darkness** In this extended figure of speech, ὀφθαλμοὺς αὐτοῦ 'his eyes' is a synecdoche standing for the total person and signifies understanding; σκοτία 'darkness' is again used metaphorically and signifies impure moral character, sinfulness; ἐτύφλωσεν 'has blinded' is an extension of the 'darkness' metaphor and means 'cause not to know' or 'be unaware'.

BOUNDARIES AND COHERENCE

The boundaries of this unit have already been discussed (under 2:3–6 for the initial boundary and 2:3–11 for the final boundary).

Semantic coherence is seen in the introduction and discussion of a new subject, but one moving along a line related to that of 2:3–6. There, obedience is a test for the believer; here, the test of love is introduced because love is the specific commandment to be obeyed. It is discussed in terms of its relationship to God as light (presented in 1:5). The contrast between the figures of light and darkness also gives coherence within 1:5–2:27. In making the contrast the author has used many negatives, particularly in v. 11. Coherence is also demonstrated by the relational structure, which consists of a *trust basis* (2:7–8), a nuclear APPEAL (2:9–10), and then a *motivational basis* (2:11). Both *bases* support the APPEAL.

PROMINENCE AND THEME

The central subject here is the mitigated exhortation to love one's brother. It is highlighted in the contrast between φῶς 'light' and σκοτία 'darkness'. The direct statement (2:10) of the importance of loving one's Christian brother is made prominent by being the positive statement in contrast to the negative statements which precede and follow it.

The vocative, the words γράφω 'I write', and the v. 7 negation—that it is not a new commandment—are used to introduce a touchy subject. Prominence is thereby given not to the unit in which they occur but to the one it supports, namely the central APPEAL. The author is carefully expressing his trust in his hearers. He reassures them that he knows that they already know and are obeying (8b) the command to love their brother as he now leads up to the advisability of obeying this command.

Since both natural and marked prominence highlight the APPEAL unit, the theme statement is derived from the HEAD proposition of the APPEAL including the HEAD of its *basis* (2:10b).

SECTION CONSTITUENT 2:12–25 (Hortatory Sub-Section: Specific appeal₃ of 1:5–2:27)
Theme: Do not love the evil manner in which other people live in the world, but continue to behave according to God's true message, since you have come to know God.

MACROSTRUCTURE	CONTENTS
TRUST BASIS	2:12–14 I am writing all these matters to you because I know that God has forgiven your sins and because you have come to know the Father and Christ, who has always existed, and because you have overcome the evil one.
NEG APPEAL	2:15–17 Do not esteem the evil manner in which other people live in the world, since you want to exist forever.
POS APPEAL	2:18–25 You know that it is the final period of this age when liars deny that Jesus is God's anointed one. But you have the power of God's Spirit and you know what is true and what is false. Therefore continue to behave according to the true message that you heard when you began to believe in Christ, in order that you may continue to live united both to God's Son and to the Father.

INTENT AND MACROSTRUCTURE

In view of the elaborate TRUST BASIS in 2:12–14, the 2:12–25 sub-section is considered a climax in this part of the discourse. Up to this point the present tense of γράφω 'I write' has been used, but from here on (beginning at 2:14a) the past tense is used. There is also a concentration of vocatives. The discourse comes to a climax with a negative content in the prohibition μὴ ἀγαπᾶτε 'do not love' (2:15a). The negative content at 2:22a is also climactic, the emotional emphasis of the denunciation of the antichrist spirit being highlighted by a rhetorical question. After the 2:15a warning command comes the encouragement of 2:23 and the prominent positive APPEAL of 2:24–25.

BOUNDARIES AND COHERENCE

The initial boundary is discussed under unit 2:3–11. As to the closing boundary, the next unit is introduced in 2:26 with ταῦτα ἔγραψα ὑμῖν 'these things I have written to you', which marks the final boundary of 2:12–25. These words correspond to the performative of 2:12.

The 2:12–25 unit consists of a TRUST BASIS (2:12–14) supporting both the NEGATIVE APPEAL (2:15–17) and POSITIVE APPEAL (2:18–25). In 2:12–14 the author expresses his trust in the readers by reminding them of their relationship to God and what they have done through this relationship. This gives coherence based on the subject of victory over deceptive snares, which is introduced in the 2:12–14 paragraph by a double reference in 13d and 14h. The second and third paragraphs are warnings against immediate dangers: 2:15–17 warns against the illusion of the world spirit in general, and 2:18–25 against the specific antichrist spirit, said to be a lying spirit. There is also a link between 2:15–17 and 18–25 in that the world is described as παράγεται 'disappearing' (2:17) and attention is called to the ἐσχάτη ὥρα 'last hour' (2:18).

One element of semantic coherence is mention of sources. In 2:14g 'the word' is from God; in 2:20 and 27 'the anointing' is from him; in 24–25 the original 'message' and 'promise' have their source in God. The negative source is 'the world', contrasted in 2:16. Because the readers have experienced the love of the Father by knowing him (2:12–14), they are now warned against forsaking that love to embrace what does not have its source in him.

PROMINENCE AND THEME

The 2:12–14 *TRUST BASIS* is quite long and has a structured poetic form, marking it as prominent. It focuses on the *APPEALS* that it supports. This intense focusing marks the 2:12–25 unit as one of the four climaxes of the letter (the others being 2:26–27, 4:1–6, and 4:7–11). John has prepared his readers for the climactic *APPEAL* in 2:24–25 by encouragement (in 2:12–14) and warnings (in 2:15–17 and 18–23). The 2:15 warning is the first occurrence of an imperative in the letter. The imperative adds marked prominence to the *APPEALS*, which are already naturally prominent. The theme statement is a summarization of the *TRUST BASIS* and the HEADS of both the negative and the positive *APPEALS* (2:15a, 2:24a).

SUB-SECTION CONSTITUENT 2:12–14 (Descriptive Paragraph: Trust basis of 2:12–25)

Theme: I am writing all these matters to you because I know that God has forgiven your sins and because you have come to know the Father and Christ, who has always existed, and because you have overcome the evil one.

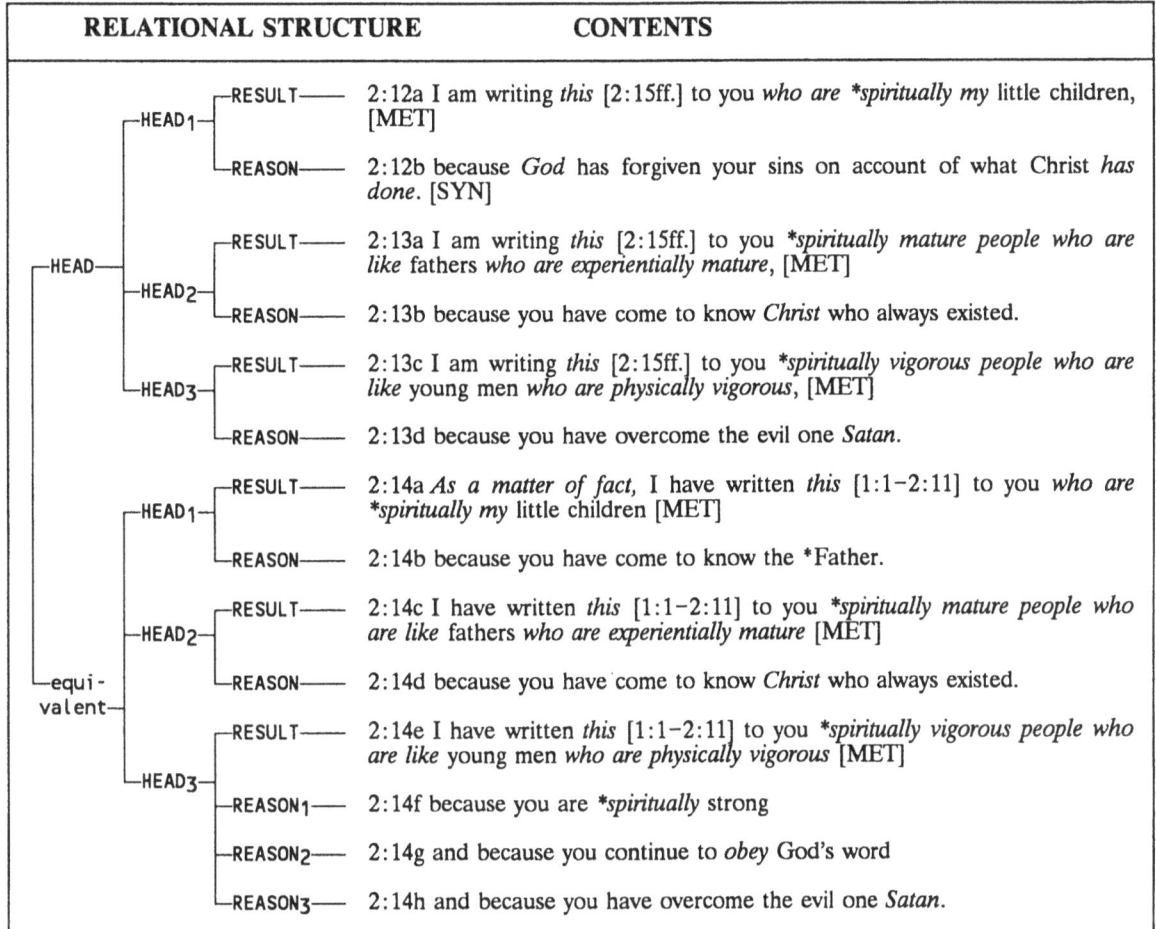

INTENT AND PARAGRAPH PATTERN

The complex 2:12–14 unit functions as a *TRUST BASIS* for the higher-level 2:12–25 unit. John is here giving strong encouragement before presenting the exhortations to overcome temptations. By an emphatic reminder of who they are and what God has done for them he provides the trust basis for exhorting them to live in the victory already won. As the new command of a new age is effective in the believers (2:8), they stand within the victory that Christ has won (5:5).

Each of the six HEADS in 2:12–14 has the same internal structure of RESULT-REASON. If one were to follow strict analytical criteria, each of the six heads would be a separate paragraph. However, these six are functioning in a very close-knit manner and are thus more easily presented as units within a large paragraph. Since the intent is to strengthen the author's trust relationship with his readers, each HEAD, if it were treated as a paragraph, would be called a causal descriptive paragraph with + REACTION + SITUATION as the principal constituents.

The form of the unit suggests two parts: 2:12–13 and 2:14. Three groups of people are addressed in 2:12–13, and these same groups are addressed in the same order in 2:14. In the first series the performative is in the present tense (γράφω 'I write') suggesting a declaration; in the second it is in the aorist (ἔγραψα 'I have written') suggesting a description.

NOTES

2:12a, 13a, 13c little children, ... fathers, ... young men Various interpretations are possible for the groups referred to. Some have taken the terms as relating to physical age or state of maturity. Both of these may apply, but neither is fully satisfactory alone, because the warnings that follow in 2:15-23 are not directed to any one particular group. Rather, the grouping is a rhetorical device to indicate qualities that ought to be true of all believers: the total dependency of children, the maturity of fathers, and the vigor of young men (supported by Dodd and Marshall). Thus, this interpretation that the address is to all the readers seems most feasible.

2:12a I am writing There are various views concerning the change of tense from the present in 2:12 and 13 to the aorist in the second part of the unit. It could be stylistic to avoid monotony, or it could be taken as the epistolary aorist by which the writer shifts to the readers' point of view. It could also be that the author was preparing the readers for the strong prohibition of 2:15, strengthening the trust relationship by stating that he had already been trusting them. (The translation of the two verb forms is not affected by either interpretation.)

There is no evidence for the theory that the aorist of 2:14 indicates that the author was interrupted in his writing and resumed later with unconscious repetition. Brooke (41-42) and others feel that such an unconscious repetition does not do justice to the author's careful choice of words. He suggests that as John paused to reflect on what he had just written and its importance, he was led to repeat these aphorisms for emphasis. After such a pause the aorist form would come naturally. This, however, hardly explains either the length or the structure of these aphorisms.

Considering that John repeatedly uses such expressions to strengthen a trust basis and soften an appeal relating to a touchy matter, the preceding explanations seem only partly adequate. Here the author is building up to an appeal concerning one of the most touchy subjects in the letter. This could explain why the author included this unit but certainly not why he structured it with such tautology, nor why the tense was shifted. It should be noted that the present tense form of γράφω does not occur again in the BODY of the Epistle, and the aorist form only at the beginning of the GENERIC APPEAL (2:26) and in the *closure* of the Epistle (5:13).

this **[2:15ff.]** The present-tense verb γράφω 'I write' requires the content of the writing to be supplied. This, in the nature of things, is something that will follow. When the tense is aorist, the content of the writing is something that was previously written (this would not be true in the case of an epistolary aorist). If the view is accepted that John was here preparing the readers for the strong prohibition of 2:15 by strengthening a trust relationship, then clearly the present-tense form refers to what John was about to write. He realized that he could enhance the trust by showing he had been trusting them all along in what he had previously written.

2:12a, 14a children Stott remarks, "If any distinct flavour is preserved between [the terms for 'little children'] τεκνία emphasizes the community of nature between the child and its parent (from τεκεῖν, to beget or bring forth), while παιδία refers to the child's minority as one under discipline (παιδεύω, to train or chastise)." These connotations are no doubt present, but are not being emphasized here. Therefore, no distinction between the two Greek words is made in the display, and the propositions containing them are considered equivalent. (See Louw and Nida 9.46 for some suggestions regarding translation.)

2:12b on account of what Christ *has done* The phrase διὰ τὸ ὄνομα αὐτοῦ 'by his name' stands for the whole of the person and work of Christ. More specifically, 'what Christ has done' means 'because Christ died instead of us'.

2:13a *spiritually mature people who are like* fathers See the first note in this unit (on 2:12a, 13a, 13c).

2:13b who always existed The Greek is ἀπ' ἀρχῆς 'from the beginning'. It seems to refer to the eternity of Christ and is rendered 'who always existed' here and in 2:14d.

2:13c *spiritually vigorous people who are like* young men See the first note in this unit (on 2:12a, 13a, 13c: little children, ... fathers, ... young men).

2:14a *As a matter of fact* This expression (a less emphatic rendering would be 'furthermore') shows the equivalence relationship with 2:12-13. Such an analysis fits with the explanation that the 2:12-14 unit is for strengthening trust with the readers. First, John gives the grounds for his trusting them; then he enhances these grounds by showing them that he has been trusting them all along, as he has been writing.

I have written See the 2:12a note on 'I am writing'.

this [1:1-2:11] The semantics of the verb γράφω 'write' requires that what is written be supplied. See the previous note on 'this' under 2:12a, 13a, 13c.

little children See the first note in this unit (on 2:12a, 13a, 13c).

2:14c fathers See the first note in this unit.

2:14e young men See the first note in this unit.

2:14g because you continue to *obey* God's word More literally, this is 'the word remaining in the believer'. (See 'united' in the Glossary.)

BOUNDARIES AND COHERENCE

The initial boundary has been discussed under unit 2:3-11. The illocutionary change to exhortation in the next unit marks the closing boundary.

The coherence of the 2:12-14 unit is seen in the symmetry of its surface structure, heightened by the repetition of the performative γράφω 'I write' (or ἔγραψα ὑμῖν 'I have written to you'), the vocatives, and ὅτι 'because'. The groups addressed are all members in Christ. Also, the author draws on the previous units and leads up to the challenge presented in the subsequent units. Motifs that occurred previously and occur again here are: forgiveness of sin (in 2:12b; cf. 1:5-2:2); experiential knowledge of God (in 2:13b and 14b-d; cf. 2:3-11); ability to overcome as the result of forgiveness and experiential knowledge of God (in 2:13d and 14f-h; cf. 2:8 where this victory was anticipated).

Due to the transitional nature of this unit there are various opinions concerning its role in the larger unit. Some commentators call it a parenthesis. According to their sense of the term *parenthesis*, this is a correct analysis because the preceding and the following paragraphs contrast, presenting the godly love of a brother (2:7-11) and the selfish love of a godless society (2:15-17), so that 2:12-14 belongs to both. But this unit has the function of expressing the author's trust in the readers so as to prepare them for the demanding challenge he will present next, a challenge to overcome definite evils.

PROMINENCE AND THEME

The performatives are prominent by virtue of their being repeated six times; the 'I write' units provide both orientation and emphasis. The REASON propositions, which point out the Christian values already possessed by the readers, might well be considered to be as prominent as the RESULT propositions. There is no surface evidence for one of these RESULT-reason units to be considered as more prominent than the others.

Although nothing in the structure indicates that the 2:12-13 unit is more prominent than the 2:14 unit, and although they are very similar to each other both grammatically and semantically, we take the second to be a re-statement of the first on the basis of marked prominence. The present tense switches to the aorist (possibly to reinforce what has already been said), and there is the repetition producing a rhetorical intensification of what was expressed in the first unit. Moreover, the first unit is supported by the second. The theme, therefore, is derived from a summary of the three RESULT-REASON propositions in the first unit (2:12-13).

> **SUB-SECTION CONSTITUENT 2:15-17** (Hortatory Paragraph: Negative appeal₁ of 2:12-25)
> *Theme: Do not esteem the evil manner in which other people live in the world, since you want to exist forever.*

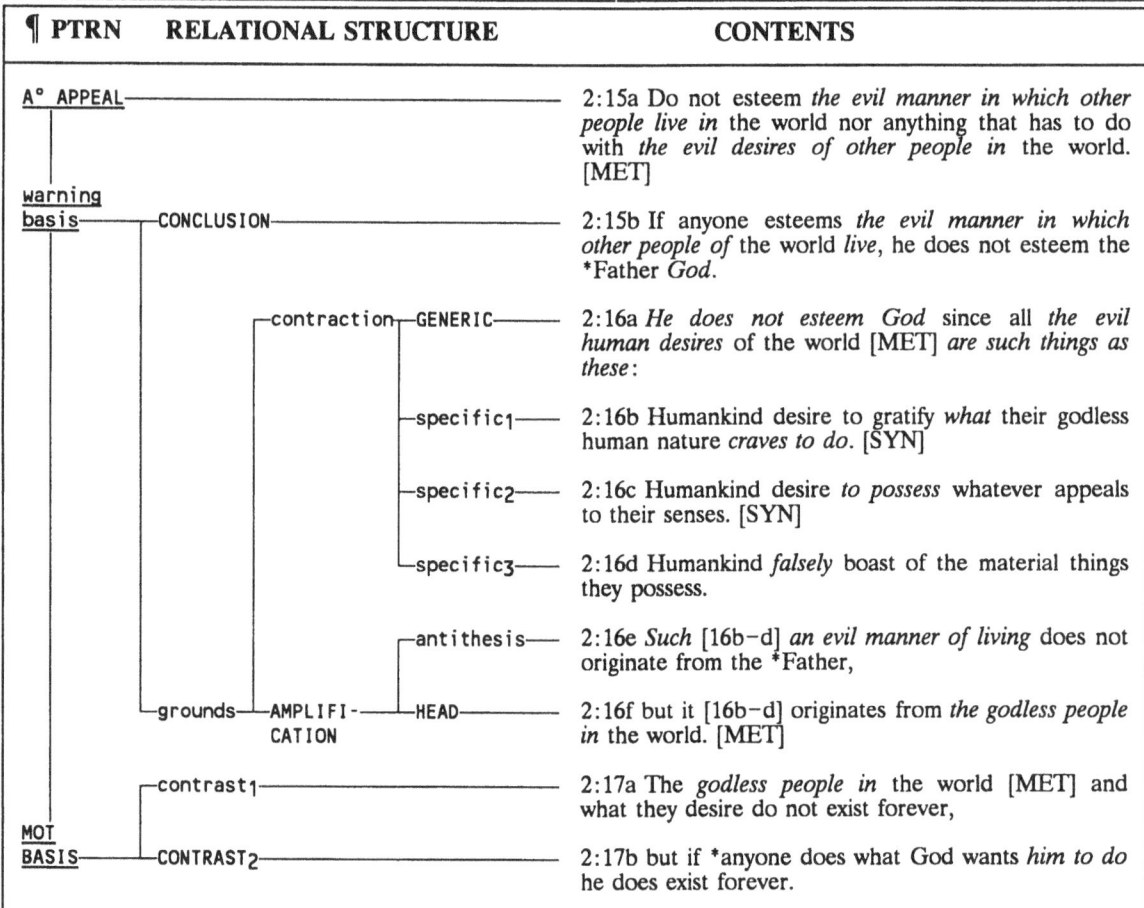

INTENT AND PARAGRAPH PATTERN

John's intent in the 2:15-17 paragraph is to affect the actions of the reader with an admonition that they not desire evil, which would cause them to sin. He wants to make certain that all the readers will continue behaving correctly.

The paragraph consists of three propositional clusters: one nuclear (2:15a) and two satellitic (2:15b-16 and 2:17). As to their communication relationship, the first is a hortatory unit, the next two grounds units. Since the primary intent is to affect behavior, it is considered a causal hortatory paragraph with + APPEAL + two *bases* as principal constituents. The *bases* are warnings to the reader that enhance the acceptability of the prohibition in the APPEAL.

NOTES

2:15a-b esteem It is important to realize that ἀγαπάω 'love' is used here with a different meaning than in most of its occurrences in the Epistle. It is not here the selfless love which led Jesus Christ to lay down his life for us (3:16), but love perverted for the selfish gratification of a person's desires as in John 12:43 ('for they loved the praise of men more than the praise of God'). Since it has to do with the personal value system, it may be expressed 'to esteem', 'place high value on', or 'set one's heart on'.

the evil manner in which other people live in the world See the note on 2:2c, where the several meanings of 'world' are given. Here in 2:15 the meaning is 'the life of human society in opposition to God'. It is a metaphor representing "mankind organized in rebellion against God" (Marshall, p. 142).

2:16a *the evil human desires* of the world Here the meaning of the metaphorical 'world' is 'evil human desires', which is different from its meaning in 15a and b.

2:16b godless human nature *craves to do* The Greek is ἡ ἐπιθυμία τῆς σαρκός 'the desire of the flesh'. It is used figuratively here to mean 'the desires of godless human nature'.

Since 'world' in 2:15 is used in the sense of 'the life of human society in opposition to God', we take the objects of desire here to refer to this same manner of living. In 5:19 John says: "the whole world is in the power of the evil one." The lifestyle of the world expresses the world spirit (see Glossary), which exerts an influence on unregenerate people causing them to do certain things. Such motivation seems to be what is intended by τά 'things' (2:15) rather than material things alone. This interpretation agrees well with 2:17b where the love of God is expressed by doing his will and with 'all things' (i.e., attitudes) in 2:16. On the other hand, the Docetists, against whom the following may warn, considered material things to be evil. Therefore, the focus is on an evil manner of living, not on matter as being evil.

2:16c desire *to possess* whatever appeals to their senses The Greek is ἡ ἐπιθυμία τῶν ὀφθαλμῶν 'the desire of the eyes', in which 'eyes' stands for sensual appeal.

2:16d *falsely* boast of the material things Examples of the use of ἀλαζονεία 'boasting' in Greek literature point to the idea of false boasting, for example, boasting of things one does not actually possess. Since in English 'boasting' connotes bragging and lacks the component 'falsely', that word is supplied in the display. What is being boasted of here is βίος 'possessions' (Louw and Nida 57.18), referring to life's external aspects, the things that support life, hence 'material things'.

2:16f, 17a *the godless people in* the world See the notes on 2:2c and 2:15a concerning 'world'.

2:17a do not exist forever The verb here is παράγεται 'pass away'. It stands in contrast to μένει εἰς τὸν αἰῶνα 'remain forever'. In this verse and in 2:8 it is usually translated as 'pass away' or 'disappear'. The interpretation that the worldly people are disappearing is based on the surface structure in which the contrast between them and those who do God's will is expressed in a parallel use of ὁ 'the one', the second occurrence being followed by δέ 'but'. The destiny of the godless people of the world is not strongly in focus, but from the parallel construction of the contrast we take it to mean that those who identify themselves with the rebellious world spirit (see 'world spirit' in the Glossary) are transient just as the world is, while those who identify themselves with God in spiritual union with him partake of his permanence.

BOUNDARIES AND COHERENCE

The 2:15-17 unit begins with a strong prohibition, the first overt command of the Epistle. The final boundary is indicated by the change of subject matter in the next unit and the introduction of the next unit with the vocative παιδία 'little children' (2:18).

In contrast to 2:12-14, which is replete with vocatives and performatives, this unit has none. The genre changes sharply from the descriptive in 2:12-14 to a forceful hortatory here.

The command and its supporting bases give the unit its coherence. The subject matter is love and the need to direct that love towards the right object. Since love for God and love for the world are mutually exclusive, this provides the *warning basis* (2:15b) for the prohibition. The contrast of destinies (2:17a-b) is the MOTIVATIONAL BASIS for the prohibition. (The prohibition could be viewed as having an antithesis in the covert exhortation of 2:17b.)

Lexical items also lend coherence: κόσμος 'world' occurs in every verse of this unit, six times in all; ἀγάπη 'love', in various forms, occurs three times in 2:15; ἐπιθυμία 'desire', which is a characteristic of the world, occurs three times, in 2:16 and 17.

PROMINENCE AND THEME

The prohibition of 2:15, being a direct command, has natural prominence. Although it is the first overt hortatory expression in the Epistle, the whole Epistle is nevertheless strongly hortative:

the commands are at first highly mitigated but surface and become more overt as the Epistle develops.... Thus, in 15b ... a covert command ... 'if any man love the world' equals 'don't love the world' and echoes in mitigated form the overt imperative of the preceding clause. (Longacre, p. 13)

The positive way of stating the 2:15a prohibition is, love God. This is also expressed covertly in 2:17b in the words ὁ δὲ ποιῶν τὸ θέλημα τοῦ θεοῦ 'the one who does the will of God'. The 17b proposition is the positive statement of the contrast and so most prominent. Therefore, the *MOTIVATIONAL BASIS* is considered to be equally prominent with the command of 2:15a, since they both convey the exhortation to love God.

The theme statement is derived from the *APPEAL* (2:15a) and the *MOTIVATIONAL BASIS*, which has the rhetorical force of a positive mitigated exhortation.

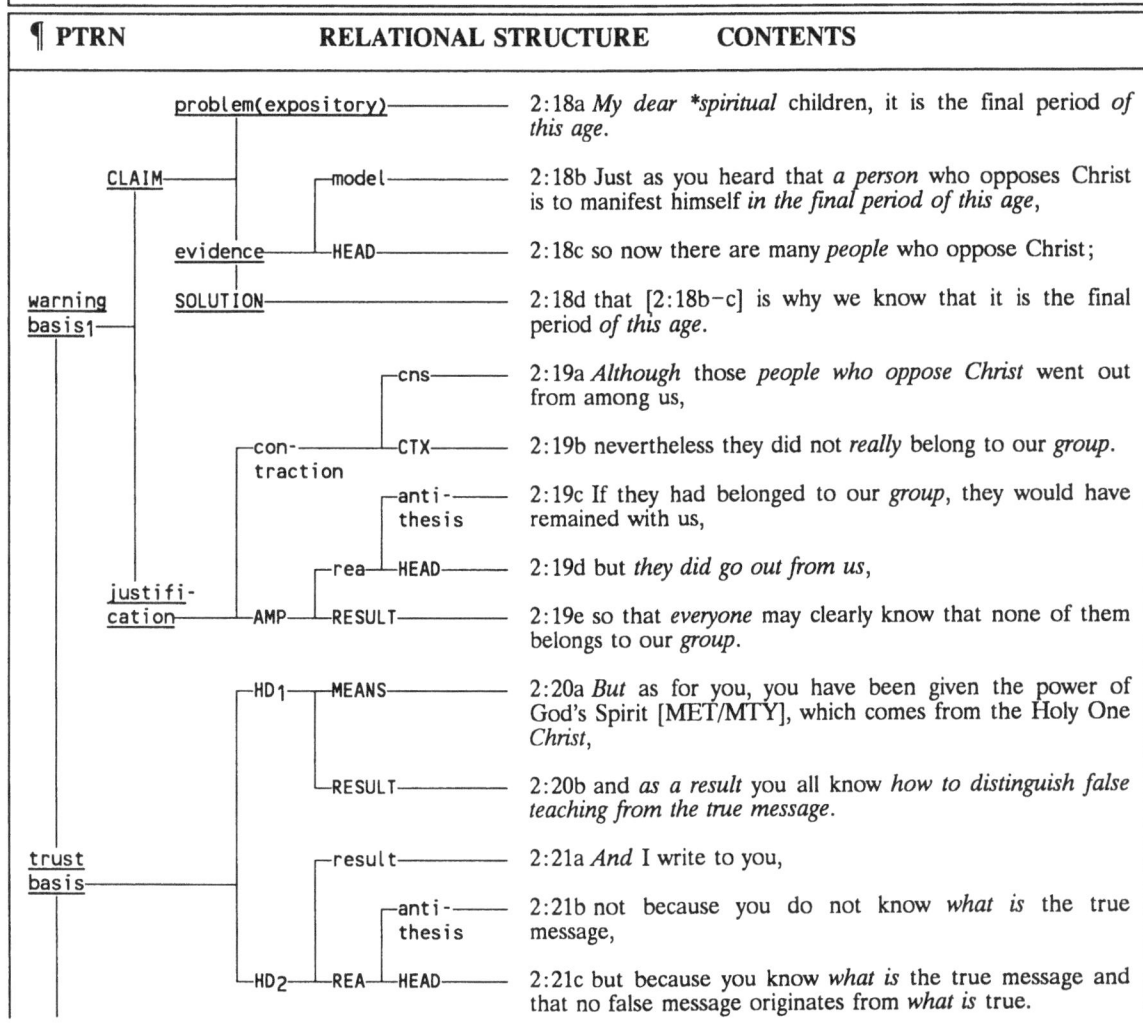

SUB-SECTION CONSTITUENT 2:18–25 (Hortatory Paragraph: Appeal₂ of 2:12–25)
Theme: You know that it is the final period of this age when liars deny that Jesus is God's anointed one. But you have the power of God's Spirit and you know what is true and what is false. Therefore continue to behave according to the true message that you heard when you began to believe in Christ, in order that you may continue to live united both to God's Son and to the Father.

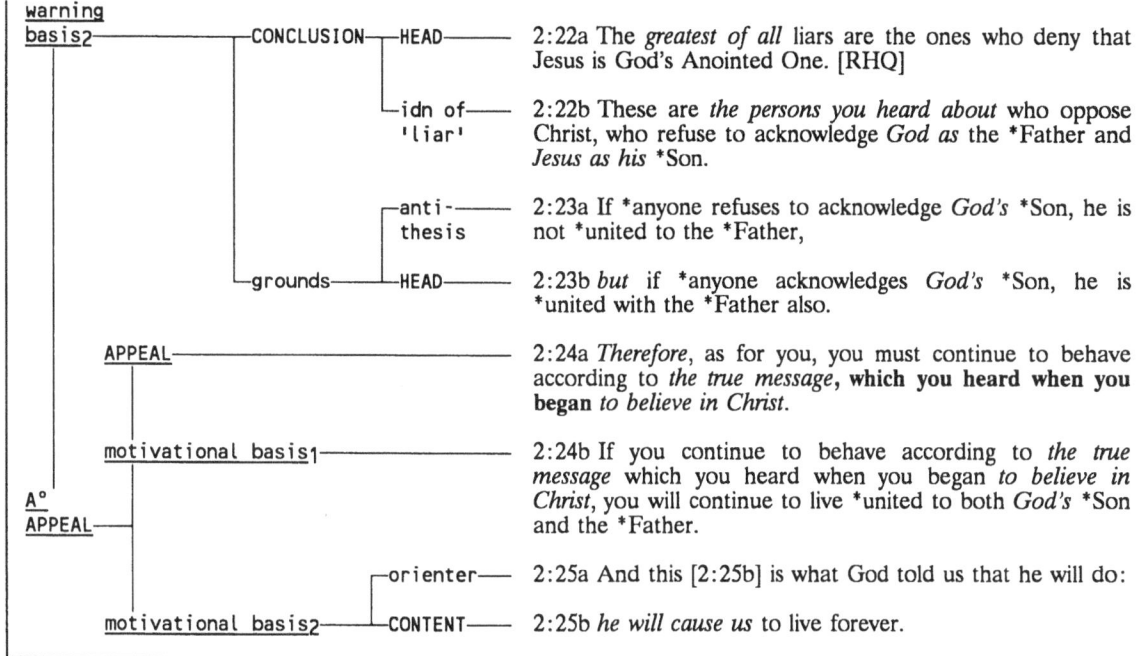

INTENT AND PARAGRAPH PATTERN

In 2:18-25 the author's intent is to affect the readers' actions, using an admonition that they continue to behave according to the message they heard when they first believed in Christ. In this first climactic part of the letter (2:12-27), John exhorts the readers regarding ethical matters (2:15-25) and then regarding doctrinal matters (2:26-27). Here in 2:18-25 he encourages ethical behavior, giving a warning against the spirit of the world. Later in 4:1-6, where the author resumes his exposure of the antichrist spirit, this spirit is identified as ἐκ τοῦ κόσμου εἰσίν 'originating from the world' (4:5), and this relationship is given as a way of detecting the spirit of error (4:6).

The 2:18-25 paragraph consists of one embedded paragraph and two propositional clusters followed by a nuclear embedded paragraph. The first three constituents are supportive units (2:18-19, 2:20-21, and 2:22-23) and the final one is nuclear (2:24-25). As to the communication relationship, the three grounds units are followed by one exhortation unit. Since the primary intent is to affect behavior, it is taken to be a causal hortatory paragraph, the principal constituents being + *bases* + *APPEAL*. The first *basis* expresses a warning, the second a trust relationship between the writer and the readers, the third another warning. These *bases* are intended to enhance the acceptability of the *APPEAL*.

NOTES

2:18a *My dear spiritual* **children** John uses the vocative παιδία 'children' as an endearment addressed to those who are figuratively his children.

the final period *of this age* There are several influences that affect the interpretation of ἐσχάτη ὥρα 'last hour': (1) the eschatological concepts of the Old Testament era, (2) the prophetic discourses of Christ, (3) the apostolic interpretation of Old Testament eschatology and Christ's prophecies, and (4) our own concept of 'last hour' in light of the past centuries of the Christian era. Successive generations of Christians have tended to understand 'the last hour' in terms of contemporary events of their own times.

The generally held interpretation of 'the end time' is that it is the whole period between Christ's ascension and his second coming. This is borne out by the repeated admonitions of vigilance by Jesus to his disciples and the warnings throughout the New Testament.

2:18b *a person* **who opposes Christ** The term 'antichrist' is used in the New Testament only by John. However, the concept is found in both Old and New Testaments in connection with references to the end of the age. It is related to the rebellion against Christ and his message, which resulted in his death. The prefix ἀντί may be translated as either 'pseudo, false' or as 'against'. The NT usage involves both. The expression '*a person* who opposes Christ' used in the display is not intended to emphasize one element over the other.

2:19d but *they did go out from us* The conjunction ἀλλά 'but' stands for an ellipsis, contrasting with the previous proposition.

2:19e *everyone* **may clearly know** The verb φανερωθῶσιν 'they be known' is in the passive voice. It is ambiguous as to whether the referent of the third person plural suffix is the antichrists as the actors or the recipients of the action. We take it to be the recipients. Who, then, is the actor? The choices are God, the believers, or other people. The last seems to be the best choice.

2:20a you have been given the power of God's Spirit The word χρῖσμα comes from χρίω 'anoint'. Commentators generally say that χρῖσμα is used here as a metonymy for the Holy Spirit, since the Holy Spirit is associated with the Old and New Testament ceremony of anointing. The ceremony of anointing in the Old Testament was a symbolic act used to appoint priests and kings for a particular office. It signified God's endowing them with powers needed for their office. A few commentaries and also Louw and Nida (37.107) take this to be metaphorical signifying assigning or appointing someone to a task and enabling them to carry it out. In Acts 1:18 Jesus told his disciples that they would receive power to be witnesses when the Holy Spirit would be given to them. The Spirit is also designated as the One enabling or guiding them into all truth (John 16:13). So we may understand χρῖσμα as the enabling that the Holy Spirit gives to the believer to properly understand the true message. Alternate interpretations are 'you have been given the Holy One (Christ)' and 'you have been given the true message (*or*, gospel)'.

which comes from the Holy One, *Christ* Commentators agree that the ambiguity of who it is who anoints can hardly be resolved, but many point out reasons for assigning that role to Christ. He is called the 'Holy One' in such Scriptures as John 6:69 and Acts 3:14. Christ promised to send the Holy Spirit to lead his disciples into all truth (John 16:7, 13). However, John also speaks of the Father as sending the Holy Spirit (John 14:16). The consensus is that though the reference is probably to Christ, the identity here of the particular divine Person responsible for the anointing is relatively unimportant. We take the 'Holy One' to be Christ.

2:20b you all know Some texts have the neuter plural πάντα 'all things' here, while others have the masculine plural πάντες 'all of you'. The majority of critical commentators have chosen the latter (as we do), arguing that the author in seeking to give confidence to his readers is stressing the fact of their knowledge rather than the extent of it. Since the object of οἶδα 'know' is clear in 2:21, many consider that a copyist in looking for an object within v. 20 may have altered πάντες to make it accusative, πάντα. As for John's purpose here, he may be refuting the secessionists' boast of knowledge or he may be emphasizing guidance into truth by the Holy Spirit (2:27c). The latter would be quite in harmony with John 16:13 as well, so that it is, therefore, possible to accept the neuter form. No clear evidence conclusively supports one view over the other. The rendering in the display follows the UBS text in accepting πάντες, which stresses the fact of that knowledge with which 'all of you' have been endowed.

know *how to distinguish false teaching from the true message* The process event 'know' requires a content. Interpretations vary according to which reading is accepted:

1. If πάντα 'things (neuter)' is accepted as the better reading (see above), then the interpretation of 'know' would be 'you know all the true teachings' (with the result that you will not be deceived).
2. If πάντες 'all (masculine)' is accepted as the better reading, then the interpretation of 'know' here would be either (a) 'all of you know the true teachings', or (b) 'all of you know how to distinguish the true from the false', which is our preference.

2:21b–c not because you do not know . . . but because you know The import of 2:20–21 is to express trust or confidence in the readers by reminding them of what they have received. Here John is characteristically careful not to give the impression that he is writing because they had forgotten the teachings or had been deceived by the false teachers. He is preparing them for the warning to not be deceived.

the true message For a broader understanding of 'truth' in this Epistle, see the 1:5b note on 'light' and the 1:6b note on 'truth'.

2:22a The *greatest of all* liars We take the rhetorical question in the surface structure to mean that ὁ ψεύστης 'the liar' is the one in whom the lie finds its most complete expression. The phrase 'greatest of all' is supplied to give this focus. The enormity of the lie can be seen in the light of 1:1–2. To deny the relationship of Father and Son sweeps away all hope of redemption because redemption depends on the eternity of the Son and his being sent by the Father.

God's Anointed One The Hebrew word 'Messiah' and the Greek 'Christ' both signify 'the anointed one' (see the 2:20a note concerning the symbolic act of anointing). 'Christ' is most frequently used as a proper name for Jesus, but in some cases it is the title for the one whom the nation of Israel was awaiting. It may be rendered 'God's anointed one', 'God's chosen one', or 'God's promised Savior'.

2:22b *the persons you heard about* This information is already given explicitly in v. 18, but repeated here in order to maintain the focus that this is not a new referent.

refuse to acknowledge *God as* **the Father and** *Jesus as his* **Son** The situation that this letter addresses was that some people claimed that the human Jesus was not the divine Christ and that the divine Christ could not have possibly been human. It was not a matter of outright atheism, denying the very existence of God. Rather, John is speaking against the false teaching and belief that do not acknowledge that the human Jesus was really God become human. It is the vital relationship between God the Father and Jesus his Son that was the central problem. Denying Jesus' relationship to God would result in denying both the Father and the Son. Thus, those who oppose Christ refuse to acknowledge the real relationship between Jesus and God (that they are equal and of the same nature) as expressed in the phrase 'Father and Son'.

2:24–25 The Greek clause order brings out the prominence that is reflected in the theme. To make this sound natural in English the order has been changed to some extent.

2:24a *the true message*, which you heard when you <u>began</u> *to believe in Christ* The Greek is ὃ ἠκούσατε ἀπ' ἀρχῆς ἐν ὑμῖν μενέτω 'that which you heard from the beginning let it remain in you'. The initial substantive clause is in sharp focus due to its position. John's appeal is that the original teaching must be adhered to, in opposition to some faddish false teaching. Supplying 'the true message' maintains the focus.

The word 'beginning' here requires a temporal point of reference, namely the time when they began to believe in Christ.

2:25a this [25b] As mentioned in the note on 1:5a, οὗτος 'this' in this Epistle refers to the following context (except for the second occurrence in 5:11).

what God told us Literally, this is 'what God promised'. A promise is a verbal expression of the speaker's commitment to do something. In many languages a word for this does not exist, but the concept can usually be conveyed by a speech margin ('he said') plus the content of what was said.

A promise is usually associated with a condition. Here the promise is given on the condition of remaining united to the Father and the Son (2:24b). It should also be noted that the pronoun αὐτός, referring to God, is emphatic.

2:25b *he will cause us* to live forever God created and sustains living beings and causes people to live eternally, hence 'he will cause us to live forever'. This is the first occurrence in the body of the Epistle of the words 'eternal life': τὴν ζωὴν τὴν αἰώνιον 'the life eternal' occurs twice (1:2, 2:25), and ζωὴν αἰώνιον 'eternal life' occurs three times (5:11, 13, 20). The reference to 'eternal life' here points back to the Epistle's introduction (1:2) and forward to the Epistle's purpose (5:13).

BOUNDARIES AND COHERENCE

The initial boundary of the 2:18–25 unit has been discussed under 2:15–17, and the final boundary under 2:12–25. A parallel construction reinforces the final boundary at v. 25: the preceding unit ends (2:17) with μένει εἰς τὸν αἰῶνα 'he remains forever', and this one ends (v. 25) with τὴν ζωὴν τὴν αἰώνιον 'eternal life'.

Several elements are introduced for the first time in this unit: ἐσχάτη ὥρα 'the last hour' (2:18, which is its only occurrence in the Epistle); ἀντίχριστος 'antichrist' (2:18, 22, occurring again in 4:3); and χρῖσμα 'anointing' (2:20, occurring again in 2:27).

Major contrasts give coherence to the paragraph. In 2:20-21 the faithful believers are contrasted with the antichrists of 18-19, as shown by the emphatic ὑμεῖς 'you'. The contrast between the lie and the truth in 2:21 is expanded in 22-23 (the respective results of denial and confession of Christ are set in juxtaposition in v. 23). Since those who deny Christ are the antichrists and those who confess him are the believers, there is contrast between 2:22-23 and 24-25. Again this is indicated by the emphatic ὑμεῖς (2:24). The pattern is one of interlocking contrasts.

Because of changes in lexical domains and in person and number in pronouns, the paragraph could be divided into three or four smaller units as follows: 2:18-19, 20-21, 22-23, 24-25. On the other hand, the smaller units may be seen as tightly bound constituents of a larger unit in view of the following features that show coherence:

1. Verse 18 begins with a vocative and introduces the warning against the antichrist spirit as manifested by those who have seceded from the community of believers now being addressed by the author.
2. Verse 20 begins with καί 'and', which shows a high degree of unity with what precedes. Here John begins his address with a forefronted, emphatic ὑμεῖς 'you'; χρῖσμα 'anointing', a metonymy for the Holy Spirit, is also forefronted. It seems that John wants to encourage his readers at this point.
3. Verse 22 with its emotional denunciation of the error of the secessionists begins with a rhetorical question, which highlights the peril of the antichrist spirit.
4. In v. 24 the readers are again addressed with the forefronted ὑμεῖς. John calls attention to the original message repeating his designation of it as 'the true message which you heard when you began to believe'.
5. Structural coherence is also based on the author's intent to affect the readers' behavior: a *warning basis* (18-19), a *trust basis* (20-21), another *warning basis* (22-23), and an APPEAL (24-25). John says, in effect: Since this is the final period of this age (18-19), and since I know that the Spirit is in you guiding you in the truth (20-21), and since you must beware of those who deny that Jesus is the Christ (22-23), I urge you to continue behaving according to the true message (24-25).

These features give coherence to the paragraph and also indicate an emotional climax at this point in the Epistle.

PROMINENCE AND THEME

What is naturally prominent in this unit is the APPEAL. However, prominence devices are used in the first *warning basis* (18-19), the *trust basis* (20-21) and the second *warning basis* (22-23):

1. Verse 18 is a chiastic structure:

   A The last hour (18a)
     B The antichrist is coming (18b)
     B' Many antichrists have appeared (18b)
   A' The last hour (18a)

2. In 2:22-24 there is a series of nominative complements introduced by ὁ 'he who', which highlights them.
3. The rhetorical question in v. 22 operates in conjunction with the nominative complements mentioned above.
4. The future tense of the APPEAL's *motivational bases* (24b, 25b) makes the *bases* prominent: the promise is that you will continue to live united to both the Son and the Father (μενεῖτε 'you will remain').

The theme statement is drawn from the nuclear propositions of each of the four paragraph pattern elements (18a, 20a, 21c, 22a, and 24a) since they are structurally prominent and also carry marked prominence.

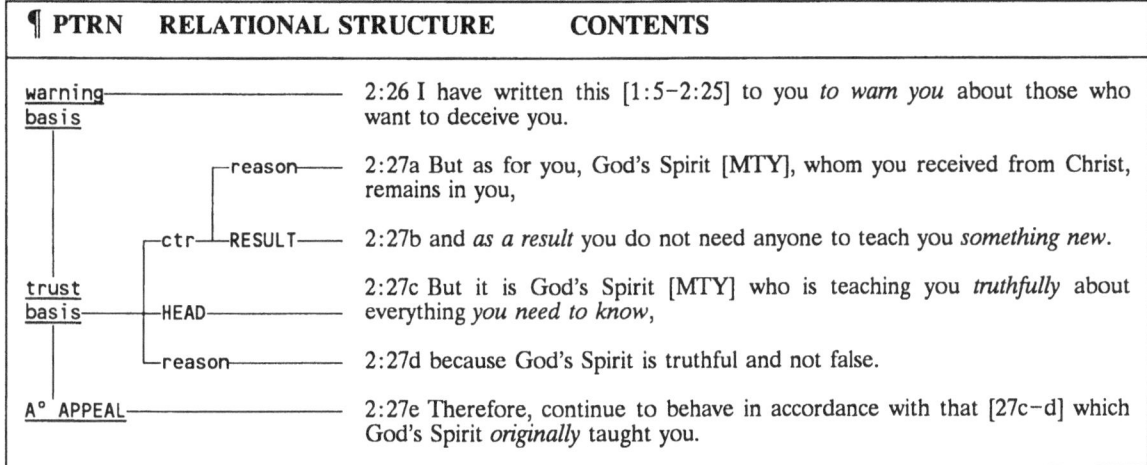

INTENT AND PARAGRAPH PATTERN

The 2:26-27 unit is a summary at the end of 1:5-2:27. John's intent here is to affect the actions of the reader using an admonition that they continue to behave according to the message they were originally taught. The paragraph consists of three propositional clusters: two supportive (26, 27a-d) and one central (2:27e). The communication relationship between them is two grounds followed by one exhortation. Since the primary intent is to affect behavior, the paragraph is considered a causal hortatory paragraph, its principal constituents being + bases + APPEAL.

NOTES

2:26 *to warn you* John is not simply writing *about* those who would deceive; rather, he is *warning against* such persons. In order that the topic of discussion, which continues from the previous paragraph, not be in doubt the words 'to warn you' have been supplied in the display.

those who want to deceive The present participle τῶν πλανώντων 'those deceiving' is taken as referring to an *attempt* to deceive—the context indicates that the effort to deceive had been unsuccessful. The expression carries the warning in 2:18-23 a step further, pointing out the intention of the secessionists.

2:27a But as for you The pronoun ὑμεῖς 'you' is syntactically emphatic and brings out the change in focus. The focus was on those who would deceive the believers; now it is on the believers. It is linked with the conjunction καί 'and': ὑμεῖς 'and you' turns the focus to 'you' (ὑμεῖς δέ 'but you' would contrast 'you' with someone else).

God's Spirit The Greek is χρῖσμα 'anointing', which is a symbolic act. It is a metonymy for the Holy Spirit. See the note on 2:20a.

2:27b, c, e teach ... is teaching ... taught What John writes is teaching, but it is within the scope of the original teaching. The anointing also is within that scope and is the witness which the Holy Spirit gives to God's truth. The witness is a safeguard against new and different teaching not included in the original message. In this sense the Holy Spirit continues to teach the believer, unfolding Christ's message so that ἀλλ' ὡς ... διδάσκει ὑμᾶς 'but as he teaches you' in 27c is the same as καθὼς ἐδίδαξεν 'just as he taught' in 27e.

2:27c God's Spirit The word χρῖσμα 'anointing' is a metonymy for the Holy Spirit (see the note on 2:20a). Since it signifies both the act of anointing and the patient, it is important to make explicit in the proposition that the anointing refers to the Holy Spirit himself, imparted to us by Christ.

truthfully This information is understood from 2:27d, which explicitly states the reason for this proposition and implied claim of truthfulness.

everything *you need to know* John is not asserting that the Holy Spirit makes the believer omniscient. Rather, the Holy Spirit teaches the believer adequate truth to prevent him from being deceived.

2:27d God's Spirit is truthful and not false There is a division of opinion whether 'it' refers to 'Christ' or to 'the anointing'. We have chosen the latter interpretation because it is in the neuter and can refer only to the 'anointing'. As before, 'anointing' is a metonymy for the Holy Spirit and in the display is rendered nonfiguratively: 'God's Spirit'.

2:27e continue to behave The present imperative μένετε 'live' focuses on the continuative aspect: 'continue to live'. A few commentators take this as indicative. However, if it were, it would be difficult to understand the paragraph as a whole: 'I am writing to you regarding those that intend to deceive you, but as for you, you have God's Spirit and you continue to behave as he has taught you'. Taking the unit as expository produces neither closure nor relational coherence (the internal relationship being neither + *evidence* + IMPLICATION nor + *justification* + CLAIM).

in accordance with The Greek is αὐτῷ 'he/it (dative)', which could be interpreted as referring to the anointing, the Holy Spirit, Christ, or the true teaching. Since there is no preceding referent except 'the anointing' (i.e., the Holy Spirit), we need not take this pronoun as masculine referring to Christ. The logical antecedent is the anointing, the Holy Spirit's ministry of teaching. Thus, we have chosen the interpretation 'remain in *it*', referring to the anointing and the Spirit's teaching.

In 2:28 the clause is repeated and the reference there is clearly to Christ (what immediately follows concerns Christ's second coming). This seems to be an intended parallelism to introduce the next major division of the letter.

God's Spirit *originally* taught you The verb ἐδίδαξεν 'it/he has taught' here raises the question of who the actor is. From 27c to here there in no grammatical antecedent except the 'anointing'; hence we take 'God's Spirit' to be the actor.

BOUNDARIES AND COHERENCE

The 2:26-27 unit begins with the deictic ταῦτα ἔγραψα ὑμῖν 'these things I have written to you'. The other evidences for the opening boundary are presented in the discussion under 2:12-25. The features of closure are presented under 1:5-2:27.

From the standpoint of surface structure, this unit, which is as a GENERIC APPEAL (or SUMMARY APPEAL) in the 1:5-2:27 section, is tightly woven. After the *warning basis*, every clause is introduced with a conjunction except for the APPEAL in 2:27e, for which 26-27d serves as *basis*. The contrast between those addressed and their opponents also gives coherence.

The 2:26-27 unit is bound together by the relational structure of two *bases* and one APPEAL. The author warns about those who would deceive (26), then emphatically turns to the fact that the readers have the Holy Spirit to teach them all truth (27b-d). In light of this warning and their trust in the Holy Spirit, John urges (27e) the readers to hang on to the original teaching.

PROMINENCE AND THEME

In the "Prominence and Theme" discussion under 1:5-2:27, reasons were presented for accepting the position taken in many commentaries and most English translations that the verb μένετε 'continue' is an imperative form. The clause καθὼς ἐδίδαξεν ὑμᾶς 'as he taught you' (2:27e) highlights the command (cf. 2:24). Thus, the overt command to continue to live united to the Spirit is prominent in the unit.

The 2:26 *warning basis* is marked as prominent by ταῦτα ἔγραψα ὑμῖν 'this I have written to you'. The *trust basis* is in sharp contrast to 2:26. The contrast causes the focus to be on the *trust basis*: καὶ ὑμεῖς 'but as for you' marks it as prominent also.

The APPEAL is the naturally prominent unit. Although the *warning basis* and *trust basis* have marked prominence, they focus prominence on the APPEAL rather than on themselves. Therefore, the theme statement is taken from the APPEAL.

DIVISION CONSTITUENT 2:28–4:6 (Hortatory Section: Specific appeal₁ of 1:5–5:12)

Theme: In order that we may be confident before Christ at his return, let us be pure, truly love one another, believe in Christ, and be very careful to test whether teachers teach people the truth or not.

MACROSTRUCTURE	CONTENTS
GENERIC APPEAL	2:28–29 In order that you may be confident that you associate properly with Christ when he manifests himself, continue to live united to Christ, doing what is right, since you want to show that God has caused you to live spiritually.
specific appeal₁	3:1–10 Do not allow anyone to seduce you to sin, because we are God's children and his children maintain themselves free from evil behavior by not continuing to sin as the devil's children do.
specific appeal₂	3:11–18 Since we have been changed from being spiritually dead people to being spiritually living people, we should love each other genuinely by helping our Christian brothers who are in need.
specific appeal₃	3:19–24 We must believe in God's Son and love each other in order to be confident that we associate properly with God and receive what we ask from him.
SPECIFIC APPEAL₄	4:1–6 Since I know you have prevailed over false teachers, I say to you, Continue to test the teaching you hear to know whether or not it is from God. You should test it by whether or not it acknowledges that Jesus Christ came in human form and by who it is that listens to the teaching.

INTENT AND MACROSTRUCTURE

John's concern throughout this high-level unit is that the readers be confident that they associate properly with God when Christ returns. His intent is to affect their behavior so that they act according to Christ's character. Several *specific appeals* build up to the climactic APPEAL for them to continue to test the teachings they hear to know whether or not they are from God. The most immediate threat to their being able to act according to Christ's character is the prevalence of false teaching.

The 2:28–4:6 section is made up of five constituent units. The first (2:28–29) is a GENERIC APPEAL bridging over from the previous section. This transitional unit is followed by four more appeals, each progressively building up to the final one. This final APPEAL (4:1–6) is part of the letter's climax.

BOUNDARIES AND COHERENCE

The opening boundary of 2:28–4:6 has been discussed under unit 1:5–2:27. The closing boundary is marked by the closing statement of 4:6d and the vocative ἀγαπητοί 'dear friends' in 4:7 as well as an imperative leading to a change in subject matter of the subsequent unit.

The 2:28–4:6 unit is held together by the indication, through *specific appeals*, of how to comply with the GENERIC APPEAL to continue united to Christ.

The explicitly stated purpose of continuing united to Christ, which is stated in 2:28–29 and 3:19, is that we might be confident before God. This purpose relates only to this unit and provides coherence to it.

Also, John's concern for his readers explicitly stated in 3:2 and 3:4–9 provides coherence. He is specifically concerned that they be like Christ and not continue sinning.

Further evidence of coherence in this section is found in the discussion of the topic of the family of God. At the unit's start the word γεννάω 'beget' occurs for the first time in the Epistle. The topic is elaborated throughout the section by frequent use of that verb and phrases such as ἔστιν ἐκ τοῦ θεοῦ 'be of God' and τέκνα τοῦ θεοῦ 'children of God', which are practically interchangeable with forms of γεννάω, and by the use of ἀδελφός 'brother', which implies family relationship. Though family terms introduced in the 2:28–4:6 unit are used again in units that follow, there is a greater concentration of them here than in any other part of the discourse.

Assurance of the family relationship is emphasized by several tests. These tests are presented more frequently here than in other parts of the Epistle, at least thirteen of them in the thirty-two verses of the section: in 2:29; 3:4, 6, 7, 8, 10, 14, 17, 21, 24; and 4:2, 6. (In citing these tests individual judgment is involved as to whether or not all remarks concerning the difference between believers and unbelievers are to be considered tests.)

PROMINENCE AND THEME

This unit focuses on a major concern relating to the author's intent for writing the Epistle, namely that the readers hold on to the true message about Jesus Christ. Structurally, the 2:28-29 GENERIC APPEAL is the most prominent unit in the section, further heightened by the *motivational basis* of 'being confident when he manifests himself' (28b-c).

However, vv. 28-29 cannot be the only source of the theme statement since it would not contrast with the theme of the previous section (1:5-2:27) except for the purpose statement. Thus, the theme statement is drawn from the GENERIC APPEAL with special attention to the purposive statement in 2:28 and from the *specific appeals* with special attention to 4:1-6 (since it is more prominent and thus one of the climaxes of the letter).

Each one of the *specific appeals* of the section has marked prominence. In 3:1-10, vv. 7 and 8 stand out because of the vocative, imperative, and contrasting relative clauses. In 3:11-18, v. 16 is prominent due to the admonition's being introduced by a demonstrative grounds proposition and emphasized by the negative example that follows. In 3:19-24, v. 23 is marked as prominent by an inclusio. It is framed by a deictic proposition and a concluding emphasis:

A This is what he commands us to do:
  B that we believe that his Son Jesus Christ is all that his name implies and love each other,
A' just as he commanded us to do.

The whole of 4:1-6 is heavy with an accumulation of features of marked prominence characteristic of a climax: vocatives (vv. 1, 4); the use of demonstrative pronouns (vv. 2, 3, 5); sharp contrasts (vv. 2-3, 6); contrasting imperatives (v. 1); and contrasting key words ('true' versus 'false' in vv. 1-6 and 'God' versus 'world' in vv. 1, 3-5).

> **SECTION CONSTITUENT 2:28–29** (Hortatory Paragraph: Generic appeal of 2:28–4:6)
> *Theme: In order that you may be confident that you associate properly with Christ when he manifests himself, continue to live united to Christ, doing what is right, since you want to show that God has caused you to live spiritually.*

¶ PTRN	RELATIONAL STRUCTURE	CONTENTS
A° APPEAL		2:28a At this time, *my dear *spiritual children, continue to live *united to Christ*
motivational basis	HEAD	2:28b in order that when Christ manifests himself we may be confident *that we associate properly with Christ*
	equivalent	2:28c and that we may not be ashamed before Christ when he comes.
axiomatic basis	grounds	2:29a Since you know that God always does what is right,
	CONCLUSION	2:29b you know that if *anyone continues doing what is right, then God has caused him to live *spiritually.

INTENT AND PARAGRAPH PATTERN

John's intent in the 2:28–29 unit is to affect the readers' actions, commanding them to behave as people united to Christ should. The unit as a whole functions as a generic command introducing a set of admonitions. Internally, 2:28–29 consists of three propositional clusters: one nuclear (28a) and two satellitic (28b–c and 29). The communication relationship between them is one hortatory unit supported by two grounds units. Since the primary intent is to affect behavior, this is a causal hortatory paragraph, the principal constituents being + *basis* + *APPEAL*.

NOTES

2:28a At this time In this letter νῦν 'now' occurs four times, in 2:18, 28; 3:2; and 4:3. In every case except 2:28 it unquestionably has an immediate temporal meaning of 'now, at this moment'. As to its meaning in 2:28, there are two opinions: (1) 'now' refers to the present circumstance of the presence of false teachers, and (2) 'now' is used to summarize or conclude the previous information. We choose the former, since the immediate temporal circumstantial meaning fits the context well and νῦν is always used this way in the Gospel of John.

Christ The referent of the pronoun αὐτῷ 'it/him' is specified as Christ. (In 2:27e the referent of αὐτῷ is taken to be the Holy Spirit; see the note there on 'in accordance with'.)

2:28b when Christ manifests himself The referent of the pronoun αὐτοῦ 'of him' and also of the third person masculine suffixes in this passage can be determined only on the basis of the actions or roles of the referent. We know from other teachings that Christ will return to judge the world. This role is also attributed to God, but 'God' does not fit this context. Commentators are unanimous in saying that here the referent is 'Christ'.

The verb φανερωθῇ 'manifest himself' is a passive form with a reflexive meaning. (Alternatively, this could mean 'when God reveals Christ'.) The eschatological reference to Christ's coming is mentioned only in these two verses in this Epistle. It may be taken in the same way as ἐσχάτη ὥρα 'the last hour' (2:18) as referring to an imminent event of unknown timing which by its imminence has a constant bearing on the whole Christian era.

be confident *that we associate properly with God* Literally, this is 'have boldness', the opposite of 'shame'. There seems to be no adequate English equivalent; the closest is 'confidence' which inherently requires some content. It is not self-confidence, but rather fearlessness because in Christ we associate properly and securely with God.

2:28c not be ashamed The preposition ἀπό 'from' used with αἰσχυνθῶμεν 'we will be ashamed' suggests a shrinking as though wanting to hide from Christ's presence.

2:29a Since The Greek grammatical structure indicates a condition-CONSEQUENCE relation.

However, we know that the protasis of the condition is true, so that this functions as reason-RESULT, here encoded as 'since'.

God As in 28b and c, the referent of 'he' in 29a and b can be determined only on the basis of the referent's actions or roles. Both God and Christ are 'righteous', but only God has the role of engendering. Because of this division of roles, commentators are not entirely agreed; but most take 'God' as the referent. In the display the third person verbal suffix is therefore specified as 'God'.

2:29b you know Commentators disagree as to whether γινώσκετε 'know' is indicative or imperative here. Given the paragraph pattern, the indicative mood fits best. The meaning would be the same even if 'know' were taken to be imperative since, generally, the imperative mood functions to give prominence to a verb of cognition rather than to signify a demand that ideas change (see the 3:1a note).

continues doing what is right It is difficult to express all the implications of the present continuous ποιῶν τὴν δικαιοσύνην 'he does righteousness'. It refers mainly to a person who behaves righteously as a way of life.

God has caused him to live *spiritually* In the Greek this is figurative: 'has been begotten'. It signifies spiritual regeneration. God is specified as the one who gives spiritual life (see the note on 29a).

BOUNDARIES AND COHERENCE

The opening boundary was discussed under 1:5-2:27. The closing boundary is indicated by the use of ἴδετε 'behold' in 3:1, introducing the next unit by directing attention to a new topic: the love of God shown in God's gift of new life and the privilege of sonship.

The relational coherence of 2:28-29 is seen in its internal structure. It starts with the nuclear *APPEAL* 'continue to live united to Christ' (28a). This is supported by the *motivational basis* 'in order that we may have confidence when he manifests himself' (28b-c) and the *axiomatic basis* 'we should be righteous like God' (v. 29).

PROMINENCE AND THEME

As an overt exhortation, the 2:28a *APPEAL* has natural prominence. The theme statement is drawn from this *APPEAL* and the HEAD propositions of the *bases*.

FIRST JOHN 3:1-10

SECTION CONSTITUENT 3:1-10 (Hortatory Paragraph: Specific appeal₁ of 2:28-4:6)
Theme: Do not allow anyone to seduce you to sin, because we are God's children and his children maintain themselves free from evil behavior by not continuing to sin as the devil's children do.

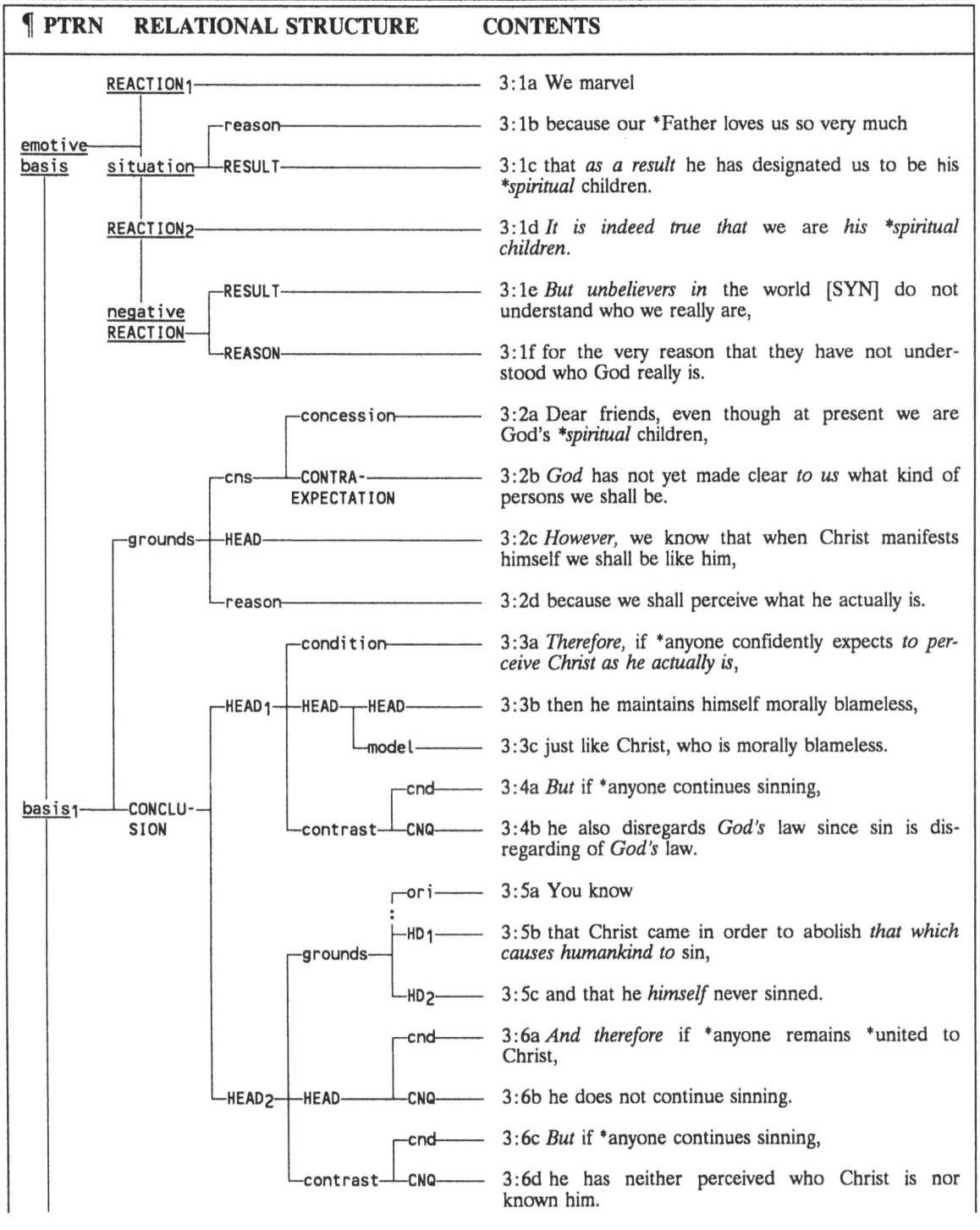

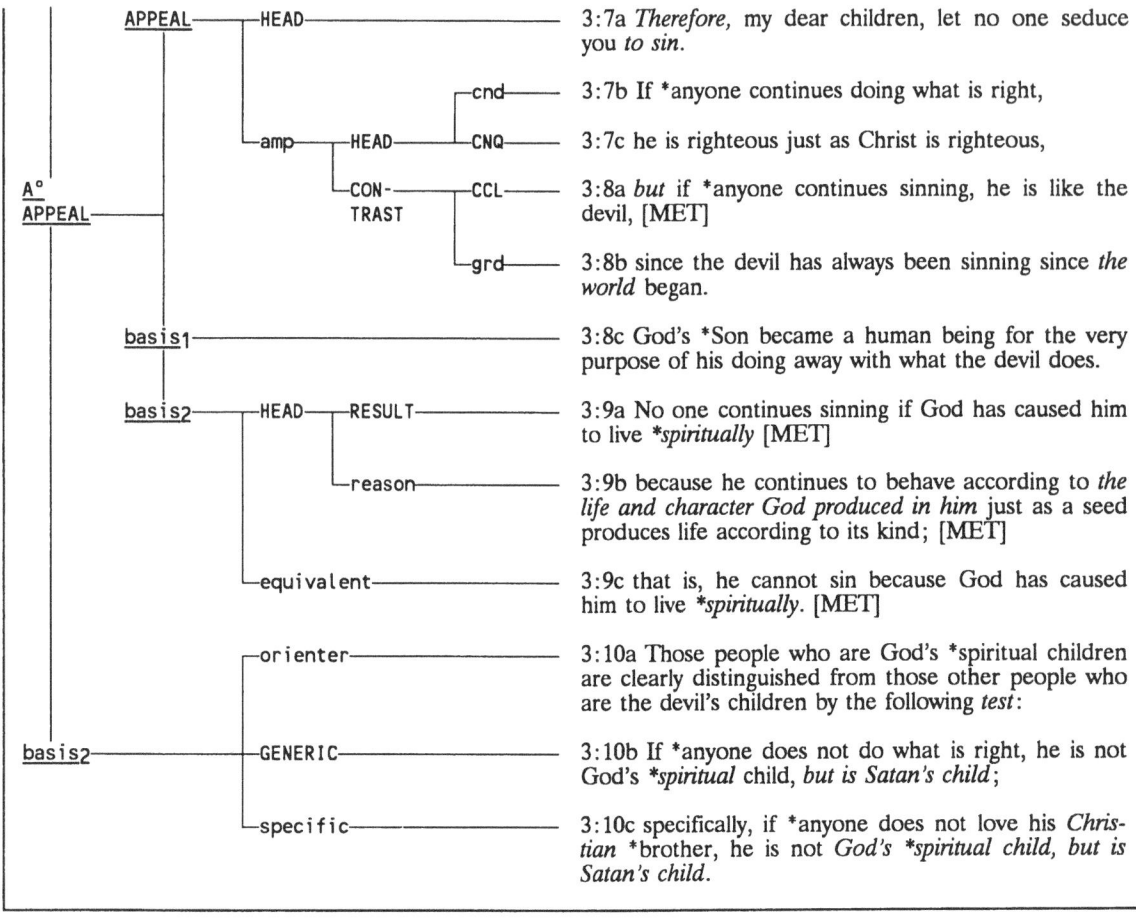

INTENT AND PARAGRAPH PATTERN

The author's intent in 3:1–10 is to affect the readers' actions, warning that they not be seduced by the false teachers into thinking that it is all right to sin. This paragraph consists of two propositional clusters and two embedded paragraphs: v. 1 (a paragraph) and vv. 2–6 (a propositional cluster) support vv. 7–9 (a paragraph), which is the central unit; and v. 10 (a propositional cluster) is the final unit, closing the sub-section by supporting the central unit and also returning to the v. 1 motif.

The communication relationship of these four units is two grounds units followed by an exhortation followed by another grounds unit. Since the primary intent expressed in the imperative verb is to affect the readers' belief system and behavior, this is taken as a causal hortatory paragraph, the principal constituents being + basis + APPEAL.

NOTES

3:1a We marvel Although ἴδετε 'take note' is an imperative, the purpose of the imperative is to draw attention to something, not to call on the readers to change their actions or beliefs.

3:1b so very much The word ποταπήν 'of what sort', an interrogative asking the nature of something, is used here as an exclamation of admiration. It is similar to a rhetorical question. There are many ways that this could be expressed such as 'how glorious', 'what amazing love', 'how greatly', or 'so very much'.

3:1c as a result Here ἵνα 'in order that' is used to signal the reason-RESULT relationship between 1a and 1c. This relationship is shown in the display as + REACTION + situation.

has designated us In this context the meaning of καλέω 'call' is to give a title or confer special privileges and responsibilities on someone. But in English and many other languages, 'call' has the central meaning of summoning someone from a distance. Other possible ways of expressing 'designate' are: 'he says we are his sons'; 'he causes us to be his sons'; 'he says to us about us, "You are my son" '; 'he entitled us to be his sons'.

3:1d It is indeed true that we are Some texts omit καὶ ἐσμέν 'and we are'. But it is classified as a B reading in the UBS text only because its omission is more easily accounted for than its addition would be (Metzger). In this analysis we accept 'we are' because διὰ τοῦτο 'therefore', which follows it, is dependent upon the clause. The expression is an emphatic reflective comment of the author's. An idiomatic way of expressing this in English would be 'and so we are!'.

3:1e But... The relationship between 3:1c-d and 3:1e-f is not at all clear since there is no overt connector and we are left with no more than the propositions 'God has caused us to be his spiritual children' and 'unbelievers do not understand who we really are'. The relationship is not restative, clarificational, or logical; rather it seems to be an emotive reaction to the tremendous truth that we have been privileged to be God's children.

unbelievers in the world Here the Greek word 'world' is a synecdoche for 'godless people' or 'unbelievers' (the second meaning of κόσμος 'world' in the note on 2:2).

understand The Greek is γινώσκει 'it/he knows'. It is rendered 'understand' by Brooke, Bultmann, Marshall, Westcott, and others. The meaning could extend to 'acknowledge', 'accept', or 'understand'.

3:1f for the very reason that The conjunction διὰ τοῦτο 'because' occurs in 1 John only here and in 4:5. In both cases it focuses prominence on the reason.

There is a difference of opinion about the direction in which διὰ τοῦτο 'for this reason' points. If it points backward, it is grounds ('for this reason') as in 4:5; but if it points forward, it is result ('as a result'). Brown (1982) says it points forward to 3:1f since this phrase regularly points forward in the Gospel of John when it is followed by an epexegetical clause introduced by ὅτι 'that'. Marshall, on the other hand, considers it important to take the phrase with what precedes for better connection with the context. However, it is questionable how unbelievers' not recognizing us could be the grounds or reason for our marveling that God shows how he loves us so deeply and freely. Therefore we favor the view that the phrase points forward. Thus, their not recognizing us is the result of their not recognizing him (the relationship between 3:1e and 3:1f). This is the relationship signaled by the combination of διὰ τοῦτο 'for this reason' and ὅτι 'that'.

God The pronoun αὐτόν 'him', which is specified in the display as 'God', could be interpreted as referring either to God or to Christ; but in this immediate context, the 'Father' is the focal topic. The Father sent Christ to reveal himself to men; in rejecting Christ they failed to understand who the Father is.

3:2a-b though at present we are..., God has not yet made clear *to us* **what kind of persons we shall be** A radical change has taken place with the gift of sonship. What we are at present and what we shall be is a matter of sequence. This is the significance of the emphatic νῦν 'now' in contrast with οὔπω 'not yet'. The conjunction καί 'and' is rendered 'but' because 'but' collocates better in English with 'yet', which follows.

The verb φανερόω 'make known' (occurring here as a passive) is transitive. An actor and a recipient of the action need to be supplied, hence '*God*' and '*to us*' in the display.

The phrase 'what we shall be' implies that we do not now know what we shall be like when Christ manifests himself again. That has not been fully explained in the Scriptures—we know only that we have nothing on earth to compare to that future state. (We do know quite well what kind of persons we are *now* as to our physical nature, our behavior, and our thoughts and desires; and this letter of First John tells us what kind of persons we *should* be as to our behavior and thoughts as a result of our sharing in God's character now that we have been made his children.)

3:2c when Christ manifests himself The text has 'he' here. Commentators differ as to whether the pronoun refers to Christ or to God. We take it to be Christ since the role of the future manifestation of himself and his 'coming' is, throughout the letter, attributed to Christ. Also, in the following context (v. 5) it is explicit that Christ is the one who came; nowhere else in the Epistle is there any reference to God's coming.

As to 'manifests himself', an alternate interpretation is 'when we appear' or 'when we are made known'. Or, in view of the immediate context (i.e., 3:2a), it could mean 'when God makes us known'. However, the larger context, especially 2:28, leads us to conclude that the actor is Christ.

3:2c–d we shall be like him, because we shall perceive what he actually is According to 2 Cor. 3:18 the believer's transformation into the likeness of Christ is in progress in this life. And according to 1 John 3:2c–d we shall be like Christ at the time when he comes because we shall perceive what he is actually like. (The Greek verb is εἰμί 'be', not γίνομαι 'become'.) While John is not denying that a process is involved (see 3:3), he speaks of a transformation to be expected at the return of Christ—the culmination of the process now going on. As the simple reading of the text indicates, that transformation results from seeing Christ as he is: human frailty reaches the potential of the glorified humanity of Christ. Another interpretation is that the believer's seeing Christ as he is will be the *evidence* that he has been made like Christ. The two views may be summarized as follows:

1. 'We shall see him as he is' refers to the culminating experience of the process of conforming believers to the image of Christ (Rom. 8:29; Phil. 1:6). The means of the believer's transformation that will come to completion at Christ's future manifestation is seeing him; it is not attainable by human effort.
2. Since we have been made like Christ, we are thereby made able to see him as he is (Matt. 5:8). Our likeness to him is the grounds for seeing him as he is.

The rendering in the display is based on the first view, which is the more simple and straightforward of the two. The fact that John must call attention to the readers' failure to demonstrate the love befitting Christlikeness (3:17) and must warn against lack of love helps to establish this interpretation.

3:3a if anyone The Greek is πᾶς ὁ 'everyone who'. It functions as a conditional: 'if anyone'. Generalized statements beginning with πᾶς 'everyone' are taken by commentators as references to people who claim special exemption or privilege for themselves.

The relationship between 3a and 3b is condition-CONSEQUENCE (HEAD). One might be tempted to think that this is another mitigated exhortation with the relationship of *EXHORTATION-grounds*. Although this is a conditional statement from a semantic point of view, its grammatical form is an embedded clause functioning as the subject of the sentence, very different from an 'if' (ἐάν) clause. While both of these forms have the same underlying semantic relation of condition, only the ἐάν clause meets the requirements for mitigated exhortation (see p. 2 re degrees of mitigation).

confidently expects The word ἐλπίς 'hope' means 'to trust/rely'. In modern English the primary meaning of *hope* is quite different, lacking the component of certainty. The rendering in the display combines the components of expectation and certainty.

to perceive Christ as he actually is The phrase 'this hope' raises the question as to what the referent of 'this' is. The immediately preceding words 'we shall perceive Christ as he actually is' fit well. Most commentators make Christ's second coming the generic referent and include many of the things that will accompany that event, the specific referent that we have mentioned being one of them. The believer's hope is to be ἐπ' αὐτῷ 'in him', and is interpreted in this verse as hope in Christ with reference to his return and to his purity.

3:3b maintains himself morally blameless The Greek is ἁγνίζω 'purify', used here in an extended figurative sense. Since the verb is in the present tense, we have expressed the meaning in keeping with this present idea.

3:4a *But* Although there is no conjunction between v. 3 and v. 4, the semantic relation is contrast.

continues sinning More literally, this is 'to continue doing sin'. It is difficult to express all the implications of the present continuous form of ποιῶν 'he does'. Here it refers mainly to a person who continues sinning as a way of life (see the note on 2:29b).

3:4b disregards *God's* law The noun 'lawlessness' here is an event. It could be rendered 'a person does not behave according to the law' or 'a person behaves disregarding the law'. The latter is the best choice from the point of view of semantic theory and also has the advantage of conciseness.

3:5b Christ came This is a specific reference to the event of Christ's becoming a human being; hence the pronoun 'he' is specified as Christ. A more literal gloss would be 'Christ appeared', but 'appeared' has the primary meaning of suddenly becoming visible to someone, which does not fit here.

in order to abolish *that which causes humankind to* **sin** The Greek is ἵνα τὰς ἁμαρτίας ἄρῃ 'in order to destroy sins'. Here 'destroy' is used with an extended meaning in the sense of 'abolish'. But since 'sins' refers to a group of events, it is not an abolishable thing. The sense of 'sins' here is, rather, 'that which (*or*, the person who) causes humankind to act sinfully'. The meaning of the clause, therefore, is closer to 'in order to abolish the cause of sinning'. Other possible, less forceful ways of expressing this are: 'Christ came in order that he might prevent humankind from sinning' or 'Christ came in order that he might enable humankind not to sin'.

3:5c he *himself* **never sinned** The sinlessness of Christ has synonymous reference to the purity mentioned in 3:3c.

3:6a *And therefore* The argument being developed in this passage has its grounds in 3:2c and its two conclusions in 3:3a–b ('Therefore . . .') and 3:6b ('And therefore'). There is no overt conjunction in the Greek showing this relationship; but since this is the logical structure, 'And therefore' is supplied.

3:6b, c continues sinning The meaning of the Greek is 'a person habitually sinning' (see the notes on 2:29b and 3:4a). Some commentators say that John is presenting an ideal for Christian behavior. The majority opinion is that the focus is on the "habit" of sinning.

3:6c *But* In v. 6, a–b and c–d are in contrast with each other. The latter is the negative of the former, hence '*but*', the preferred word in English for showing contrast.

3:6d neither perceived . . . nor known Here an extended figure is used involving the words ὁράω 'see' and γινώσκω 'know'. This is not seeing or knowing in the ordinary sense, as one knows his neighbor, but rather perceiving and understanding the person of Christ on a spiritual level.

Christ The Greek pronoun 'he' is specified as Christ.

3:7a *Therefore* In the Greek there is no conjunction to join this clause with previous ones. However, the clause is introduced by a vocative, which John frequently uses to introduce a direct exhortation. The exhortation here is clearly the APPEAL based on all that was said in vv. 1–6, and the *basis*-APPEAL relationship is properly shown by 'therefore'.

seduce you *to sin* The Greek is μηδεὶς πλανάτω ὑμᾶς 'let no one lead you astray', a figure meaning 'to deceive by affecting the ideas' or 'to seduce by affecting the emotions, ideas, and ultimately the behavior'. In view of the immediate context (esp. 3:1, which is emotional, and 3:2–6, which is expository, as well as 3:7b–8:b), we take the verb to mean more than simply affecting ideas. It means affecting behavior as well. The verb 'seduce' requires that the effect of seducing be supplied: sin.

3:7c righteous A possible alternative to 'righteous' is 'to be declared right by God', but this hardly seems correct since the issue being addressed in the context is living in an appropriate relationship with God by behaving according to what God intended. A better alternative would be 'he is in a proper relationship with God just as Christ is'.

3:8a like the devil The Greek is ἐκ τοῦ διαβόλου ἐστίν 'he is from the devil'. If taken literally, this would mean that a person's origin is from the devil. But this is a figurative use meaning 'a person has a character similar to that of the devil'.

3:8b since *the world* **began** Scripture does not give a clear account of the origin of the devil, but we know he acted in his present role before the expulsion from Eden. The events in Eden could be considered the beginning of the world.

3:8c became a human being See the 5b note.

doing away with The more literal rendering would be 'destroy', which collocates better with material things (e.g., 'destroyed the house'). Here the word refers to undoing the effects of some previous action.

what the devil does This is no neutral activity. It specifically refers to all the evil actions of the devil in assaulting man's heart, mind, and soul, and God's physical creation.

3:9a continues sinning See the 4a note.

if God has caused him to live *spiritually* Commentators are agreed that γεγεννημένος ἐκ τοῦ θεοῦ 'born from God' here is used metaphorically, as represented in the display.

3:9b he continues to behave according to For the meaning of μένω 'remains' in the phrase 'remains in him', see 'joined together' in the Glossary. Here μένω is to continue living or behaving according to a stated characteristic. As to ἐν αὐτῷ 'in him', it is clear from the immediate context that the referent is the child of God, who should continue to show the same characteristics as the Father: the seed remains in him, the believer. Some commentators say that the referent of 'in him' is God, but this is not supported by the context.

the life and character God produced in him just as a seed produces life according to its kind In the Greek 'God's seed' is a metaphor that specifies neither the referent nor the point of similarity between referent and image. In our rendering the image, 'seed', is retained and the referent and point of similarity are supplied. Commentators tend to confuse the referent and point of similarity of this metaphor, suggesting various referents such as 'the principle of life', 'the Word of God', 'the children of God', or 'the Holy Spirit'. But spelling out the metaphor makes it clear: Just as seed develops and produces its own kind, so the character imparted by God to the believer develops and produces its own kind (i.e., godly behavior). It could be restated as 'God's children continue to show the characteristics of their spiritual Father'.

3:9c he cannot sin This proposition might seem to be asserting something different from 9a. The 9c statement has long been debated: Is it a statement of ideal, or is habitual sin the focus? In our analysis we favor the second interpretation (as does NIV: "he cannot go on sinning"). We have therefore shown the relationship between 9a and 9c as "equivalent" in the display.

3:10a God's spiritual children The topic of the metaphor 'children' is the believers, and the point of similarity between the topic and image has to do with the source of life: just as the source of the physical life of children is their biological parents, so the source of believers' spiritual life is God. In order to present the proposition in parallel terms, as it is in the Greek text, 'God's spiritual children' and 'the devil's children' are expressed as a contrast. In the metaphor 'the devil's children', the topic is unbelievers and the source of their spiritual life is the devil.

clearly distinguished ... by the following test Again there is the problem as to the referent of 'by this' in ἐν τούτῳ φανερά ἐστιν 'by this it is made known'. As discussed in the note on 2:3a, we take the referent to be the following context. The meaning 'clearly distinguished' is well supported by both commentators and lexicons in this context. We have supplied 'test' from the context.

3:10b but is Satan's child Proposition 3:10a is a preface to the 10b test by which to distinguish God's children from the devil's children. Here John elliptically states only one side of the inference ('he is not God's *spiritual* child'). The total inference includes 'but is Satan's child'.

3:10c specifically The conjunction καί 'and' shows that 10b and c are closely related to each other without specifying the relationship. The relation that seems most appropriate is that of GENERIC-specific. The generic seems to be prominent since it restates the motif of this paragraph that we not continue sinning. By means of the specific John is turning the attention of the hearer to the need to love one another. The last clause of v. 10 is anticipatory (tail-head link), leading into the subject matter of the next paragraph (3:11–18).

is not *God's spiritual child, but is Satan's child* Not only does καί 'and' show a close semantic tie between clauses, but it is often associated with ellipsis. The previous proposition, 10b, makes reference to 'God's spiritual child'. In 10c this element and the element 'Satan's child' are ellipsed in the Greek but are supplied in the display.

BOUNDARIES AND COHERENCE

The opening boundary of 3:1–10 coincides with the closure of 2:28–29. The evidence for the boundary has already been discussed under that unit. The final boundary of 3:1–10 is marked by the summary in v. 10 bringing moral purity and family relationship together. The next unit (3:11–18) is opened by the emphatic and anaphoric deictic ὅτι αὕτη 'because this'. There also is a change in topic from sinning to loving.

In determining boundaries we have given consideration to systems of division used by various commentators. Here commentators differ as to the boundaries and coherence. We agree with the many who combine 3:11–12 with 3:13–18 because the subject of love is in focus and Cain is taken as a negative example of one who did not love his brother. Additional arguments for this position are:

1. The central topic of 3:1–10 is righteousness in contrast to sinning. Love is mentioned only as a motivational basis for being righteous (i.e., its mention is supportive and not central).
2. The central topic in the unit that follows (3:11–18) is love in contrast to hate, murder, and death, for all of which Cain provides a key illustration.
3. The mitigated exhortation to love each other in v. 11 is a most appropriate lead-in to the central issue of 3:11–18.
4. The author is preparing the readers for the exhortation to not be surprised if the people of the world hate them. He emphasizes the reason that Cain hated his brother: it was because Cain did evil and his brother did not. Likewise, the people of the world who do evil hate those who do not do evil.
5. Grammatically, it is not a forced position for ὅτι 'because' to introduce a paragraph break.

Arguments in support of placing 3:11–12 with 3:1–10 are:

1. The subject of love was already introduced in 3:1, where the love of God is God's motive for making believers his children. So the concept of love has an important bearing on the 3:1–12 section.
2. The example of Cain is appropriate for showing the distinction between τὰ τέκνα τοῦ θεοῦ 'the children of God' and τὰ τέκνα τοῦ διαβόλου 'the children of the devil' (3:10), because the basis of Cain's murderous act was that his deeds were evil and Abel's were righteous (v. 12). Thus, the negative illustration completes the discussion of the origin of actions.
3. The exhortation in v. 11 is 'we should love each other' with the negative example in v. 12 linked to it by grammatical contrast: οὐ καθώς 'not like'.
4. As for lexical markers, neither ὅτι 'because' (v. 11) nor καθώς 'as' (v. 12) are likely boundary indicators since they are subordinate conjunctions.

It is our view that 3:11–12 is a transitional unit linked to both the preceding and the following units, but with a stronger linkage to the one that follows it.

Semantic coherence for 3:1–10 is seen in the contrast of the behavior of those who have been born of God and those who belong to the devil. Lexical items concerning behavior are: ποιῶν τὴν δικαιοσύνην 'does what is right' (3:7, 10); δίκαιος 'righteous' (twice in 3:7); ποιῶν τὴν ἁμαρτίαν 'commits sin' (3:4, 8–9); and ἁμαρτάνω 'sin' (3:6, 8–9). Lexical items concerning the family relationship are: τέκνα 'children' (3:1, 2, 7, and twice in 10); ἐκ 'from', meaning source (3:8, 10); υἱός 'Son of God' (3:8) in reference to Christ; and γεννάω 'beget' (twice in 3:9).

Semantic coherence in the unit is also found in the fact that believers are called 'children of God' and in the consequent implication of moral purity. The fact that believers are now in the relationship of children to God carries the promise of their bearing the family likeness of moral purity (3:3c).

Also adding to coherence are the terms that occur contrasting moral qualities that result from the believer's relationship to God and those that result from sin. Terms for moral purity occur in 3:3b–c, 5c, 6a, 7c, 9a–b, 10b; terms for sin occur in 3:4, 5b, 6b–c, 8a–b, 8c, 9a–c. These terms do not occur after v. 10.

There are several other lexical forms that give coherence to the unit. Three contrasts are stated, each of which begins with πᾶς ὁ 'everyone who'. The first of these (3:3 and 4) contrasts the one who gladly awaits what God has promised, purifying himself, with the one who does not know God and gives himself to sin. The second of these (3:6a–b and 6c–d) contrasts the one who remains united to Christ with the one who continues sinning. The third of these (3:9 and 10) contrasts the one whom God has caused to live with the one who is related to the devil. The simple ὁ 'he who' in (3:7b and 8a) introduces a further contrast. It contrasts the one who continues doing what is right with the one who continues sinning.

As to structural coherence, the 3:1–10 paragraph, which has four distinct constituents (3:1, 3:2–6, 3:7–9, and 3:10), is viewed by some commentators as two separate paragraphs (1–6 and 7–10) since 1–6 is supportive of 7–10. But 1–6 cannot stand alone as a semantic unit; rather, in supporting the *APPEAL* it completes a hortatory paragraph pattern. Therefore, we consider 1–10 to be a single paragraph (in a sense a "complex paragraph") consisting of three *bases* (3:1, 2–6, 10) and an *APPEAL* (3:7–9). The 7–9 *APPEAL* in turn has its own *bases* and *APPEAL*. This semantic structure provides the unit's coherence.

Further structural coherence is seen in the inclusio of 3:1 and 3:10, where the family relationship is brought out at the beginning and close of the unit by such terms as τέκνα τοῦ θεοῦ 'sons of God' and ἀδελφὸν αὐτοῦ 'his brother'.

PROMINENCE AND THEME

The 3:1–10 unit begins with a strong emotional response to the fact that God has designated us to be his sons. Although ἴδετε 'take note' is an imperative form, its rhetorical force ought not to be taken as hortatory (intended to affect behavior). Rather, it is an emotional expression.

After expressing this emotion, John repeatedly emphasizes the believer's responsibility to behave according to the family character of not sinning. This motif of not sinning occurs in 3:3b, 4a, 6b–c, 7b–c, 9a, 9c, and 10b and is so prominent in this unit that it must be expressed in the theme statement.

Three pairs of πᾶς ὁ 'all who' introduce contrastive units in vv. 3–4, v. 6, and vv. 9–10. These pairs of contrasts are not apparently for the purpose of marking prominence; rather, they are a poetic device that lends coherence.

The nuclear part of the *APPEAL* is μηδεὶς πλανάτω ὑμᾶς 'let no one lead you astray'. This relates to ideas as well as actions. From the immediate context it is clear that the implied result is 'to sin'. It is interesting to note that the surface form is imperative, which implies an intent to affect behavior (hortatory), while the verb itself and its complement entails affecting ideas (expository) as well. The subject matter lies between expository and hortatory in intent, but the unit is in any case definitely hortatory in view of the clear reference to the readers' behavior.

The *naturally* prominent segments convey the greatest significance. Therefore the theme statement is taken from the HEAD proposition of the *APPEAL* (3:7a) and from *the REACTIONS* (3:1a, d) of the *emotive basis* and from the HEADS (3:3b, 6b) of the next *basis*.

SECTION CONSTITUENT 3:11–18 (Hortatory Paragraph: Specific appeal₂ of 2:28–4:6)

Theme: Since we have been changed from being spiritually dead people to being spiritually living people, we should love each other genuinely by helping our Christian brothers who are in need.

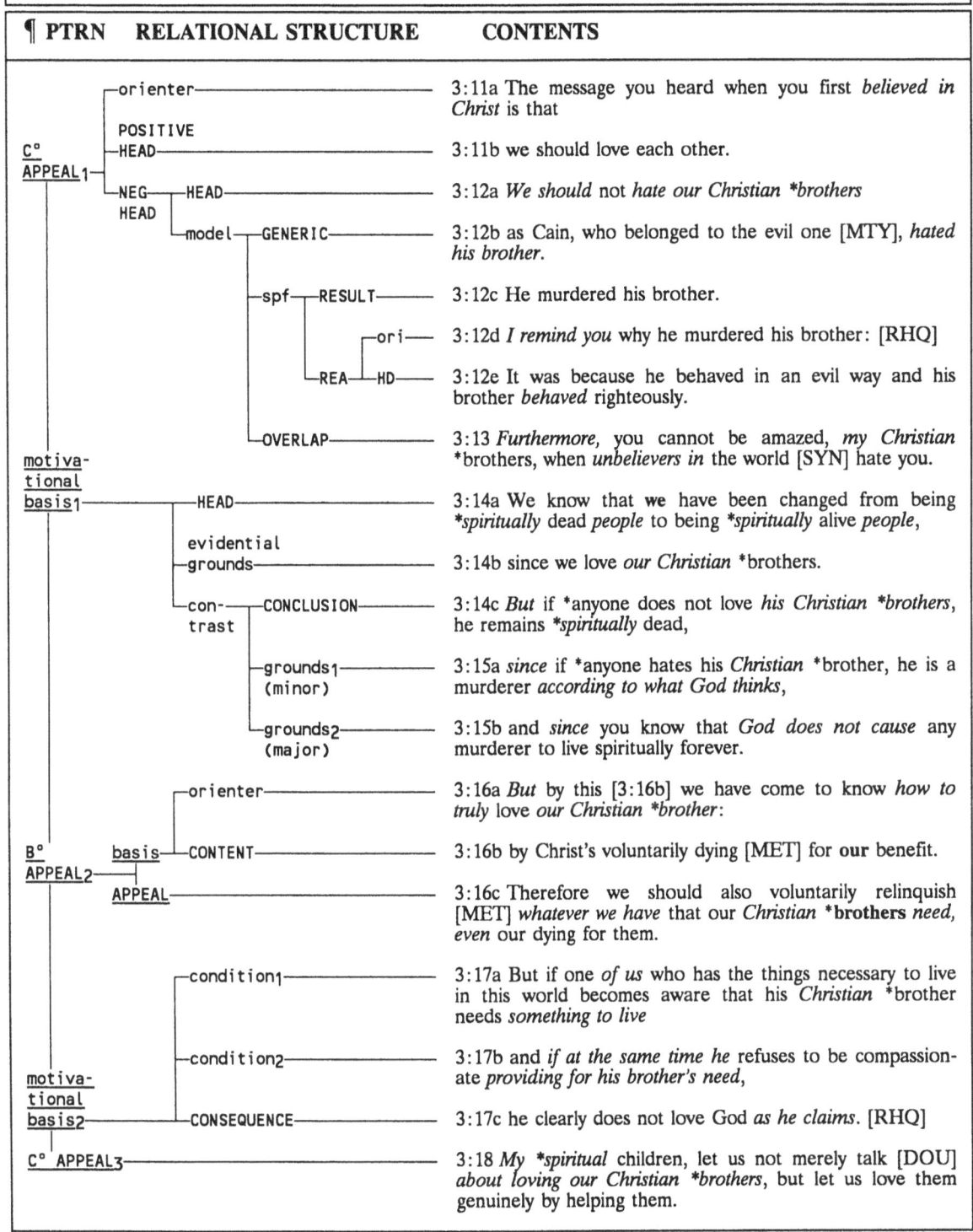

INTENT AND PARAGRAPH PATTERN

John's intent in the 3:11–18 unit is to affect the readers' actions by two C° APPEALS and one B° APPEAL to love the Christian brothers genuinely. We take 3:11–18 to be a single paragraph consisting of one embedded paragraph and three propositional clusters: 3:11–13 is an APPEAL, followed by a *basis* (3:14–15), followed by an APPEAL (3:16), which in turn is followed by a second *basis* (3:17) and yet another APPEAL (3:18). Their communication relationship is an exhortation unit followed by a grounds unit followed by an exhortation unit followed by a second grounds unit and an exhortation unit. Both motivational grounds units support the exhortation that precedes and follows. Since the paragraph's primary intent is to affect behavior, the genre is causal hortatory, the principal constituents being + *basis* + APPEAL.

NOTES

3:11a The initial ὅτι 'for, because, that is' links this unit with the previous one (3:1–10), in which the last proposition ('specifically, anyone does not love his *Christian* brother') is transitional, introducing the topic of 3:11–18. This interclausal conjunction subordinates the clause that follows it to the main independent clause, but its function here at the beginning of 3:11 is unusual. Versions and commentators make paragraph breaks here without ever discussing the unusual use of ὅτι, apparently assuming that it functions like γάρ 'because' between paragraphs. We view this linkage as a surface phenomenon that could be represented by a nearly meaningless English 'for'. However, from a semantic point of view, ὅτι needs no lexical representation aside from the paragraph juncture and the thematic shift.

when you first *believed in Christ* See the note on 2:7b.

3:11a–b we should love In the construction αὕτη ἐστίν ... ἵνα 'this is [the message] that [we should love each other]', αὕτη 'this' is a cataphoric pronoun acting as a prominence device to bring the content introduced by ἵνα 'that' into focus. (This same construction occurs also in 3:23 and 5:3.) The focus is on the word 'message/command', which functions as an exhortation with the least degree of mitigation (see the discussion on mitigation in the Introduction).

3:12a We should not *hate* The conjunction that links 11b and 12a is οὐ καθώς 'not just as, not like'. It assumes the previous 'we should love each other', suggesting a contrastive action or behavior. (This has been made explicit in the display.)

3:12b belonged to the evil one The metaphor ἐκ τοῦ πονηροῦ 'from the evil one' is essentially the same one as in 3:10a (see the note there on the 'devil's children'). Here τοῦ πονηροῦ 'of the evil' is a metonymy standing for 'the devil'.

3:12d *I remind you* The Greek rhetorical question here functions to emphasize the reason for Cain's act of murder. This proposition of itself cannot present the reason for Cain's murdering his brother, since the 'why' only points to the next proposition where the specific reason is presented.

3:12e It was because The rhetorical question in 12d followed by ὅτι 'because' and the forefronting of τὰ ἔργα αὐτοῦ πονηρὰ ἦν 'his works were evil' makes this proposition very prominent. The cleft construction 'it was because', though somewhat ungrammatical in English, shows this prominence.

3:13 It is difficult to know how this verse functions in the paragraph. It seems to be an incidental comment between the APPEAL and *motivational basis*. In the display it is shown as an overlap with Cain's hateful behavior, the underlying thought of which is: Do not hate as Cain hated his brother because he was evil; furthermore, you cannot be amazed when evil people hate you too.

you cannot be amazed The Greek imperative here is not a true appeal for action. Rather, it functions as an orienter with a very expressive force.

my *Christian* brothers Only in this place does John address his hearers as 'brothers'. Elsewhere he addresses them as 'beloved' or 'children'. Having just spoken of the brothers Cain and Abel, John calls his audience 'brothers'. It is suggested that he does so to associate himself more closely with the readers as one who also suffers as an object of the hatred of the ungodly.

when *unbelievers in* the world hate you This is not a future conditional event as the literal rendering of εἰ μισεῖ 'if it hate' might indicate. Rather, it is a statement of present fact. The meaning here is often referred to as a first class condition.

For the meaning of κόσμος 'world' see the second meaning in the note on 2:2c.

3:14a, c It is difficult to determine the relative prominence between 3:14a and 14c. The two are contrastive, the first being positive and the second negative. Although the positive part of a contrast is frequently the more prominent, here the negative part is more fully developed, and either part *could* serve as a good motivational basis for loving each other. But what helps us see that 14a is more prominent than 14c is that *'remains* spiritually dead' in 14c does not cohere as grounds for 'love each other'. (Notice that 14c does not say that if one hates, he will *become* spiritually dead, but rather that if one hates he is *already* spiritually dead.)

3:14a we The pronoun 'we' is syntactically prominent and therefore stands in contrast to the word 'world' (i.e., 'people').

have been changed from The Greek is μεταβεβήκαμεν, literally 'have passed over', that is, passed over to a different state of being.

3:14c–15b This propositional cluster forms a syllogism consisting of a conclusion (14c), a minor premise (15a), and a major premise (15b).

3:14c love *his Christian brothers* In some Greek texts τὸν ἀδελφὸν αὐτοῦ 'his brother' appears after ἀγαπῶν 'love'. This is probably an addition: there are superior texts which do not have it (it is not in the UBS text). That it is an addition by copyists is considered more likely than that it is an omission (Metzger). But whether the reading is accepted or rejected, the meaning is the same. The focus of the 3:11–18 paragraph and particularly of 3:13–15 is on the Christian brother.

3:15a *according to what God thinks* In law a murderer is a person who has unlawfully *killed* another person. However, John says that a person who *hates* a fellow Christian is a murderer. This definition is not according to human thinking or standards. Thus, 'according to what God thinks' is supplied.

3:15b *God does not cause* any murderer to live spiritually forever The Greek is οὐκ ἔχει ζωὴν αἰώνιον 'does not have eternal life', suggesting that eternal life is a possession. But in semantic theory a state of being is something that is experienced, not possessed. Hence it is rendered here as an experience, 'living forever'; and it is an experience that God can cause in another. The phrase ἐν αὐτῷ μένουσαν 'it remains in him', which focuses on the state of being, further supports this rendering. The implication is that a murderer has not experienced this state that God causes in some other people, although he may potentially experience it.

3:16a this [3:16b] See the 1:5a note.

have come to know The verb γινώσκω 'know' often conveys the sense of knowing from experience or learning. Since it is in the perfect tense it may be interpreted as 'having learned' in contrast to οἶδα 'know' in 3:15b, which refers to recalling a matter already known. Although the components of meaning overlap in these two verbs, the former frequently assumes the underlying experience or learning process by which one learns, while the latter assumes the ability to perform, process, and recall what one already knows. In 3:15b John is reminding the hearers of what they already know, namely that no murderer has eternal life. In 3:16a, in contrast, he is advising the hearers how it was that they came to experience something, namely being loved by God: it was through Christ's loving us and dying for us.

know *how to truly* love *our Christian brother* The noun ἀγάπη 'love' represents an event and requires an actor and a goal: 'someone loves someone else'. Here John focuses on the genuine manner of believers' love for other people.

3:16b Christ's voluntarily dying for our benefit The Greek is ἐκεῖνος ὑπὲρ ἡμῶν τὴν ψυχὴν αὐτοῦ ἔθηκεν 'that one on our behalf laid down his life', a metaphor. Again, ἐκεῖνος 'that one' refers specifically to Christ (see the note on 2:6b); 'laid down his life' means that by an act of his own will he allowed himself to be killed, hence 'voluntarily dying'. The Greek word order is significant: ὑπὲρ ἡμῶν 'for us' is in the emphatic position, hence 'he laid down his life for *us*'. The same word order is used in 16c: 'we should lay down our lives for our *brothers*.

3:16c voluntarily relinquish *whatever we have that our Christian* brothers *need, even* **our dying for them** The Greek is καὶ ἡμεῖς ὀφείλομεν ὑπὲρ τῶν ἀδελφῶν τὰς ψυχὰς θεῖναι 'we also are obligated to lay down our lives on behalf of the brothers'. The metaphor 'lay down our lives' parallels the one in 16b—it is what Christ himself has done. The meaning seems to be relinquishment by an act of the will of anything (including one's life or livelihood) for the good of a Christian brother. But what believers are to do 'on behalf of the brothers' is markedly different from what Christ did 'on our behalf' (ὑπὲρ ἡμῶν). Christ suffered the punishment that we deserved in order to give us eternal life; we are to suffer the cost of helping our Christian brothers live adequately both physically and spiritually, as made clear by what follows.

3:17–18 Verse 17 is conjoined to v. 16 by δέ 'but' and presents a contrastive *basis* for the APPEAL of 16c. However, v. 17 presents a contrastive *basis* for the APPEAL of v. 18 as well, and it is more closely linked lexically and by semantic domain to v. 18 than to v. 16. In effect, v. 17 supports both the APPEAL in 16c and the one in v. 18. In the display v. 17 has been placed as a *motivational basis* between the two APPEALS to show its function as a transitional unit supporting both of them.

3:17a the things necessary to live in this world Commentators are divided as to the meaning of τὸν βίον τοῦ κόσμου 'the life of the world'. Some suggest that βίον, meaning 'life, wealth, possessions, or recourse for subsistence', here refers to wealth and that John is urging the rich to share. Another interpretation is that it refers to the things necessary to maintain life and that John is urging everyone to share according to his means. This latter interpretation is preferable.

The meaning of 'world' here is the fifth one in the note on 2:2c, 'the goods that support human physical life'.

becomes aware The verb θεωρέω 'see, look at, observe' in this context specifically means 'come to understand'.

needs *something to live* The verb phrase 'to have a need' must be treated as a unit expressing an experience-type event. It refers to a person's lacking what is necessary for life whether socially, economically, or for health.

3:17b refuses to be compassionate *providing for his brother's need* The Greek 'closes his bowels regarding him' is a dead metaphor that means 'refuses to be compassionate'. It is not merely an emotional reaction toward a person with a need, but an emotional reaction coupled with an action.

3:17c Verse 17 finishes with a rhetorical question pointing out the incongruity of claiming to love God, yet at the same time not expressing love to a Christian brother.

love God *as he claims* The genitive form in the phrase 'God's love' can be interpreted either as 'he loves God' or 'God causes him to love other people'. The latter would be rendered 'God has not caused him to love other people'. But this would shift the focus from refusal to show compassion to God's ability to affect behavior. The first interpretation is preferable because there is an underlying assumption here that this is a person who claims to love God and at the same time refuses to express practical compassion toward his Christian brother.

3:18 let us not merely talk *about loving our Christian brothers* Some commentators say that μὴ ... λόγῳ μηδὲ τῇ γλώσσῃ 'neither by word or by tongue' is deliberately paired off with 'deed' and 'truth'. Others say that 'tongue' is a synonym for 'word', a contemptuous use, and thus a forceful means of expressing that situation where love in action does not accompany words. The latter is the preferred interpretation: the doublet form here is clearly a prominence marker, as it so frequently is in the New Testament.

The literal rendering of the clause is 'let us not love by word nor by tongue', meaning 'let us not merely talk about loving our Christian brothers'. This construction places great prominence on the clause that follows, 'but let us genuinely love them by helping them'.

let us love them genuinely by helping them The Greek is ἐν ἔργῳ καί ἀληθείᾳ 'in deeds/work and truth', in which 'deeds' signifies actions (hence 'helping') and 'truth' signifies genuineness, sincerity, and lack of hypocrisy.

BOUNDARIES AND COHERENCE

The initial boundary of this unit has been discussed in detail under 3:1–10. The indicators of the closing boundary include:

1. The change of topic in 3:19 to confidence in prayer.
2. The summary-type APPEAL in 3:18 that concludes the unit.
3. The introductory ἐν τούτῳ 'by this' in 3:19, which, though it points back to what *has* been said, mainly points forward to the new topic (the same phrase in 3:16 points only to the content immediately following).
4. The tail-head linkage created by the repetition in 3:19 of the word ἀλήθεια 'truth' which also occurs in 3:18.
5. No more occurrences of the πᾶς ὁ 'anyone who' contrasts that characterize the previous unit.

Semantic coherence in 3:11–18 depends on the contrast between God's love and the hatred of the world spirit. Love is almost synonymous with spiritual life in 3:14, and hatred is equated with murder and death in 3:15. Another contrast is that of the quality of God's love (3:16) as contrasted with professed love that is not demonstrated by action (3:17–18).

Lexical items that belong to the domain of love are: ἀγαπῶμεν τοὺς ἀδελφούς 'we love our Christian brothers' (3:14); ἐκεῖνος ὑπὲρ ἡμῶν τὴν ψυχὴν αὐτοῦ ἔθηκεν 'Christ voluntarily died for our benefit' (3:16a); ἡμεῖς ὀφείλομεν ὑπὲρ τῶν ἀδελφῶν τὰς ψυχὰς θεῖναι 'we should relinquish whatever we have to supply our Christian brother's need' (3:16b); ἀγαπῶμεν ... ἐν ἔργῳ καὶ ἀληθείᾳ 'let us love our Christian brothers ... truly' (3:18). Lexical items that belong to the domain of hatred are: πονηρός 'evil' (3:12, twice); μισῶ 'hate' (3:13, 15); θάνατος 'death' (3:14, twice); ἀνθρωποκτόνος 'murderer' (3:15, twice); κλείσῃ τὰ σπλάγχνα 'closes the heart, refuses' (3:17).

Death is a strong motif running through this unit: Cain murdered his brother (3:12c); we have been changed from being dead people (3:14a); anyone who does not love, remains spiritually dead (3:14c); anyone who hates his brother is a murderer (3:15a); murderers cannot live forever (3:15b); Christ showed us true love by voluntarily dying for us (3:16b); we must voluntarily relinquish what we have for our brothers, even to dying for them (3:16c).

Structurally, the unit is held together by three APPEALS, all of which deal with the need to love each other. An inclusio, ἀγαπῶμεν 'let us love' in v. 11 and in v. 18, further supports the structural coherence.

PROMINENCE AND THEME

The three APPEALS have an equal degree of natural prominence except that the second has less mitigation than the first and third. The first seems to be more generic than the others; it also has the greatest detail and development; and it is introduced by a complex orienter in 3:11a. The third APPEAL, with the vocative in 3:18 calling for the reader's attention, is a kind of wrap-up of the subject of loving genuinely, emphasizing its importance. (There is a vocative in 3:13 but with a different function; it creates identification between the author and the readers, as has already been discussed.)

The theme statement is drawn from a synthesis of the three APPEALS together with the first *motivational basis*.

SECTION CONSTITUENT 3:19-24 (Hortatory Paragraph: Specific appeal₃ of 2:28-4:6)
Theme: We must believe in God's Son and love each other in order to be confident that we associate properly with God and receive what we ask from him.

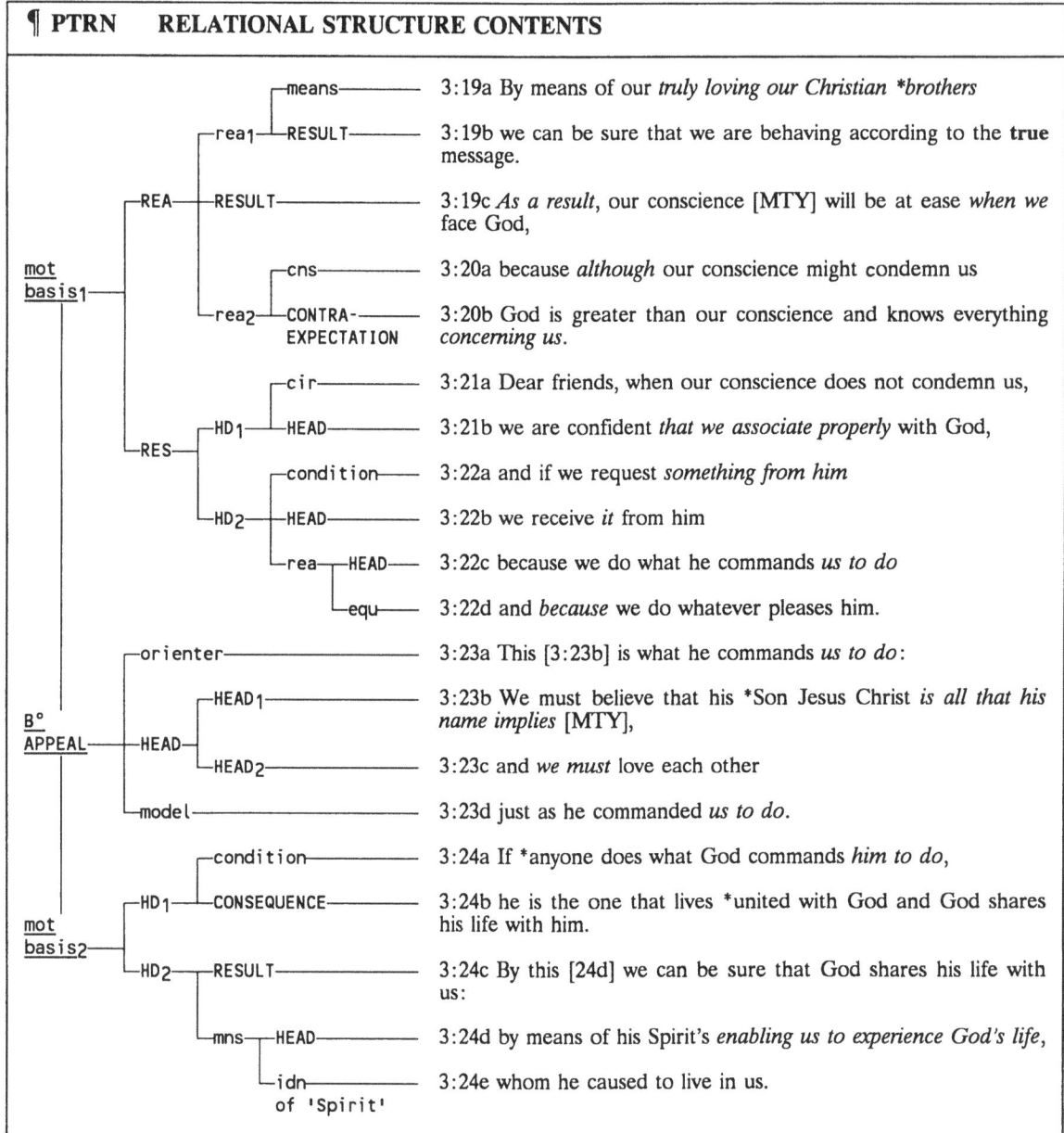

INTENT AND PARAGRAPH PATTERN

The author's intent in the 3:19-24 paragraph is to affect the readers' actions by an APPEAL urging them to continue to believe in God's Son Jesus Christ and to love each other. The paragraph consists of three propositional clusters: the first, 19-22, supports the central one in v. 23, which is followed by another supportive one in v. 24 (v. 24 relates back to everything that was said about being united to Christ in 2:28-29). The communication relationship is a grounds unit followed by an exhortational or conclusion unit followed by a second grounds unit. This paragraph could be considered either causal hortatory or causal expository. We take it to be causal hortatory since its primary intent is to affect behavior as seen in 3:23, where John speaks of 'the commandment' and expresses its content with ἵνα plus the subjunctive. The principal constituents of the paragraph are + *basis* + APPEAL.

NOTES

3:19-20 We take 3:19-20 to be the reason for 3:21-22. It presents two reasons that assure believers that they are united to God: awareness of the love put within us by God (3:19a; cf. 3:18) and awareness of the grace of God that accepts our humanness because of Christ, who sacrificed himself for us (3:20b; cf. 2:2). On this basis God is greater than our conscience. A further indication that 3:19-20 is the reason for 3:21-22 is that the vocative ἀγαπητοί 'dear friends' (v. 21), which often begins a new thought, occurs after the *basis* has been laid and introduces the concepts that lead up to the APPEAL in 3:23 (the most generic appeal in the Epistle, in that it encompasses most of the other appeals).

3:19a By means of our *truly loving our Christian brothers* As stated in the note on 2:3a, ἐν τούτῳ 'by this means' usually refers to what follows, but here we have taken it to refer to what precedes because of the near unanimity of commentator opinion. The referent according to this interpretation is 'we truly love our Christian brothers'. The rendering in the display is based on this interpretation.

Based on the other interpretation, that ἐν τούτῳ 'by this' refers to the following context (which would be consistent with the meaning of the phrase in all its other occurrences in the Epistle), the rendering would be as follows:

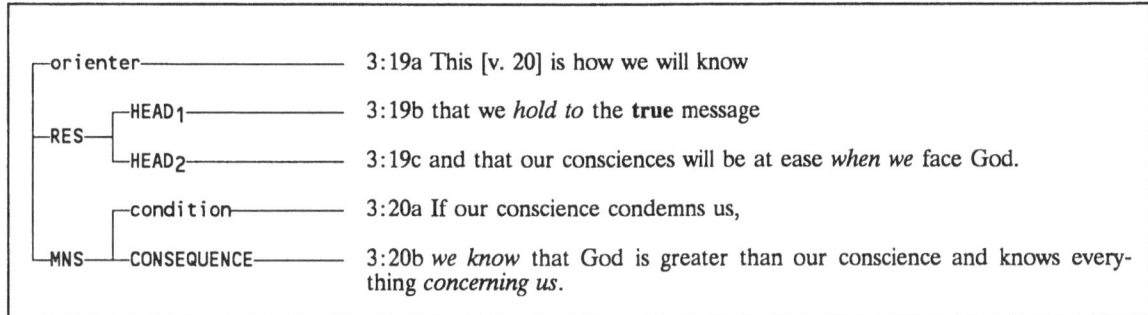

3:19b we can be sure In the 19a-b means-RESULT relationship, 19a is the means of our being *assured* that we are saved and behaving properly, not the means by which to be saved.

we are behaving according to the true message The Greek is ἐκ τῆς ἀληθείας ἐσμέν 'from the truth we are', which indicates that the true message is the source of how we behave or live (the first meaning in the note on 1:6b). The phrase 'from the truth' is forefronted and therefore prominent.

3:19c *As a result* The conjunction καί 'and' indicates a close semantic tie with the previous clause without specifying the relation. It seems to fit the immediate context best if we take καί as signaling a reason-RESULT relation.

our conscience will be at ease A literal rendering would be 'shall persuade/reassure our heart'. Commentators are divided as to whether the meaning of πείθομαι in this context is 'be persuaded' or 'be certain'. We prefer 'be certain, be at ease', a rare usage but not singular. It not only fits the context best but is the choice of most commentators. Louw and Nida (25.166) say in reference to its usage here that it means "to exhibit confidence and assurance in a situation which might otherwise cause dismay or fear." This meaning (according to Louw and Nida 25.158) is very similar to that of παρρησία 'courage' in 2:28. It should be noted that the verb tense is future, which leads to the question whether this will happen at the time of the final judgment or whether it is a more immediate concern relating, for instance, to prayer. We prefer the latter interpretation although it has been left ambiguous in the rendering.

In this context 'our heart' means 'our conscience', but in many languages 'heart' is not used as a metonymy for the center of emotions and thinking processes. Whatever the equivalent term is in a given language should be used in translating (e.g., 'lungs', 'kidneys', 'mind', 'stomach', or even just 'we/our/us').

when we face God The Greek has 'before him'. Commentators generally agree that this is not a reference to judgment of the believer, but to either the believer's position of living under God's continual observation or addressing God in prayer.

3:20a although Brooke translates ὅτι here as "whereinsoever." (Several commentators and versions agree.) He calls attention to a similar use of ὁ τὶ ἄν in the Gospels as justifying the adoption of it here. Some translations simply ignore the ὅτι and translate the ἐάν 'if' that follows it (as in the alternate display above). Probably the meaning is clear with either of these translations, but a little more accurate if ὅτι is not ignored (it *is* well attested). We take ὅτι ἐάν as indicating concession.

3:20b God is greater That God is greater in rank and understanding is not questioned, but did John say this to inspire confidence or as a warning? The majority of commentators agree on the meaning 'Since God is greater than our accusing conscience, we can be confident that he understands and loves us'. However, the minority opinion, with good reason, understands this as 'Since God is greater than our accusing conscience, we had better behave according to his desires'.

knows everything *concerning us* The comprehensive statement γινώσκει πάντα 'he knows all things' includes the knowledge of our fallen nature and of the provision through God's grace by which he sees us in Christ and forgives us when we 'miss the mark' (1:9; 2:1). Alford is one of those commentators who see God's knowing here as that of a judge who would be more severe than one's own conscience. But other commentators reject this as being out of harmony with the main teaching of the passage and of the Epistle as a whole: In 1:9 the author declares that God is faithful and just to forgive confessed sin. In 3:1 attention was called to the amazing love by which we have received sonship. In 3:16 the depth of the love of Christ is pointed out. The purpose of the Epistle is that the readers experience the joy of fellowship (1:3–4) and the assurance of eternal life (5:13). In view of all this, we consider that God's knowing everything has to do with God as merciful (though this is not specified in the display).

3:21–24 As Longacre (pp. 26, 28) has pointed out, this unit closes with the largest and clearest chiastic structure in the letter:

> A If our heart does *not know anything against us* (i.e., if we have confidence), (v. 21)
>
> B We receive from him, because *we do what he commands us*. (v. 22)
>
> C This is *what he commands us*: (3:23a)
>
> D We are to believe in the name of his Son Jesus Christ and love each other. (3:23b-c)
>
> C· This is just *as he commanded us*. (3:23d)
>
> B· *The one who does what he commands* lives united to God. (v. 24)
>
> A· His Spirit *causes us to know that we are united to God*. (v. 24)

The D in the chiasm must be taken as a single unit because faith and love are viewed as a single action counted for righteousness and because ἐντολή 'command' is in the singular.

3:21a when our conscience does not condemn us Our conscience can no longer condemn us when Christ's love in us enables us to truly love others, thus meeting the full requirement of God's command.

3:21b we are confident *that we associate properly with God* Commentators agree that the context is prayer (see v. 22). However, παρρησίαν ἔχομεν πρὸς τὸν θεόν 'we have confidence before God' harks back to 2:28b and, more specifically, to 3:19c. The reference is to a continual assurance regarding our relationship with God. Concerning 'confident', see the note on 2:28b.

3:22a we request *something from him* The word 'something' is supplied as the content of 'request' and 'from him' as the person of whom the request is made.

3:22c we do what he commands *us to do* This is not a slave's obedience: it is spontaneous. Doing what God commands is the response of love to the grace of God demonstrated in the believer. The event signified by 'command' requires a content and a recipient of the action, hence 'us to do'.

3:23–24 Three new concepts are presented here. (1) It is the first mention in the Epistle of πιστεύω 'believe'. (2) The reciprocal aspect of being united to God is introduced: God's Spirit lives in the believer and the believer lives in God. (3) The fact of the Holy Spirit's having been given to us is mentioned for the first time.

3:23a he commands See the note on 22c. Here in 23a a problem arises as to whether

God or Christ is the referent of αὐτοῦ 'his'. The choice affects the interpretation of the whole of v. 23 and especially of 'command'. If 'he' refers to God, then the command is to 'believe and love', but if it refers to Christ, the command is only to 'love'. In the display 'he' is taken to refer to God.

3:23b believe that his Son Jesus Christ *is all that his name implies* The command begins with the charge to believe. Faith is the belief and acceptance of the fact that all Christ claims to be is true: πιστεύσωμεν τῷ ὀνόματι τοῦ υἱοῦ αὐτοῦ 'believe on the name of his Son' means to believe in his character and the significance of his incarnation, 'name' being a metonymy for the total personality. The literal meaning of the name 'Jesus' is Savior, and the title 'Christ' signifies that he was anointed by God for a special purpose. The phrase 'Son of God' indicates his position in the Godhead. In this first section alone, references that amplify this significance are 1:2 (he was with the Father and was revealed to men); 1:3 (we are joined together to be with him and with the Father); 1:7 (his sacrifice cleanses all our sins); 2:1 (he is the believers' advocate); 2:2 (his atonement is for all men); 2:6 (his conduct is the standard for our conduct); 2:13-14 (he is the pre-existent One from eternity); 2:23-25 (acknowledging him as God's Son and Christ ensures eternal life); and 2:27 (believers have been taught to continue to live united to him).

3:23c love each other If we accept Christ as what he claims to be, we are accepted by God into his family, and his love in us is the manifestation of this acceptance. Confidence in the person of the Son results in loving other believers with the kind of love that characterizes the family relationship.

3:23d as he commanded If the agent of the command is 'God', as we take it, 23d is related to both 23b and 23c and the three together mean 'we must believe in his Son and love each other just as God commanded us'. If the agent of the command is 'Christ', then 3:23d is related only to 3:23c; this would give the meaning 'we must love each other just as Christ commanded us'. The Greek grammatical structure is ambiguous as to whether 23d supports b and c or just c; however, the chiasm in this verse lends strong support to taking the command in 23a as the same command in 23d, in which case 23d is related to both 23b and c.

3:24b lives united with God and God shares his life with him The Greek is ἐν αὐτῷ μένει καὶ αὐτὸς ἐν αὐτῷ 'he remains in that one and that one in him'. This is difficult to express in propositional form. For one thing, it expresses two concepts, since 'remaining in' cannot by the nature of the participants be a reciprocal experience. The meaning of a human's remaining in God seems to be that the human maintains a close social relationship with God by partaking in God's moral purity. The meaning of God's remaining in a human seems to be that God continues to consider him or her with favor. The Greek phrase may be seen as a doublet. If it is, the meaning would be that a human and God experience a special social interrelationship, and this concept would be prominent due to the doublet form.

3:24d-e his Spirit . . . whom he caused to live in us The word πνεῦμα 'spirit' is not qualified, but is simply identified as 'given to us'. It can therefore refer only to God's Spirit.

BOUNDARIES AND COHERENCE

A sandwich structure marks the boundaries of the 3:19-24 unit: ἐν τούτῳ γνωσόμεθα 'by this we will know' (3:19a) introduces the unit; ἐν τούτῳ γινώσκομεν 'by this we know' (3:24) closes it; and the content of knowledge in both instances is practically the same. The tail-head linkage referred to in the discussion of the 3:11-18 sub-section also marks the initial boundary.

Another tail-head linkage marks the final boundary: πνεῦμα 'spirit' in 3:24 is repeated in 4:1, serving to introduce the next topic. The linkage is strictly lexical since the referent is quite different in each case (in 3:24 'spirit' refers to God's Spirit, whereas in 4:1 it refers to teachers who teach falsely about God). That the following unit begins with the vocative ἀγαπητοί 'dear friends' (in 4:1)—introducing another delicate subject—is another indication of the closure of the 3:19-24 unit.

Among commentators there is much greater consensus concerning the coherence of this unit than of many others in the Epistle. The chiastic structure of vv. 21-24 strengthens the unit's coherence (see the note on 21-24).

The topic of this unit is confidence, introduced in 2:28, and words in this domain lend lexical coherence: γινώσκω 'know' (3:19, 20, 24); πείθω 'reassure' (3:19); παρρησία 'confidence' (3:21); and πιστεύω 'believe' (3:23). Confidence is based on the family relationship pictured in 3:22: the obedient child coming to his father with his requests.

This unit is central to two major concerns of the author: that we have confidence before God (19, 21) and that we know God experientially (19, 24). These concerns, especially the latter, tie the unit together as an inclusio.

The relational structure of the unit demonstrates its coherence: there is a *motivational basis* in 19-22 ('since we can approach God with confidence'); an *APPEAL* in v. 23 ('we must believe in his Son Jesus Christ and love each other'); and another *motivational basis* in v. 24 ('it is the one who does what God commands him to do who lives united to God').

PROMINENCE AND THEME

The HEAD proposition of the 3:23b-c *APPEAL* has natural and also marked prominence:

1. Structurally, it is the center of the chiasm.
2. The demonstrative αὕτη ἐστίν 'this is', referring to the command, is forefronted in 23a; and in 22c and 24a τὰς ἐντολὰς αὐτοῦ 'his commands' is forefronted. This prominence heightens the prominence of the content of the 23b-c command itself.
3. Because it is repeated four times in 3:22-24, ἐντολή 'command' is prominent.
4. The content of the command contains the full name 'his Son Jesus Christ', specified as the object of the faith commanded.
5. Structurally, the *APPEAL* of a unit is its most prominent part.

The theme statement is derived from the first *motivational basis* and the *APPEAL*.

SECTION CONSTITUENT 4:1-6 (Hortatory Paragraph: Specific appeal₄ of 2:28-4:6)
Theme: Since I know you have prevailed over false teachers, I say to you, Continue to test the teaching you hear to know whether or not it is from God. You should test it by whether or not it acknowledges that Jesus Christ came in human form and by who it is that listens to the teaching.

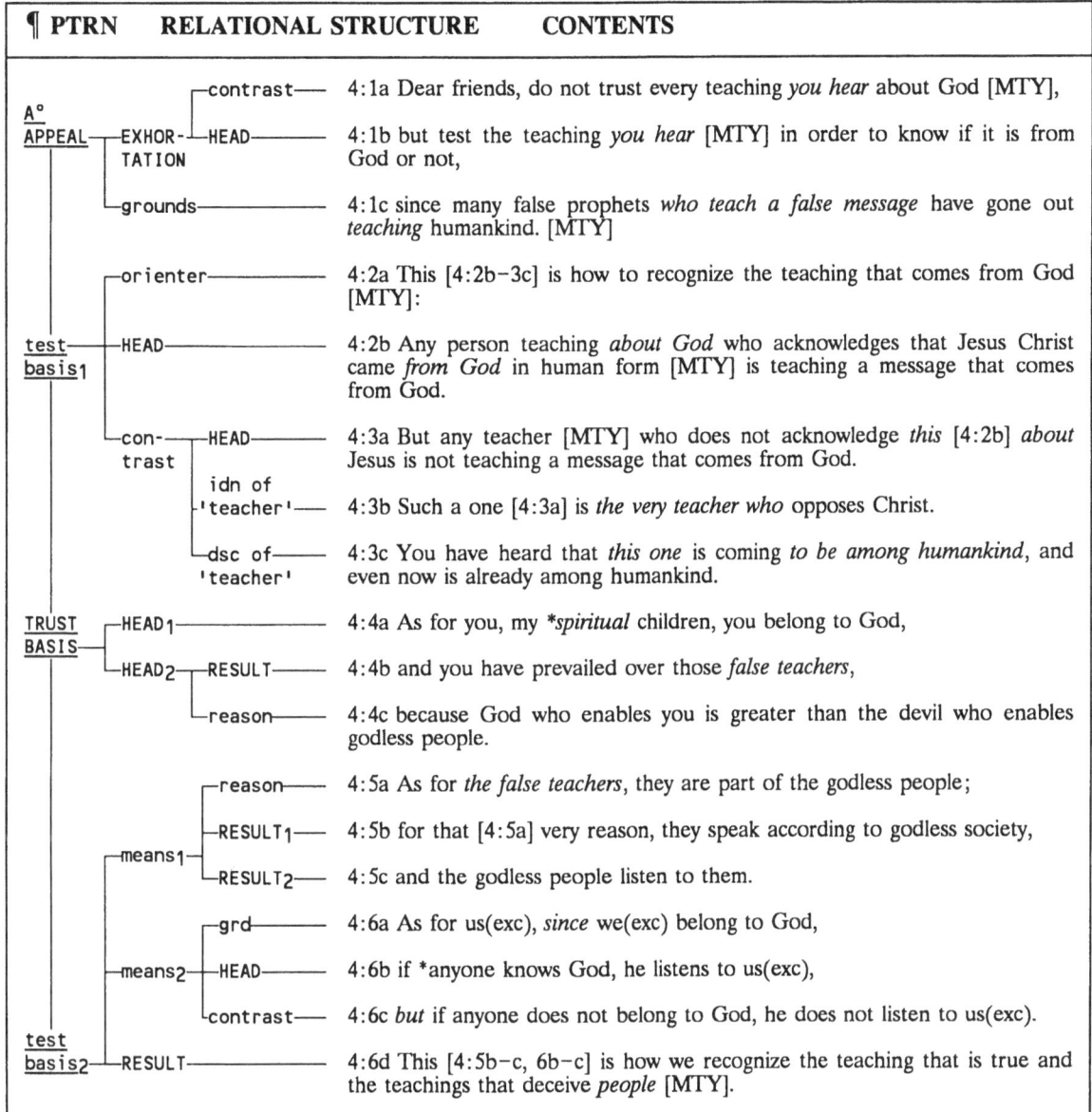

INTENT AND PARAGRAPH PATTERN

John's intent in the 4:1-6 paragraph is to affect the readers' actions by a warning command that they not believe every teaching but test its truthfulness. The paragraph consists of four propositional clusters: the first (4:1) is central; the other three (4:2-3, 4:4, and 4:5-6) support the central one. Their communication relationship is that the first is exhortational, the second means, the third grounds, and the fourth means. Since John's primary intent is to affect the readers' behavior (as clearly demonstrated by the imperative verb in v. 1), this is considered a causal hortatory paragraph, with the principal constituents + *bases* + APPEAL.

NOTES

4:1a every teaching *you hear* about God The context of 4:1-6 is the contrast between true teaching and false. In the early church God's Spirit was particularly associated with the function of speaking or teaching God's truth. Prophets spoke under the control of the Spirit. The word 'spirit' here (and in 1b, 2a, 2b, 3a, and 6d) is a metonymy for the person who speaks about God and what he teaches about God (Bullinger, p. 543).

4:1b test the teaching *you hear* John provides tests not to discern whether their motivation is from God or not, but rather whether they speak a true or false message in order to know whether the message comes from God.

See the note on 4:1a about 'spirit'.

4:1c many false prophets *who teach a false message* The multiplicity of 'spirits' activating the many prophets can be attributed either to the great number of false prophets or to the many evil spirits who activate them. There is but one Spirit of God (4:2a). It is possible for a number of spirits to activate those who are willing to accept their teaching and speak for them. In view of the many diverse erroneous teachings that result, the test in 4:2b of confessing, or refusing to confess, allegiance to the incarnate Christ is valid.

have gone out Commentators disagree as to the meaning of ἐξέρχομαι 'go out'. Some suggest that this means movement from one sphere to another, that is, that these were Christian prophets who left the church to teach in the sphere of the world. Others suggest that the meaning is that they went into the world empowered by Satanic teaching and still others that they simply appeared teaching among humans. We have chosen the last interpretation.

humankind The meaning of κόσμος 'world' here is 'human beings' rather than 'other people opposed to God' as some would suggest. See the note on 2:2c.

4:2a recognize The Greek verb is variously translated 'know', 'come to know', and 'recognize', all of which are acceptable. The problem arises as to whether the form here is indicative or imperative. In view of the main appeal in v. 1 to 'test the teaching', the most appropriate function of what follows is to enable the reader to test the teaching by providing him with some specific tests. So we have taken this verb to be indicative as have the majority of commentators.

See the note on 4:1a about 'spirit'.

4:2b came *from God* in human form The literal rendering here is 'has come in the flesh'; there is no explicit indication of the origin of Christ. The word 'flesh' is a metonymy for 'human being', but this is in no way an assertion that Jesus, the anointed one, simply showed up as another human being.

is teaching a message that comes from God The Greek is literally 'it is from God' focusing on the origin of the message. Jesus came to the world of humans from his divine origin and became a human being. Recognition of this is the crucial test of true God-inspired teaching.

See the note on 4:1a about 'spirit'.

4:3a does not acknowledge Instead of μὴ ὁμολογεῖ 'not acknowledge' some manuscripts have λύει 'annul'. It is on the basis of "overwhelming external support" that UBS accepts the longer reading (Metzger). The verb λύει has been suspected of being a scribal gloss because it is so directly slanted against the Docetic teaching of the patristic period. Therefore we take μὴ ὁμολογεῖ to be the true text.

See the note on 4:1a about 'spirit'.

4:3b *the very teacher who* opposes Christ The teachers motivated by spirits that refuse to confess the incarnation of Christ are identified as representatives of the antichrist spirit, which is in opposition to Christ himself. (The word 'teacher' is supplied from 3a.)

4:3c is coming *to be among humankind* ... is already among humankind The verb 'come' requires a location. The location is specified in the following clause as 'the world', which we take to mean 'humankind' (see the notes on 2:2c and 4:1c).

4:4a As for you The pronoun 'you' is forefronted in the Greek; it is in contrast with the previous topic of the 'false teachers'.

you belong to God Different shades of meaning can be implied by 'you are of God': 'you are children of God', 'you have your motivating source of action and life from God', or more simply 'you belong to God'.

4:4b prevailed over The verb is 'have overcome, have prevailed over'. The manner of prevailing is not expressed. Implicitly it is by relying on the true teaching and not accepting the false teachings.

those *false teachers* We take the referent of αὐτούς 'them' (masculine neuter plural accusative) in 4b to be 'false prophets' in 1c, which is the only masculine plural form in the preceding context. (The whole paragraph deals with these false teachers.) Alternatively, the masculine singular τὸ τοῦ ἀντιχρίστου 'the spirit of the antichrist' could be the referent since it is closer—John could possibly have in mind 'those who oppose Christ' since the antichrist spirit has been semantically identified with the false prophets and teachers.

4:4c enables The literal rendering is 'he [God] that is in you' and 'he that is in the world'. (See the discussion in the Glossary at the end of the entry on 'joined together', where the word 'in' is treated, esp. being 'in' someone.) In these constructions the focus is on having mutual characteristics. The form 'you are in God' is far more usual than 'God is in you', which occurs here. Certainly this involves having mutual characteristics, but the total context of this paragraph points more specifically to God's strengthening and enabling of the believer and his belief system.

godless people The word κόσμος 'world' in this context means 'godless people' (the second meaning in the note on 2:2c).

4:5a As for *the false teachers* The word 'they' is forefronted in the Greek; it contrasts with the previous topic of 'you' (the believers).

4:5b speak according to godless society The word κόσμος 'world' here means 'godless human society' (see the note on 2:2c). The source or motivation of the false teachers' speech is human society in opposition to God.

4:5c godless people See the note on 4:4c.

4:6a–c us(exc) . . . we(exc) Because of the expressed contrast between the true and false teachers in vv. 5 and 6, we interpret these pronouns as exclusive.

4:6a As for us(exc) The Greek pronoun is forefronted; it contrasts with the previous topic, 'false teachers'. John is referring to himself and other Christian teachers. He is not alienating himself from the audience but from the false teachers. He includes himself with the true teachers, since he makes reference to other people listening to a teaching.

belong to God See the note on 4:4a.

4:6d This [4:5b–c, 6b–c] The phrase ἐκ τούτου 'from this' is anaphoric, referring back. (It is different from ἐν τούτῳ, which most commonly refers forward.) The question remains as to its scope: Does it refer to what immediately precedes it (5–6c), or is it more inclusive? Since 6d and 2a form a structural inclusio, we take the position that 'this' specifically refers to vv. 5–6c. Proposition 2a immediately precedes the test to which it refers, while 6d immediately follows the test to which it refers. Observe the chiasm:

A 'by this we know' (4:2a)
 B the first test presented (4:2b–3c)
  C the trust (4:4)
 B' the second test presented (4:5–6c)
A' 'from this we know' (4:6d)

the teaching that is true The prophet who is activated by God's Spirit speaks the truth because God is the 'Spirit of truth'.

See the note on 4:1a about 'spirit'.

BOUNDARIES AND COHERENCE

The initial boundary of the 4:1–6 unit is indicated by the tail-head linkage and vocative (see the discussion under 3:19–24). The closing boundary is marked by a deictic (4:6d) referring to what preceded (other evidences of this boundary are discussed under 2:28–4:6).

The structure of the unit is that of an inclusio: 4:2a and 4:6d are essentially the same. (Cf. ἐν τούτῳ γινώσκετε τὸ πνεῦμα 'this is how you can know the spirit' in 4:2a and ἐκ τούτου γινώσκομεν τὸ πνεῦμα ... 'this is how we know the spirit' in 4:6d.) That this is a paragraph is recognized by almost all commentators, but its external coherence is not a matter of complete agreement. Several consider it to be a parenthesis because it seems to be an amplification of the last clause of 3:19–24. Others see it as a development of the concept of faith introduced in 3:23. In our analysis, we see πνεῦμα 'spirit' in 3:24 and repeated in 4:1 as introducing the 4:1–6 unit. (It is John's style to move from one topic to the other like this.) The unit presents the fourth of the four *specific appeals* encompassed by the generic appeal in 2:28–29, namely to continue to live united to Christ (see the 2:28–4:6 display).

Words in the domain of discerning provide lexical coherence to the 4:1–6 unit: δοκιμάζετε 'test' (4:1); γινώσκω 'know' (4:2,

6); ψευδοπροφῆται 'false prophets' (4:1); ἀλήθεια 'truth' (4:6); and πλάνης 'deception' (4:6). The phrase ἐκ τοῦ θεοῦ 'from God' occurs six times (once each in vv. 1, 2, 3, 4, and twice in 6).

This unit consists of an *APPEAL* (v. 1), a *test basis* (vv. 2–3), a *TRUST BASIS* (v. 4), and a second *test basis* (vv. 5–6). It could be summarized like this: Test the teaching you hear to know if it is from God or not (v. 1) by whether it acknowledges that Jesus Christ came in human form (v. 2); I say all this since I know you have prevailed over the false teachers (v. 4); another test of false teaching is that godless people listen to it (v. 5). In the *TRUST BASIS* John expresses his confidence in the readers, assuring them that they are quite unlike the false teachers. The *TRUST BASIS* coheres in the text by virtue of the contrast the readers are to the false teachers just described.

PROMINENCE AND THEME

In the higher-level structure of which 4:1–6 is a part, it is such a prominent unit that it is a climax in the letter (as mentioned under 2:12–25 and 2:28–4:6).

Internally, it has its own prominence structure: The prohibition against relying on false teachers and the contrastive command to test them (4:1a) are structurally prominent as in any hortatory unit. Supporting this *APPEAL* are the grounds (4:1b), an enabling test (4:2b), a statement of trust (4:4a), and a test to enable the reader to comply with the *APPEAL* (4:6b).

There are also prominence features in the *TRUST BASIS* (v. 4) and the second *test basis* (vv. 5–6). These include the explicit use of the pronouns ὑμεῖς 'you' (v. 4a), αὐτοί 'they' (v. 5a), ἡμεῖς 'we' (v. 6a), and their forefronted position in the sentences. Another prominence-marking feature is the chiastic form of the contrast set forth by the pronouns:

A You belong to God. (4:4a)
  B They belong to the world. (4:5a)
A' We belong to God. (4:6a)

These marked-prominence features are associated with this the *first part* of the Epistle's second climax. (Keep in mind that 2:12–27 is the first climax in the Epistle, and 4:1–11 the second. The next unit, 4:7–11, is the *second part* of the second climax.) These features do not affect the theme because they relate to the prominence structure of the entire letter, not the internal structure of this paragraph; and it is the structural prominence of the paragraph that determines the theme. The theme is drawn from the *TRUST BASIS* and the two *test bases*, together with the HEAD of the *APPEAL*.

> **DIVISION CONSTITUENT 4:7–5:12 (Hortatory Section: Specific appeal₂ for 1:5–5:12)**
> *Theme: In order to be assured that we behave according to God's character we must love each other. We must do so since, as God's Spirit testifies, Jesus came to cause us to live spiritually forever.*

MACROSTRUCTURE	CONTENTS
APPEAL₁	4:7–11 My dear friends, let us love each other, since God shows us how to love.
appeal₂	4:12–21 In order to be assured that we behave according to God's character and that we love God and our Christian brothers just as he intended us to, we must love our Christian brothers, because God loved us first.
basis	5:1–12 If a person believes that Jesus is God's Anointed One, he is one whom God has caused to live spiritually and he loves his Christian brothers. He also overcomes the evil of human society. We know this is true because God's Spirit testifies that Jesus came to save humankind.

INTENT AND MACROSTRUCTURE

John's concern throughout the 4:7–5:12 unit is that people have eternal life (4:9) and that the readers be confident that they associate properly with God when Christ returns to judge the world (4:17). His intent is to affect the behavior of the believers so that they love each other as God showed them and thus know they have eternal life and relate properly to God.

As to the unit's macrostructure, it is hortatory and is composed of two APPEALS and a *basis*. The appeals are (1) love each other (4:7–11) and (2) we must love our Christian brothers because God loved us first (4:12–21). These appeals are made on the basis that God causes us to live spiritually and God's Spirit assures us that Jesus came to save us (5:1–12). The grammatical forms of the 4:7–11 and 4:12–21 appeals, although quite different, make them somewhat mitigated.

The 4:7–11 unit, which immediately follows the third climactic unit of the letter (4:1–6), is the fourth climactic unit.

BOUNDARIES AND COHERENCE

For the opening boundary of the 4:7–5:12 unit, see the discussion of the closing boundary of 2:28–4:6. It should be noted that boundaries for this section are debatable because the markers are open to various interpretations. However, the primary criterion for establishing boundaries is the coherence of the unit's semantic content; and at 4:7 not only does the subject change, but also the argument: it changes to poetic expression as the author presents his declaration 'God is love'. For emphasis he launches his discussion of this topic with alliteration and a chiastic structure (see the note on 4:7–8). We take the alliteration to be a marker of the opening boundary: ἀγαπητοί, ἀγαπῶμεν ἀλλήλους 'dear friends, let us love each other'.

The closing boundary is co-terminous with that of the higher-level unit, 1:5–5:12 (see the discussion under 1:5–5:12).

Structural coherence within the 4:7–5:12 section is seen in its two APPEALS and their *basis*. The first APPEAL (4:7–11), to love each other, is supported by the fact that God has shown his love to us. The second *appeal* (4:12–21) is essentially the same as the first. The *basis* is that we have many benefits from believing in Christ: God has caused us to live eternally, we love fellow Christians, we obey what God commands us, we overcome the world spirit (see Glossary), and we know what is true (5:1–12).

The 4:7–5:12 unit recalls previous themes and motifs: 5:1–12, in particular, is "a sort of a whirlwind windup of the book" (Longacre, p. 37), the topic of which is overcoming the world spirit—the victory which leads to eternal life—echoing 2:17 and 25. In 4:15–16 'love' and 'faith' are shown to be interdependent means for the life of union with God, which is eternal life. In 5:6–12, to conclude his argument that Jesus is God's gift of love by which eternal life is realized, the author strengthens his own witness by pointing out God's divine witness.

Semantic coherence in the 4:7–5:12 section is found in the continuing, but more direct, emphasis on the theme of God's gift of eternal life through his Son, which was introduced in the prologue (1:2). Two strands, love for each other (4:7–11) and faith in God's Son (4:12–21), are intertwined in the development of this theme.

A comparative study of lexical items used in the three sections of the BODY of the letter indicates that though the third section (4:7–5:12) is shorter than either of the other two, there is a greater concentration of the use of ἀγαπάω 'love' and its derivatives in it. Also, words in the domain of belief are more numerous. Words in the domain of living united to Christ are about equal in number in the second and third sections, though the comparison is difficult to make because in the third section a greater variety of terms is used to express the concept. The heavy concentration of these lexical items in this unit adds to its coherence and closure character.

PROMINENCE AND THEME

Although both *APPEALS* in the 4:7–5:12 section are structurally prominent, the first one, 4:7–11, has special prominence because it is the fourth climax, that is, the second part of the Epistle's second double climax (the first part being 4:1–6). In a sense, this is the climax of the whole Epistle.

In the 4:7–11 unit there are many marked-prominence features characteristic of a climax: (1) vocatives in vv. 7 and 11; (2) a chiasm in vv. 7–8:

  A Love has its source in God. (4:7b)
    B Everyone who loves his Christian brothers has been caused to live by God. (4:7c)
    B' The one who does not love his Christian brothers does not even know God. (4:8a)
  A' It is God's nature to love everyone. (4:8b)

(3) alliteration at the beginning of the unit (ἀγαπητοί, ἀγαπῶμεν ἀλλήλους 'dear friends, let us love one another'); (4) the use of demonstrative pronouns and other deictics (e.g., ἐν τούτῳ 'by this' in 9a and 10a); (5) contrasts introduced forcefully by negatives or by οὐχ ... ὅτι 'not that' together with ἀλλ' ὅτι 'but that' in 8a and 10; (6) a high concentration of the key word 'love' (fifteen times); (7) the lexical density of concepts mentioned earlier: being born of God, being in God, knowing God, demonstrating godly character, the coming of God's unique Son to the world, salvation through the Son, propitiation for sins, remaining united to God, loving completely.

The 4:7–5:12 section is made up of two *APPEALS* and a *basis*. Although both *APPEALS* are structurally prominent, the first, which is the Epistle's main climax, is more prominent than the second. The theme statement is derived from all three of these constituents, with special prominence on the first.

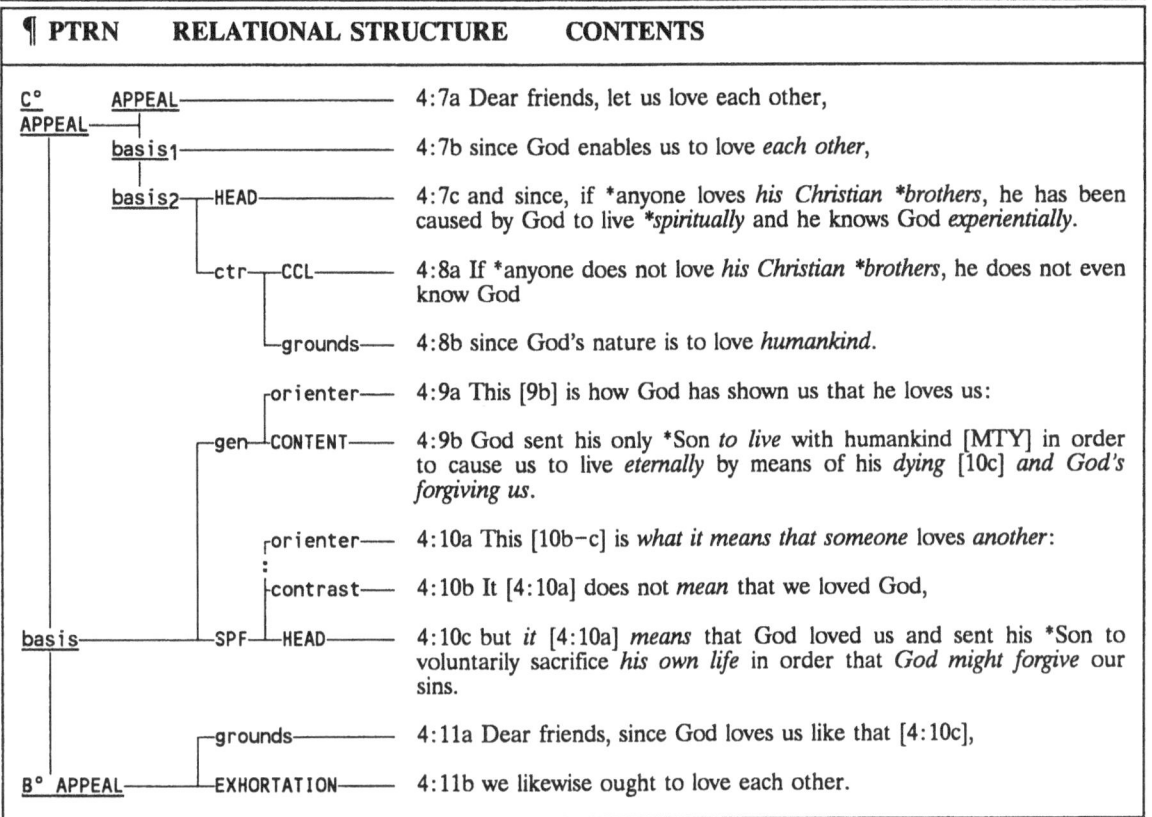

INTENT AND PARAGRAPH PATTERN

John's intent in the 4:7–11 paragraph is to affect the actions of the reader using a command that they love each other. The paragraph consists of three propositional clusters: two nuclear (4:7–8 and 4:11) and one satellitic (4:9–10). Their communication relationship is two hortatory units supported by a grounds unit. Since the primary intent is to affect the behavior, this is considered a causal hortatory paragraph, the principal constituents being + basis + APPEAL.

NOTES

4:7–8 The chiastic structure of vv. 7–8, described under 4:7–5:12 in the "Prominence and Theme" section, demonstrates the coherence of these two verses and makes the passage prominent.

4:7b God enables us to love *each other* Literally, this is 'love is from God'. It means that God is the source of our ability to love others. Since love is an event that requires a goal, a goal is here supplied from the context ('each other' from 7a).

4:7c has been caused by God to live *spiritually* A literal rendering of the Greek is 'has been born from God'. The context shows that physical birth is not in view here; what is referred to is God's causing us to live eternally, that is, to associate properly with God, as a child with a father in a family.

4:8b God's nature In the phrase 'God is love', 'love' is a noun. Stated as an event, it is 'God loves humankind'. But the meaning is not only that God loves humankind, but that he does so according to his nature or character. In other words, 'God loves humankind; that is just how God is' or 'God behaves lovingly towards humankind'.

love *humankind* In the Greek the object of 'love' is not given. According to the immediate context 'humankind' is the implicit object of God's love. The generic and universal statement is that God loves all beings that have self-consciousness and respond to his loving them.

4:9b An alternate rendering with the same meaning would be: 'God sent his only Son to this world in order that his Son *might die for us* in order that we might live *eternally*'.

sent his only Son *to live* **with humankind** The destination of the sending is 'the world'. Here 'world' means 'people/humankind', not simply planet earth. The focus is that Jesus was sent to live within human society.

by means of his *dying and God's forgiving us* This is the central part of God's commissioning of his Son (ἀπέσταλκεν 'sent him'): Jesus died in order that God might forgive humankind, causing humankind on that basis to live eternally. Although dying is not expressed explicitly in the text until 10c, it was central to John's teaching, as his readers knew.

4:10 An alternate rendering of v. 10 is 'The following tells *how we know what it really means for someone* to love *another*: God loved us *so much that* he sent his Son to voluntarily sacrifice *his own life* in order that *God may forgive* our sins. Certainly, we have not loved God like that.'

4:10a *what it means that someone* **loves** *another* The clause ἐν τούτῳ ἐστὶν ἡ ἀγάπη 'in this is love' refers to the following context as new information, but it also builds on the previous context as old information. The deictic ἐν τούτῳ 'in this' points to the following context. Although 'love' is an event requiring an actor and goal to be supplied, the rendering in the display leaves the actor and goal unspecified in order to maintain the play on words. (They could be supplied from the following context.)

4:10c to voluntarily sacrifice *his own life* The Greek is 'propitiation, expiation, or sin offering'. The same word is in 2:2 (see the note there). The strong connection with love in this unit makes it important to emphasize the voluntary nature of the sacrifice and the great cost involved in true love.

in order that *God may forgive* **our sins** The expiation, or sin offering, has the purpose of being 'for our sins'. The required case frames have been made explicit in the display.

4:11a like that [4:10c] Commentators agree that οὕτως 'like this' refers to the immediately preceding context. But some think that it points to the extent of God's love, others to the manner in which God loves us, and still others that it encompasses both the extent and manner. But they all agree that it means 'God loved us at a great personal cost', since no man can do what Christ did for us.

4:11b likewise The relationship between 4:11a and 4:11b is grounds-EXHORTATION, but there is also a strong secondary relationship of model-HEAD (i.e., 'we should love each other according to the pattern of God's loving us').

BOUNDARIES AND COHERENCE

The initial boundary of the 4:7–11 paragraph coincides with that of the 4:7–5:12 section and has already been discussed there. Note that 4:7–11 is marked by an inclusio:

A Love each other. (7a)
  B Love is from God. (7b)
  B' God so loved us. (11a)
A' We likewise must love each other. (11b)

This sandwich structure, together with the paragraph pattern of an APPEAL, a *basis*, and a second summary APPEAL, defines the unit.

The next unit starting at 4:12 has several features that support the boundary between v. 11 and v. 12:

1. The content changes: from loving others because God has enabled us to do so to loving others in order to be assured of our relationship with God.
2. As frequently is the case between large units, there is no conjunction.
3. The aorist is typical of 4:7–11, whereas no aorist verb occurs in the next unit.

Some commentators have judged the vocative ἀγαπητοί 'beloved' of 4:11 to be the beginning of a new paragraph, but a vocative does not necessarily have the function of introducing a paragraph. The use of the vocative there is to mitigate the exhortation.

Some form of ἀγάπη 'love' occurs thirteen times in the 4:7–11 unit; there is not one propositional cluster in which it is not included. The unit is introduced by the alliterative ἀγαπητοί, ἀγαπῶμεν ἀλλήλους 'dear friends, let us love each other' in v. 7. Then in vv. 9 and 10 ἐν τούτῳ 'by this' is used to introduce two parallel statements: first, a generic statement of the meaning of God's love; then, a more specific restatement of it. All of these features lend coherence to 4:7–11.

PROMINENCE AND THEME

The 4:7–11 paragraph is the second part of the Epistle's second double climax (see the discussion under 4:7–5:12); hence it is very prominent in the higher-level structure. Internally, 4:7–11 has its own prominence structure: The exhortation of 4:7a is structurally prominent, and is supported by the *basis* statements of 4:7b–c. To clarify the meaning of the verb ἀγαπάω 'love' in v. 7, an illustration is given in a generic form in 4:9 and in a specific form in v. 10. The vocative ἀγαπητοί 'dear friends' occurs twice (4:7, 11), each time leading into a prominent exhortation, thereby placing marked prominence on them.

The structurally prominent constituents in the paragraph are the *APPEALS* in 4:7–8 and 4:11. Both are introduced by the vocative ἀγαπητοί, as just mentioned, drawing attention to their contents. The 7b proposition aptly summarizes the *basis* of vv. 9–10. The theme is taken from the two *APPEALS*, since they are prominent, and the vocative and the 7b proposition, since it summarizes the 9–10 *basis*.

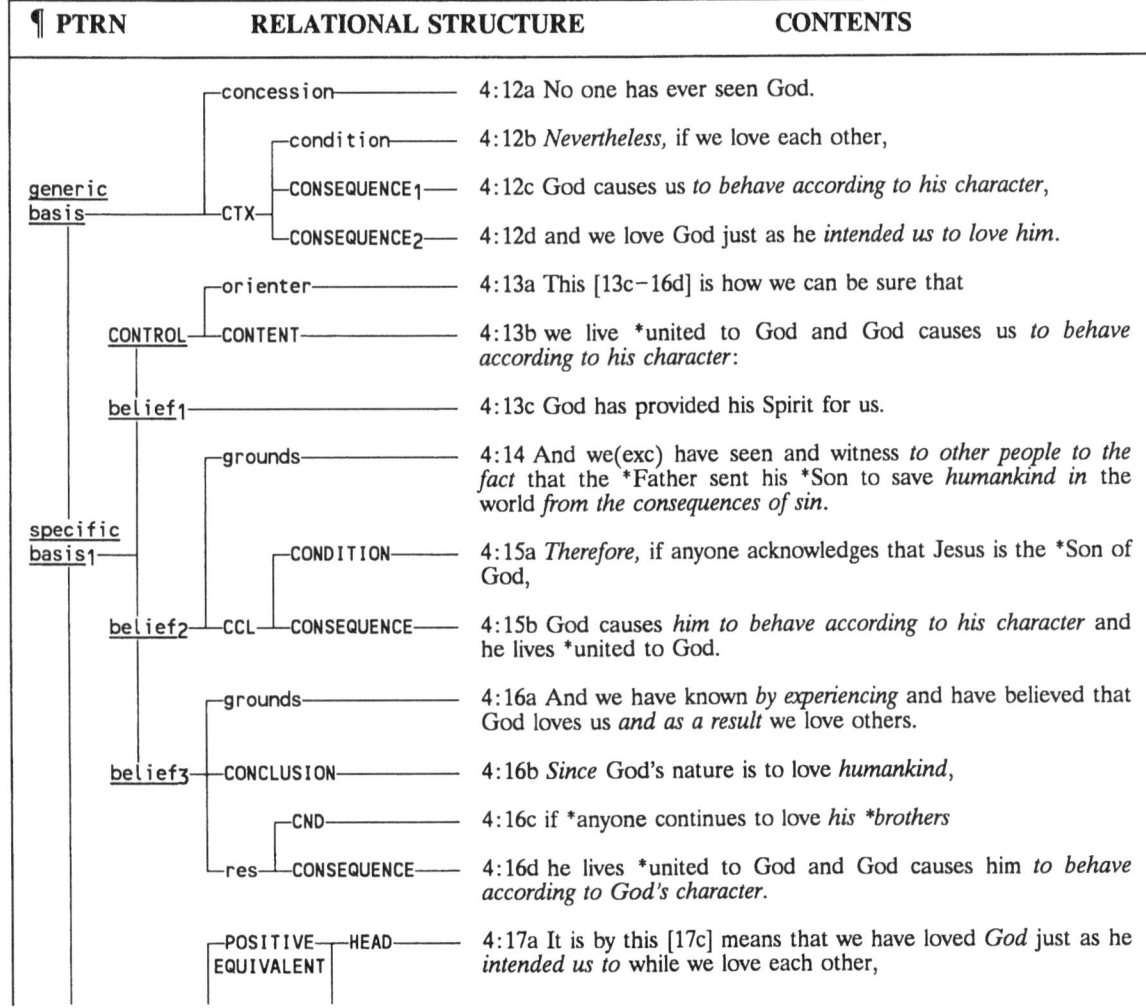

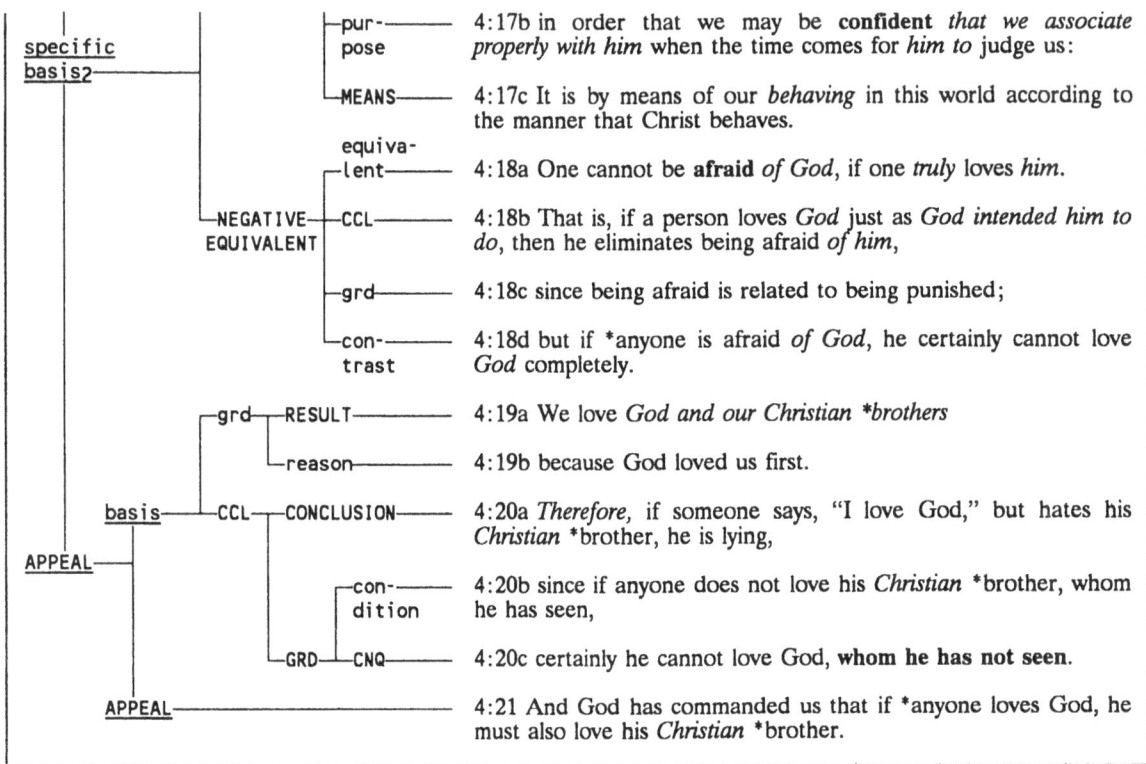

INTENT AND PARAGRAPH PATTERN

The author's intent in the 4:12-21 paragraph is to affect the actions of the readers using an admonition (in 4:21) that they help each other in practical ways, thus showing real love. It consists of three supportive units (4:12, 4:13-16, and 4:17-18) and one central APPEAL (4:19-21). Their communication relationship is three grounds units followed by one exhortational unit. Since the primary intent is to affect the behavior (clearly demonstrated by the allusion to a command in 4:21), the unit is considered causal hortatory, the principal constituents being + basis + APPEAL.

For further details regarding the structure of the constituent units, see the discussion under "Boundaries and Coherence" (p. 84).

NOTES

4:12a No one has ever seen God The relationship to its context of the axiomatic statement that no one has ever seen God is uncertain. However, the rendering in the display is based on our natural expectation that we would have to observe someone before we could know and imitate his behavior and character. Nevertheless, contrary to that expectation, God does cause us to behave according to his character; that is, he directs our behavior and we honor him just as he has intended us to. An alternate interpretation is: 'although no one has ever seen God, other people will observe his character when we love our fellow Christians'. The problem with this latter interpretation is that it requires that the conditional clause be considered prominent, that is, principal in the argument. This would be possible only if 12a alone were the *generic basis* of the 4:21 APPEAL (and 12b-d, another *specific basis*.)

4:12b-d The relationship between 4:12b and the two following propositions is that of condition-CONSEQUENCE as clearly signaled by ἐάν 'if'. The argument is 'if it is true that we love each other, then it is also true that God controls our behavior'. If this were taken to be a first-class conditional clause, the meaning would be 'since we love each other, it is evident that God controls our behavior'. This does not seem appropriate in the context since the total argument is that we should love each other. (It is not a deduction as though we were already loving each other.)

4:12b Nevertheless The Greek text has no conjunction to show the connection between 12b-d and 12a, but since the thought is that Christians behave according to God's character even though they have never seen him, an adversative is supplied in the display.

4:12c God causes us *to behave according to his character* The topic of God's remaining in us believers is taken up and developed more fully in 4:13–16. Some form of ὁ θεὸς ἐν ἡμῖν μένει 'God remains in us' is repeated there three times, in 13b, 15b, 16d. This could be stated in propositional form as 'God shares his manner of behaving with us', 'God's character remains in us', 'God's character controls our manner of behaving', or 'God causes us to behave according to his character'. We have chosen the last as the most adequate. The actor is 'God'; 'remains' is rendered as 'causes us to behave according to his character'. The sphere of the control is 'in us'.

4:12d we love God just as he *intended us to love him* There are many differences among commentators concerning ἡ ἀγάπη αὐτοῦ ἐν ἡμῖν τετελειωμένη ἐστίν 'the love of him is perfected in us'. Differing interpretations of 'the love of him' are: 'God loves us', 'God's loving us results in our loving others', and 'we love God'. There are also differences concerning 'is perfected': one view is 'God's purpose for loving us is completed'; another, 'you have done what God intended'. Interestingly, there is no discussion regarding 'in us'. From our viewpoint 'in us' could mean 'us (agent)', 'in reference to us', 'God has caused us to love', or 'God intends that we love'. All the above, when combined, result in a jungle of interpretations. The immediate context is a statement of the condition that must be met if God's character is to control us. The context both before and after this clause is 'because God loves us, we love him, and because he has commanded us to love us, we must love each other'. Therefore, in rendering 12d we equate 'the love of him' with 'we love God', 'is perfected' with 'we have done just as God intended us do', and 'in us' with 'God intends that *we* love'.

4:13a, c The word ὅτι 'that' occurs twice in v. 13, each time with a different referent. The clause introduced by this particle in its first occurrence is the content complement of the previous verb. The clause introduced by this particle in its second occurrence is the content complement of ἐν τούτῳ 'by this'. So it means 'we can be sure that we live united to God by means of his providing his Spirit for us'. If the second clause were a second content complement of the verb, it would be introduced by καί 'and' rather than by ὅτι. The second ὅτι introduces three conjoined means units (4:13c, 14, and 16a), each introduced by καί showing their equal status and parallel function. Thus, the meaning is 'we can be sure that we live united to God by means of his providing his Spirit for us, and by means of the apostles' telling us, and by means of God's enabling us to love others' (see the second paragraph of "Intent and Paragraph Pattern" after the 4:12–21 display).

4:13a This [13c–16d] The deictic ἐν τούτῳ 'by this' refers to the following context.

4:13b See the note on 4:12c.

4:13c has provided In many languages the meaning of 'give' is limited to handing over some physical object. The rendering here avoids the primary meaning of 'give' and expresses more exactly the secondary meaning, which in this context is what is intended.

his Spirit This is an abbreviated way of expressing that God's Spirit is a means for assurance that believers are united to God. It can be restated as 'we can be sure that we live united to God by God's Spirit's reassuring our consciousness'.

4:14 we(exc) The plural here is understood as referring to John and the apostles, as in 1:2–3, and not including the readers.

to other people to the fact The event 'witness' requires that a message and the recipient of the message be supplied. The recipients are 'other people'. The message is the historical fact made explicit in the following context.

sent his Son See the note on 4:9b.

to save *humankind* **in the world** *from the consequences of sin* The literal rendering is 'savior of the world'. A savior is a person who rescues another from some harmful event and makes his life secure. The verb form means 'to rescue from danger and restore to a former state of safety and well being' (Louw and Nida 21.18). The term was used by ancient rulers in describing themselves as the defenders of the people. Semantically, 'savior' is a personified abstraction of the event 'save, rescue', hence the shift from a noun to a verb in the display. Many harmful events could be supplied within this religious context as required by the event 'save', but in order to be brief and general we have supplied 'from the consequences of sin'.

Here the metonymy 'world' stands either for humankind in general or for godless people (see the note on 2:2c).

4:15b See the note on 4:12c.

4:16a we Here 'we' could be inclusive or exclusive; either fits the context quite well, as most commentators agree. Inclusive has been chosen for the display since 'we(exc)' is the unusual in this letter.

by experiencing Because of the experiential aspect and the perfect tense of ἐγνώκαμεν 'we have known', the knowing is attributed here to experience with God.

God loves us *and as a result* we love others The Greek is τὴν ἀγάπην ἣν ἔχει ὁ θεὸς ἐν ἡμῖν 'the love which God has in us'. Commentators are divided as to whether this means 'God loves us' or 'the fact that God loves us is the source by which we love other people'. But to have God's love ἐν ἡμῖν 'in us' can be said to include both God's loving us and our loving others; hence in the display both ideas are presented.

4:16b God's nature is to love See the note on 4:8b concerning 'God's nature'.

4:16c continues to love *his brothers* The phrase 'remain in the love' can mean 'God continues to love him', 'he continues to love God', or 'he continues to love his Christian brothers'. Commentators prefer to leave the ambiguity; but if in a given language the translator must make a choice, the best is the one in the display. If the receptor language allows ambiguity, then that might be the choice; however, rendering the abstract noun 'love' as an event does not lend itself to ambiguity. Since v. 16 is a summary of the Epistle's main climax (4:7-11), in which the author exhorts the readers to love each other, and since the paragraph's *APPEAL* is to show genuine love toward our Christian brothers, we take this conditional clause to be 'he continues to love his Christian brothers'.

4:16d God causes him *to behave* See the note on 4:12c.

4:17-18a In this passage love is contrasted with fear, for which love has no place. Love based on faith produces confidence, not fear.

4:17a by this [17c] As the referent for ἐν τούτῳ 'by this', commentators and versions offer three different possibilities: (1) what precedes it in 16c-d, namely 'if anyone continues to love *his brothers*, he lives united to God and God causes him *to behave according to God's character*'; (2) the purposive clause that follows it in 17b, namely 'in order that we may be confident *that we associate properly with him* when the time comes for *him to* judge us'; and (3) the resumptive ὅτι clause that follows it in 17c, namely 'by means of our *behaving* in this world according to the manner that Christ behaves'.

These three views can be displayed as follows:

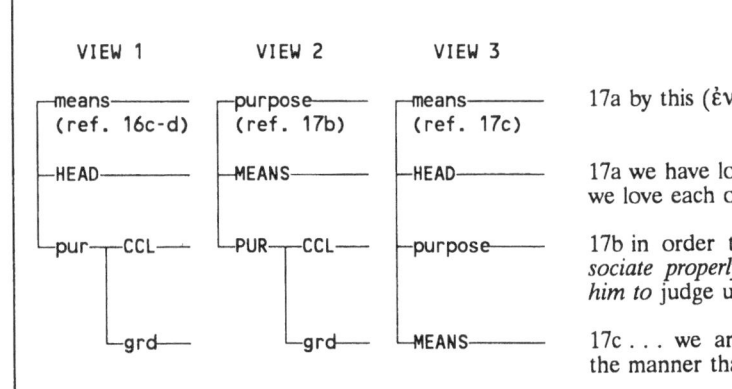

A few commentators and versions hold to the first view. The great majority of commentators and versions hold to the second. Of those we consulted, only David Smith (*The Expositor's Greek Testament*) and Longacre (p. 33) hold to the third. But the third view is the most consistent in light of our note in 2:3a. It maintains a means relation for ἐν τούτῳ, which is its function when followed by a resumptive ὅτι, the meaning being 'by this means'. This is the view reflected in the display of the 4:12-21 paragraph.

we have loved *God* **just as he** *intended us to* **while we love each other** There are several difficulties with τετελείωται ἡ ἀγάπη μεθ' ἡμῖν 'love is perfected with us'. The problems are similar to those in 4:12d (see that note), where τετελείωται 'is perfected' is rendered the same as here. In this context ἡ ἀγάπη 'love' refers to an active event, not just an emotion or state. It can mean 'we love God' or 'God loves us'. In view of the following statements that there can be no fear in love and God's love is always perfect, we have decided that the meaning here is 'we love God'.

The major difficulty in interpretation is the meaning of μεθ' ἡμῖν 'with us'. There is no consensus among the commentators. The simplest view is that it refers to 'our loving each other within the fellowship of believers'.

4:17b <u>confident</u> *that we associate properly with him* The word 'confident' is forefronted in the clause, thus prominent. Here it echoes 2:28 (see the note there) where the coming of Christ calls for confidence rather than shrinking in fear.

when the time comes for *him to* **judge us** The phrase ἐν τῇ ἡμέρᾳ τῆς κρίσεως 'in the day of judgment' refers to the time when God will judge all humankind. Because of reference to the coming of Christ, the phrase 'the day of judgment' here is interpreted as the final judgment rather than the daily correction of the Holy Spirit. The fact that believers will stand confidently before him indicates that the reference is more specifically to the judgment of believers.

4:17c *behaving* The words 'as he is so are we' refer to the believers' likeness to Christ. The rendering in the display is in terms of 'behaving'—living with God on the basis of a mutually loving relationship and in harmony with that relationship.

in this world It is ambiguous in the Greek whether 'in this world' is linked with both 'he' (Christ) and 'we' (believers), or only the latter. (The literal gloss is 'just as that-one is and we are in the world this'.) The theological and contextual arguments do not seem to solve the problem. From a grammatical point of view, since 'in this world' immediately follows 'we are', and since 'this' follows 'world' ('in world this'), we take it that John is contrasting believers' being in the world with the fact that Jesus is not now in this world.

Christ The Greek pronoun here refers to Christ. See the note on 2:6b.

4:18a <u>afraid</u> This word is forefronted in the clause and is thus prominent.

one *truly* **loves** *him* In order to include the implicature that to love God we must obey his commandments, especially the one to love each other, the rendering here is 'truly loves'. This follows the interpretation on which the rendering in 4:17a is based ('we have loved God . . . while we love each other').

4:18d he certainly cannot love *God* **completely** Literally, this is 'the one that fears has not been perfected in love'. The concept 'perfected' is an abstraction of an event, so is best rendered as an adverb. However, it is nuclear to the clause and therefore prominent. The rendering 'certainly cannot' attempts to restore this focus. The event 'love' requires both an actor and a goal, here made explicit. The preposition 'in' expresses the sphere of 'perfected'.

4:19-21 In this passage true love for God is contrasted with the love of those who claim to love God but show, by hating their Christian brother, that they do not.

4:19a-b we ... because God The free pronoun forms ἡμεῖς 'we' and αὐτός 'he' (specified in the display as 'God') are forefronted in the Greek. The forefronting emphasizes that this is a contrast between our love and God's.

4:19a we love The verb ἀγαπῶμεν 'we love' can be taken either as hortatory subjunctive or as indicative. We consider it indicative.

love *God and our Christian brother* In the Greek the verb ἀγαπῶμεν 'we love' occurs without an expressed object in some texts and with it in others. UBS scholars (Metzger) and several commentators feel that the correct reading is the one without the object since copyists would tend to feel the need to supply an accusative object here and thus corrupt the text. Many modern English versions translate 'we love' with no object. Commentators generally interpret this as an all-inclusive love that includes love for God and the Christian brother. However, in view of the larger context and the force of the whole letter, it might be taken to refer quite specifically to loving our Christian brother (even though the immediately preceding context deals with loving God). Either rendering, 'we love our Christian brothers' or 'we love God and our Christian brothers', is acceptable in this context.

4:20a if someone says As in 1:6 and 2:4, this expression introduces a false claim, which is called a lie.

he is lying The Greek 'he is a liar' refers to speaking falsely. Here, more specifically, it refers to inconsistency between what a person claims about himself and his manner of behaving.

4:20b-c There is a chiasm in the Greek (see the discussion under "Boundaries and Coherence" on p. 89). Since the chiastic order of the Greek cannot be preserved in English, it is not represented in the display.

4:20c certainly he cannot love God In 4:20a the claim to love God is called a lie, which gives marked prominence to the denial in 20c, and this prominence is expressed by 'certainly'. The UBS text omits the πῶς 'how' that makes this clause a rhetorical question in some texts. The rendering in the display is based on this omission.

As to the meaning of 'cannot', it could mean that the person is incapable of loving God or that he does not love God because he does not love his brother. Although both interpretations fit the context, most commentators choose the former, as do we.

whom he has not seen This clause comes first in the Greek and is therefore prominent; it is in sharp contrast to what immediately precedes it ('the brother whom he has seen'). English structure will not allow switching the order of the clauses, so the prominence is shown by bold type in the display.

4:21 God has commanded An alternate interpretation is 'Christ has commanded'. This is not an important difference, but we have taken the opinion of the majority of commentators in our rendering here.

BOUNDARIES AND COHERENCE

The opening boundary of 4:12-21 has been discussed under 4:7-11. The closing boundary is marked by a tail-head linkage: The reference to loving the brother in 4:21 is carried over to 5:1, where it is expressed more explicitly as loving the one who has been begotten as a brother.

Coherence in the unit is seen in the idea of confidence before God when he judges us as the overriding purpose for living united to God and loving our Christian brothers. Coherence is further demonstrated by the occurrence of lexical items in the domain of faith: γινώσκω 'know' in 4:13, 16; θεάομαι 'behold' and μαρτυρέω 'witness' in 4:14; ὁμολογέω 'acknowledge' in 4:15; πιστεύω 'believe' in 4:16; παρρησία 'confidence' in 4:17. Also, some form of ἀγάπη 'love' occurs fifteen times in this unit (though not at all in vv. 13-15).

The relational coherence is as follows: After the *generic basis* (4:12) the argument is developed that if we live united to God by believing that Jesus is his Son (4:13-16, the first *specific basis*) and since we do love God (4:17-18, the second *specific basis*), we must therefore love our Christian brothers (4:19-21, the *APPEAL*).

The first *specific basis* (4:13-16) is an embedded paragraph. It consists of one principal unit (4:13a-b) and three supportive units (4:13c, 14-15, and 4:16). Their communication relationship is a result followed by three means, but it is labeled as an embedded paragraph pattern of control-beliefs. This could be taken as either a straightforward explanation of how we know that God causes us to behave according to his own character or as an emotive presentation of the writer's belief system, which is the means for controlling his behavior. Because of the personal reference to John's own experience with Jesus, the emotive intensity of the lexical items employed, and the expression of a belief system, this embedded paragraph has the characteristics of a volitional expressive paragraph in which the author intends to affect the emotions of his audience. Hence this embedded paragraph is taken as a volitional expressive, the principal constituents being + *belief* + CONTROL.

The *APPEAL* unit (4:19-21) is also an embedded paragraph. It consists of one supportive unit (4:19-20) and one principal unit (4:21). Their communication relationship is grounds-EXHORTATION. This embedded paragraph is causal hortatory, the principal constituents being + *basis* + *APPEAL*.

If this 19-21 embedded paragraph were interpreted as expository, many problems would arise as to how the whole (4:12-21) paragraph hangs together because none of its constituents stands alone. However, viewed as a hortatory unit, they do form a coherent semantic paragraph.

If the 12-21 paragraph were to be interpreted as expository, it would consist of three evidential units and an inference. This would, of course, affect the meaning and structure of the whole paragraph. The meaning would be as follows:

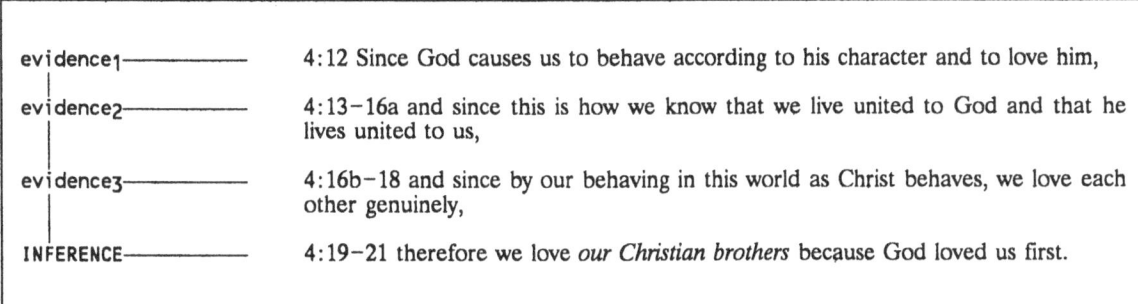

But the basic problem with this analysis is that the constituents of the unit do not cohere.

We realize that our decision regarding a long-debated exegetical problem is based on a semantic criterion. But this criterion does present strong support for our considering 4:12-21 and its 4:19-21 constituent as hortatory.

There are some unusual structural (grammatical disturbances) and rhetorical features in 4:12-21 due to its immediately following the main climax of the letter (4:1-11). It forcefully summarizes and focuses back on the climax.

Here, instead of using a chiastic structure—his favored device—John uses a parallel structure. The two brief clauses of v. 12 (the *generic basis* for the *APPEAL*) are A and B of the parallel presentation. The two *specific bases* that follow (they are expansions) are A' and B'. This could be viewed as follows:

A God causes us to behave according to his character (v. 12c)
B we love God just as he intended us to love him (v. 12d)
  A' we live united to God and God causes us to behave according to his character (v. 13b)
  B' we have loved God just as he intended us to while we love each other (v. 17a)

The first *specific basis* (4:13-16) focuses on and summarizes 4:1-6; the second *specific basis* (4:17-18) focuses on and summarizes 4:7-11, the climactic paragraph. The first *specific basis* is an emotive embedded paragraph, therefore prominent. The second *specific basis* is presented as positive and negative equivalents of the 12d statement (12d is B, 17-18 B').

The *APPEAL* in 4:19-21 focuses on John's major concern that the Christians genuinely love each other. The *APPEAL* contains a chiasm in 20b and 20c:

A The one who does not love his Christian brother (v. 20b)
  B whom he has seen, (v. 20b)
  B' not having seen God, (v. 20c)
A' certainly cannot love him. (v. 20c)

PROMINENCE AND THEME

The 4:12-21 paragraph is postclimactic; and, as might be expected, it evidences turbulence. The structural prominence is clear: there is the principal *APPEAL* (4:19-21), supported by a generic *basis* (4:12) and two *specific bases* (4:13-16 and 4:17-18). The significant prominence features are as follows:

1. High lexical density of allusions to previous motifs and themes.
2. Deictic pronouns and conjunctions.
3. The chiasm of vv. 20-21.

Most of these features show up at the nucleus of each of the paragraph's constituents.

The theme statement is drawn from the most prominent elements of the paragraph: The concept of perfected or fulfilled love in the second *specific basis* (4:17–18) is marked as prominent by the repetition of the word 'love' (three times) and by the deictic ἐν τούτῳ 'by this'. The *basis* of the APPEAL is marked as prominent by the fact that the 20b–c grounds statement is a chiasm (discussed under "Boundaries and Coherence"). The APPEAL (4:21) is marked as prominent by the forefronting of ταύτην τὴν ἐντολήν 'this command'.

SECTION CONSTITUENT 5:1–12 (Expository Sub-Section: Basis of 4:7–5:12)
Theme: If a person believes that Jesus is God's Anointed One, he is one whom God has caused to live spiritually and he loves his Christian brothers. He also overcomes the evil of human society. We know this is true because God's Spirit testifies that Jesus came to save humankind.

MACROSTRUCTURE	CONTENTS
application	5:1–5 If a person believes that Jesus is God's Anointed One, he is one whom God has caused to live spiritually and he loves his Christian brothers. He obeys God's commands, and he overcomes the evil of human society.
PRINCIPLE	5:6–12 If a person believes in and lives united to God's Son, he is one whom God has caused to live spiritually forever. We know this is true because God's Spirit testifies that Jesus came to save humankind.

INTENT AND MACROSTRUCTURE

Having presented all the major exhortations summed up in the double climax (4:1–6 and 4:7–11), John now turns to a brief exposition of the bases and benefits of living according to Christ's character. This part of the letter concludes the whole presentation; it can be considered the denouement of the letter.

The 5:1–12 section is made up of two paragraphs: one descriptive (5:1–5), one expository (5:6–12). The latter states a *PRINCIPLE*, the former an *application* of it. The macromeaning is: God has caused those who believe in God's Son to live spiritually forever (*PRINCIPLE*); they show this by loving their Christian brothers, obeying God, and overcoming the world spirit (*application*).

BOUNDARIES AND COHERENCE

The opening boundary (between 4:21 and 5:1) was discussed under unit 4:12–21, and the closing boundary under unit 4:7–5:12.

The structural coherence is seen in the display. Another aspect of coherence has to do with the subject matter. Now approaching the end of the Epistle, John delivers the last thrust, the irrefutable witness of God to his Son (5:6–12).

PROMINENCE AND THEME

The theme of 5:1–12 is based on structural prominence since features of marked prominence appear only in the *PRINCIPLE*, 5:6–12 (see the discussion under that unit).

> **SUB-SECTION CONSTITUENT 5:1-5 (Descriptive Paragraph: Application of 5:1-12)**
> *Theme: If a person believes that Jesus is God's Anointed One, he is one whom God has caused to live spiritually and he loves his Christian brothers. He obeys God's commands, and overcomes the evil of human society.*

¶ PTRN	RELATIONAL STRUCTURE	CONTENTS

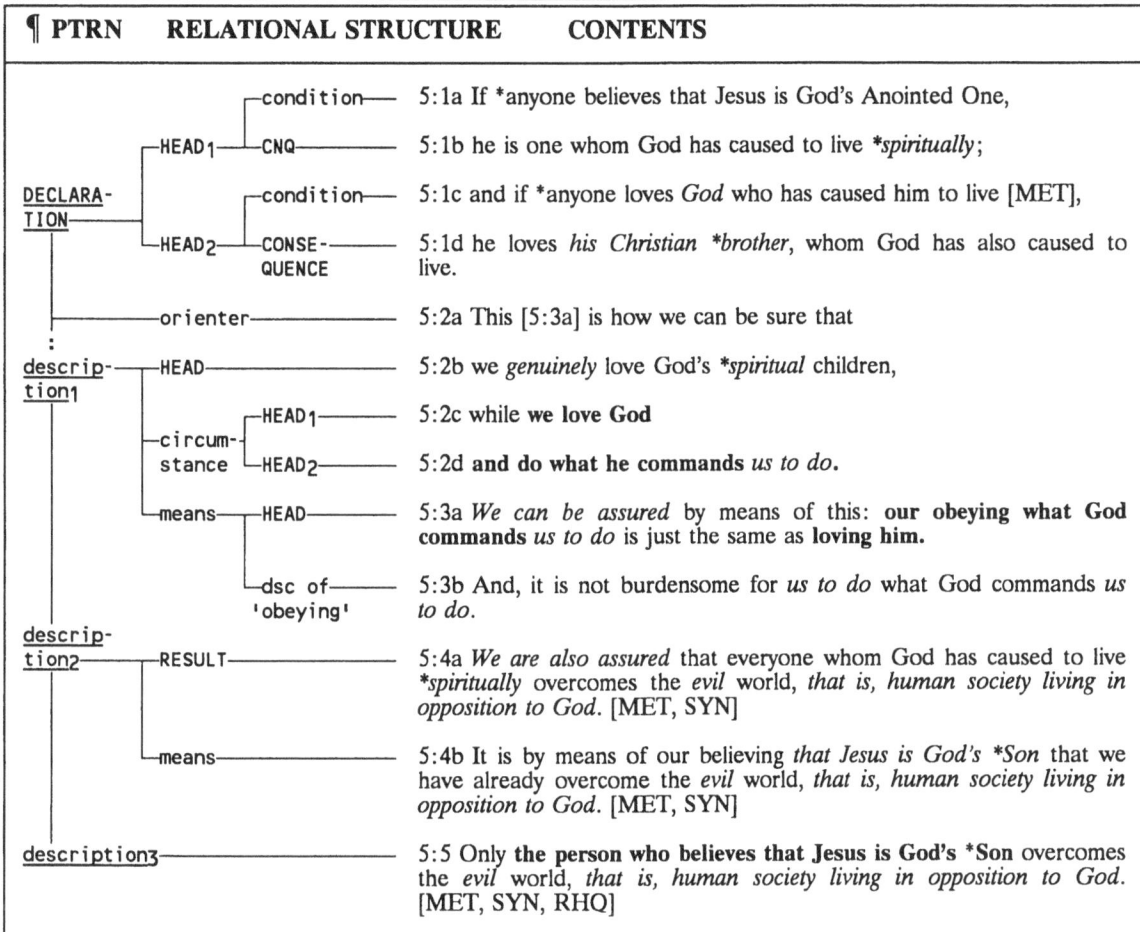

INTENT AND PARAGRAPH PATTERN

As John concludes the main message of this letter, his intent is to affect the readers' emotions with a summary of all the previous instructions. He wants to make certain that they understand that believing in Christ and loving their Christian brothers is part of being God's children. This paragraph has four constituents: v. 1, vv. 2-3, v. 4, and v. 5. The communication relationship is one generic statement followed by three specific ones. Since the primary intent of this paragraph is to affect the emotions (as indicated by its denouement character and its many prominence markers), this is considered a volitional descriptive paragraph, the principal constituents being + *description* + DECLARATION.

NOTES

5:1a God's Anointed One The Hebrew word 'Messiah' and the Greek word 'Christ' both signify 'the Anointed One'. Anointing was a symbolic act (see the note on 2:20a). The most frequent use of 'Christ' is as a proper name to refer to Jesus, but in some cases (as here) it is used as the title of the One whom the nation of Israel was awaiting. It may also be rendered as 'God's Chosen One' or 'God's promised savior'.

5:1c God who has caused him to live Literally, this is 'parent'. The topic is God, the image 'parent', and the point of similarity 'one who causes to live'. Here, of course, the metaphor refers most specifically to God's being one who causes us to live spiritually/forever.

5:1d he loves *his Christian brother*, whom God has also caused to live An alternate interpretation is 'he loves Christ whom God caused to live in the world', but only a few English translations support this interpretation.

The textual question as to whether or not καί 'also' should be accepted seems to revolve around the probability of its being a scribal addition carried over from 4:21. But if v. 1 is accepted as an aphorism (see the comments under "Coherence"), the conjunction does not fit well. For this reason we omit καί.

5:2a This [5:3a] A few commentators take ἐν τούτῳ 'by this' as pointing to the preceding context; however, following most commentators, we prefer to preserve the pattern in the Epistle of its pointing to the following context (see the note on 2:3b). Indeed, the meaning is virtually the same. There *is* a significant difference, though, among those who take it to refer forward. Some say 'this' in 2a refers to 2c–d; some say it refers to 3a. But to say that 'this' refers to 'while we love God' does not cohere properly—it mixes a means signal in 2a with a circumstance in 2c–d (ὅταν 'when' introducing 2c–d can not signal means). It would cohere much better of we take 'this' to refer to 3a: 'loving God is the same as obeying his commands'. The analysis in the display is based on this view. (The introductory γάρ 'for' in 3a is taken as signaling only a loose logical relationship, allowing it to be a means relation.)

Proposition 2a serves as orienter for the next two *description* units (5:2b–3b and 5:4). These are the two contents of what we know, each introduced by ὅτι 'that is'.

5:2b *genuinely* This refers back to 3:18 (see the note there).

5:2d do The difference between the textual variants ποιῶμεν 'we do' and τηρῶμεν 'we honor' is not significant for the translator. The rendering in the display is not intended to reflect a particular textual preference.

5:3a *We can be assured* The word γάρ 'for' frequently shows a logical relationship such as grounds-CONCLUSION, reason-RESULT, or even means-RESULT. The analysis here is based on means-RESULT.

the same as The construction αὕτη ἐστίν ... ἵνα occurs three times in the Epistle, in 3:11, 3:23, and 5:3. In all cases αὕτη 'this' points forward to the ἵνα clause as an equivalent restatement of the predicate nominative of 'this is'.

5:4a everyone whom God has caused to live *spiritually* In English it is not acceptable to say 'whatever God has caused to live' in reference to persons. Therefore, 'whatever' is rendered 'everyone whom'. However, the Greek neuter expression supports the broadest interpretation by its general and abstract form. This has been interpreted by commentators as emphasizing the victorious power rather than the victorious person (Stott), so that the victory is to be attributed to God's begetting. Thus it would mean 'everyone whom God has caused to live spiritually overcomes the evil world by means of his being caused to live spiritually'.

evil* world, *that is, human society living in opposition to God The word 'world' is used here (also in 4b and 5) in the third of the senses in the note on 2:2c: 'the evil of human society in opposition to God' (see *world spirit* in the Glossary).

5:4b have *already* overcome The word 'already' is supplied to emphasize the aorist active form of the participle. Different interpretations regarding the victory include the victory of Christ (John 16:33) or the individual experience of new birth, which brings the believer into the benefit of that victory.

evil* world, *that is, human society living in opposition to God See the note on 4a.

5:5 Only the person The rhetorical question 'who ... except for' expects the answer 'nobody'. The words in bold in the display are prominent due to their being the closing segment of a chiasm, restating 1a (see the discussion under "Boundaries and Coherence" that follows).

evil* world, *that is, human society living in opposition to God See the note on 4a.

BOUNDARIES AND COHERENCE

The opening boundary is discussed under unit 4:13–21. Another marker of the boundaries is the inclusio of ὁ πιστεύων 'the one who believes' (in 5:1a and 5:5).

The closing boundary is marked by a tail-head construction: the deictic phrase οὗτός ἐστίν 'this is', in 5:6, points back to 'the Son' in 5:5. Although v. 5 is included in the next unit by some commentators because of its declaration of the Son of God, we recognize it as the second part of the inclusio and as transitional: The focus of effective power of faith here in 5:1-5 changes to the divine witness to the Son in the next paragraph.

The coherence of the 5:1-5 paragraph comes from its chiastic structure. Many of the motifs developed throughout the body of the letter are again taken up here as a summation of the letter. The chiasm is as follows:

- A the one who believes that Jesus is the Christ (5:1a)
  - B be born from God (5:1b)
    - C love those born from him (5:1d)
    - C' we love the children of God (5:2a)
  - B' the one born by God overcomes ... (5:4a)
- A' the one who believes that Jesus is the Son of God (5:5)

Because it is a summation of previous motifs, this paragraph evidences many unusual uses of conjunctions and other discourse signals. Verse 1 is a generalized statement in which the actors are unspecified or unidentified as simply πᾶς ὁ 'all who' (1a starts with πᾶς ὁ 'all who', and 1c is conjoined by the parallel καὶ πᾶς ὁ 'and all who'); there is no doubt that the whole verse is an aphorism. Verses 2-4 are the specific applications of the v. 1 generalizations; in 2-4 the actors are specified as 'we' (coinciding with the units C' and B' in the chiasm).

The beginning of v. 2 presents further unusual relations and constructions: 2a begins with ἐν τούτῳ γινώσκομεν 'by this we know'. The referent of 'this' is a problem, but we take it to be 'loving God is the same as obeying his commands' in 5:3a (see the note on 5:2a).

There is another problem in 2a: what is it that we know or are sure of? Since ὅτι 'that' in 2b introduces the clause 'we love the children of God', it is obvious what it is that we are sure of. However, at the beginning of 4a there is another ὅτι, so the content of the knowing or assurance could be 4a as well as 2b. But the ὅτι in 4a could be interpreted as introducing a reason clause supporting 3b; it would then mean 'his commands are not burdensome *because* all who are born from God overcome the world'. While this is a coherent and acceptable interpretation, it would subordinate the C' part of the chiasm. Another possibility is that ὅτι 'because/that' is here introducing a statement parallel to 2b: 'we are sure (2a) that we love the children of God (2b) and that all who are born of God overcome the world (4a)'. This latter interpretation seems to fit best as to coherence, use of the conjunction, and congruence with the chiasm.

Another unusual construction is in 3a and it is paralleled in 4b (αὕτη ... ἐστιν ἡ ... 'this ... is the ...'). Since 3a is the means of 2b, we take 4b as the means of 4a.

In v. 5 'believing that Jesus is God's Son' is equated with 'overcoming the world', thereby tying 'overcoming the world' in 5:4b to 'believing that Jesus is God's Anointed One' in 5:1a, an effective summation device. The reference in v. 5 to Jesus as God's Son is not only summational, but also transitional: it forms a tail-head construction with the next paragraph.

This 5:1-5 paragraph starts out with an emphatic DECLARATION (5:1) about believing in the Son and loving Christian brothers (cf. 3:23). This is followed by three concise *descriptions*, which allude to previous motifs: 'loving genuinely and obeying his commands', 'overcoming the evil world spirit', and 'the one who believes that Jesus is God's Son overcomes the world spirit'.

The figure of a weaving has been used to describe this Epistle. In this particular unit it is as though the artisan were tying off the threads as he brings together major motifs in foregoing units. Faith, love, and victory are brought together and clearly related to the Epistle's overall purpose: being joined together with God by the common ground of his moral character. Faith gives evidence of God's begetting, which results in love and victory.

Key words are frequently repeated in the paragraph, as might be expected near the close of a discourse, giving it internal coherence as well as coherence with the entire letter. The words ἀγάπη or ἀγαπάω 'love' occur in 5:1c, 1d, 2b, 3a; πίστις/πιστεύω/γινώσκω 'faith/believe/know' in 5:1a, 2a, 4b, 5; νίκη/νικάω 'victory/overcome' in 5:4a, 4b (twice), 5; and γεννάω/τέκνα 'beget/children' in 5:1b, 1c, 1d, 2b, 4a.

PROMINENCE AND THEME

The structural prominence of this paragraph is: a *DECLARATION* (v. 1) supported by three *descriptions* (vv. 2–3, v. 4, and v. 5). The theme is drawn from the HEADS of the *DECLARATION* and a summation of the *descriptions*.

The third *description* has two features of marked prominence: (1) It is the close of the chiasm, ὁ πιστεύων ὅτι Ἰησοῦς ἐστιν ὁ . . . 'the one who believes that Jesus is . . .', which restates v. 1. (2) It is an emphatic rhetorical question marked by εἰ μή 'if it isn't'.

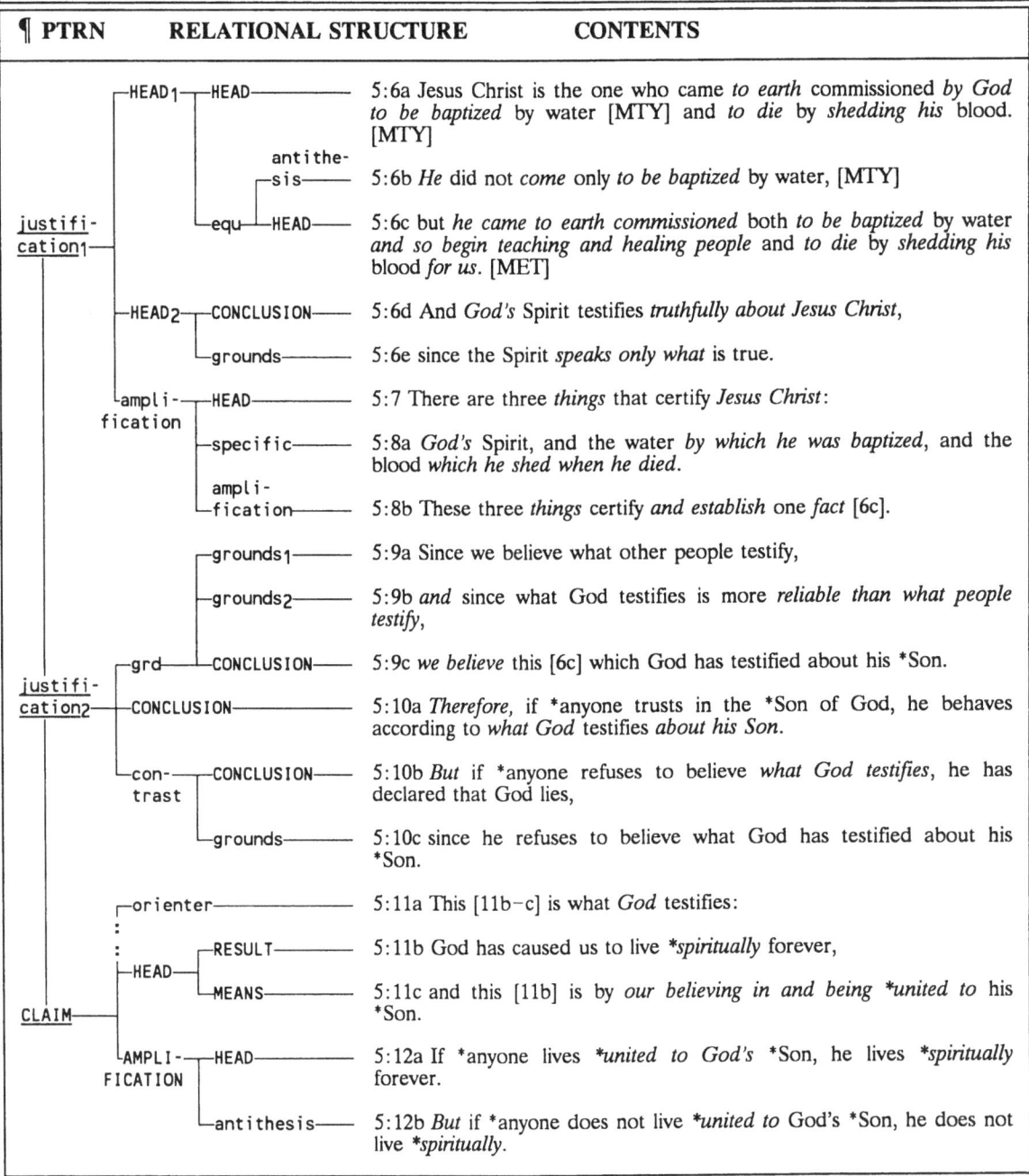

SUB-SECTION CONSTITUENT 5:6–12 (Expository Paragraph: Principle of 5:1–12)
Theme: If a person believes in and lives united to God's Son, he is one whom God has caused to live spiritually forever. We know this is true because God's Spirit testifies that Jesus came to save humankind.

¶ PTRN	RELATIONAL STRUCTURE	CONTENTS
justification₁	HEAD₁ — HEAD	5:6a Jesus Christ is the one who came *to earth* commissioned *by God to be baptized* by water [MTY] and *to die* by shedding his blood. [MTY]
	antithesis	5:6b He did not *come* only *to be baptized* by water, [MTY]
	equ — HEAD	5:6c but *he came to earth commissioned* both *to be baptized* by water *and so begin teaching and healing people* and *to die* by shedding his blood *for us*. [MET]
	HEAD₂ — CONCLUSION	5:6d And *God's* Spirit testifies *truthfully* about Jesus Christ,
	grounds	5:6e since the Spirit *speaks only what* is true.
	amplification — HEAD	5:7 There are three *things* that certify *Jesus Christ*:
	specific	5:8a *God's* Spirit, and the water *by which he was baptized*, and the blood *which he shed when he died*.
	amplification	5:8b These three *things* certify *and establish* one *fact* [6c].
justification₂	grounds₁	5:9a Since we believe what other people testify,
	grounds₂	5:9b *and* since what God testifies is more *reliable than what people testify*,
	grd — CONCLUSION	5:9c *we believe* this [6c] which God has testified about his *Son.
	CONCLUSION	5:10a *Therefore,* if *anyone trusts in the *Son of God, he behaves according to *what God* testifies *about his Son*.
	contrast — CONCLUSION	5:10b *But* if *anyone refuses to believe *what God testifies*, he has declared that God lies,
	grounds	5:10c since he refuses to believe what God has testified about his *Son.
CLAIM	orienter	5:11a This [11b-c] is what *God* testifies:
	HEAD — RESULT	5:11b God has caused us to live *spiritually forever,
	MEANS	5:11c and this [11b] is by *our believing in and being *united to his *Son.
	AMPLIFICATION — HEAD	5:12a If *anyone lives *united to God's *Son, he lives *spiritually forever.
	antithesis	5:12b *But* if *anyone does not live *united to God's *Son, he does not live *spiritually.

INTENT AND PARAGRAPH PATTERN

John's purpose in 5:6-12 is primarily to explain that there is ample proof that Jesus came to the earth to save humankind. The paragraph is composed of three propositional clusters (vv. 6-8, vv. 9-10, and vv. 11-12). The communication relationship between these propositional clusters is two grounds units followed by a conclusion. The paragraph could be considered either volitional or causal, and either expository or descriptive. Since the author does not present differing evidences, but marshals only that which supports his CLAIM, we take this to be a volitional paragraph and, since the primary intent is to affirm a known truth (thus affecting ideas), also expository. The principal constituents are + *justification* + CLAIM.

NOTES

5:6a Jesus Christ is the one The Greek is οὗτός 'this one', which focuses prominence on the immediately preceding referent.

came *to earth . . . to be baptized* **by water and** *to die* **by** *shedding his* **blood** The words 'water and blood' in connection with the incarnation of Jesus Christ have been much discussed. First of all, we are given to understand that ἐλθών 'came' is a historical aorist and that ἔρχομαι, the verb from which it is derived, is used with reference to Christ's having come *commissioned by God to accomplish a particular task*. On this basis we must seek for the interpretation of 'water and blood' in the historical events relating to Christ's task of redemption. This rules out the interpretation that understands 'water and blood' as referring to the sacraments. Another theory, that 'water and blood' refers to the incarnation in general (based on the supposition that the author speaks against Docetists who denied the human body of Jesus), cannot be accepted because it depends on a symbolic and not a historic referent for 'water'. Still another theory, that equates *both* the water and the blood with the death of Jesus (cf. 'blood and water' in John 19:34), is also inadequate; for even though in this theory (which could here have been used against the Docetic heresy known to exist at the time we assume John wrote the Epistle) a historical event is in view, the argument against it is that here again 'water' must be understood in a symbolic sense, as in the previously mentioned interpretation. While the blood and water which flowed from Jesus' side are beautifully symbolic, in 1 John 5:6 the author is presenting more than a metaphor.

In our view the words 'water' and 'blood' each refer to a *separate event* as indicated by the fact that each noun is preceded by the preposition and article in 5:6c. The most acceptable interpretation is that 'water' is a metonymy standing for Jesus' baptism in the Jordan and that 'blood' is a metonymy standing for his sacrificial death on the cross. Jesus' baptism at the beginning of his ministry was attested in John 1:34 by the remark "And I have seen and have borne witness that this is the Son of God"; his death was attested by a similarly significant statement at the end of his earthly ministry (John 19:35). Therefore, we take 'water and blood' to refer to the historical events of Christ's baptism and crucifixion.

blood Manuscripts vary here. Some have πνεύματος 'spirit', some αἵματος 'blood'. Strong evidence supports the latter; the former is probably a scribal error that substituted the reading of John 3:5 for the original (Metzger). The UBS text accepts αἵματος as correct.

5:6b He did *not come* **only** *to be baptized* **by water** The phrase οὐκ ἐν τῷ ὕδατι μόνον 'not only by water' is succinct: much is implicit.

5:6c both *to be baptized* **by water** *and so begin teaching and healing people* **and** *to die* **by** *shedding his* **blood** *for us* The historical event of Jesus' baptism in the Jordan by John is presented in all the Gospels as a symbolic act initiating his ministry. According to the records, he ministered to people by teaching and miracles of mercy. The culmination of what God commissioned him to do was dying in order to redeem all who would trust in him. The focus here is not on the two events of his baptism and crucifixion as temporal and spatial points in history, but rather on the totality of what Christ came to do, having been commissioned by the Father. The propositions are therefore worded to supply more comprehensive information so as to avoid a punctiliar interpretation of the historical events.

5:6d *God's* **Spirit testifies** The importance of the Holy Spirit as the witness is primary in this discussion. He was present at the baptism of Jesus (John 1:33), and the writer of Hebrews declares that it was "through the eternal Spirit" that Jesus offered the blood of his sacrifice (Heb. 9:14). The significance of the Spirit as witness here is that the author is giving the strongest possible witness for his declaration. The Holy Spirit *is* truth and his is the witness of God himself. His witness is of far more importance than that of men (see 5:9b).

truthfully about Jesus Christ The clause 'the Spirit is the witness' expresses who the actor of the event 'witness' is; the content and the manner need to be supplied. The content, 'about Jesus Christ', is based on 6c; the manner, 'truthfully', is based on 6e.

5:6e *speaks only what* **is true** The word 'truth' here implies a communication. An alternative is 'speak truthfully'.

5:7-8 Since the expansion of the Greek text at this point is not well supported by either external or internal evidence, we follow the UBS text, which omits the expanded text and rates the omission as very certain ("A").

5:7 three *things* **that certify** That there are three witnesses fulfills the requirement of Deut. 19:15.

5:8b *and establish* **one** *fact* The Greek is εἰς τὸ ἕν εἰσιν 'it is toward one'. This can mean either that the three become one certification or that the three agree to establish one truth.

5:9b more *reliable than what people testify* The witness of God is greater, stronger, and more acceptable than a human witness because of God's trustworthy character and because, as Brooke (p. 138) says, "God, and God alone, is fully competent to speak" concerning his Son.

5:9c we believe Commentators agree that there is a logical gap or ellipsis between 5:9a-b and what follows. This (we believe) supplies the missing part of the syllogism.

this [6c] Opinions on the significance of the deictic αὕτη 'this' in this context are diverse. Does it refer to the witness of the three in 6c, or to vv. 7-8, or to 'what God has testified about his Son' that immediately follows it, or to more than just one of these? Our own preference is to take it to refer to the previous context, namely 6a-b, since if it referred to the following context, it would be quite tautologous: 'we must believe what God testifies, since God has testified about his Son'.

5:10a-b In the Greek sentences 10a and 10b both begin with the same relative construction. They are not joined by a conjunction, and 10b is a negation of 10a. Thus 10a and 10b are contrasting units. Usually, in such a construction, the negated unit supports the positive unit, as is the case here. Thus the first unit is the prominent one.

5:10a behaves according to *what God* **testifies** *about his Son* The Greek is 'have the testimony in himself', in which 'the testimony' refers to 'that which God has testified about his Son' in 9c. The phrase 'have in himself' as used throughout 4:7-5:12 indicates that the person's behavior is controlled by the message. It is not just a passing assent to the message. The implication is that the person has a deep conviction and certainty regarding the truth of the message and behaves according to it. The Epistle addresses from beginning to end the issue of behaving according to the very character of God and Jesus Christ. To refuse to believe or deny the message is not confined to a confessional formula but to a behavior consistent with the message.

5:10b *what God testifies* The verb 'believe' requires a content, which in this context is 'what God testifies'.

5:11a This [11b-c] Here the deictic αὕτη 'this' refers to what follows, its expected use.

5:11b has caused us to live *spiritually* **forever** Commentators generally agree that ἡμῖν 'to us' refers to John and the letter's addressees, not humankind in general. Although 'eternal life' certainly is offered and available to all who will believe, here John is talking specifically about those who already have been caused (ἔδωκεν in the aorist) to live spiritually. Verse 12, which amplifies 11b, gives additional, and contrastive, information about 'living spiritually forever'. (It could be taken as a specific application or deduction of v. 11 only if the verb δίδωμι were future or present tense.)

5:11c The double use of the deictic pronouns in 11a and 11c mark this MEANS proposition as prominent.

by *our believing in and being united to* **his Son** The Greek is 'this life is by/in his Son'; in other words, the Son is the means of our being caused to live forever. Since the whole impact of the letter is that by believing (focal in 5:10) and being united to God's Son we thereby are caused to live forever, this implied information is supplied in the display.

5:12a–b In the Greek the two contrasting sentences 12a and 12b are almost identical (except that 12b contains 'not'). They are joined without a conjunction. In such a construction the negated unit usually supports the positive unit, which is the case here. Thus the first unit is the prominent one. (The same construction is in 10a and 10b.)

BOUNDARIES AND COHERENCE

The opening boundary of the 5:6–12 unit was discussed under unit 5:1–5. The closing boundary coincides with that of the body of the letter and was discussed under 1:5–5:12.

This unit coheres structurally because of its expository genre. Here there are no exhortations, not even mitigated ones. The exposition is developed with the CLAIM and supported by two *justifications* of that CLAIM. The CLAIM is that God has caused believers to live spiritually forever (5:11). The first *justification* is that God proved to us that he commissioned his Son Jesus to enter the world to save humankind (5:6–8). The second *justification* is that we can be totally assured that God's message about his Son is true (5:9–10).

The paragraph's semantic coherence is seen in the discussion of God's witness to his Son (see 5:6d, 9b, 11a.). It is God's own witness to this vital truth that is in focus here. His witness is declared to be greater than human witness (5:9b); in fact, it is the source of human witness (5:9c). Thus there are echoes here of previous passages: 1:1–3, which focuses on John's witness; 4:14, where John's "seeing-and-telling" is referred to as a means of believers' jointly participating in the moral character of God; and 2:24–25, where this joint participation is related to eternal life (as in 5:11–12).

This harking back to previous motifs signals that the discourse is nearing its end. Here, 5:6a, which says that God is witness to Christ's coming in human form, points back to the prologue, which introduces τοῦ λόγου τῆς ζωῆς 'the word of life' (1:1) and announces the revelation and source of that 'life' (1:2).

Lexical items in the domain of witness are: μαρτυρέω 'witness', in 5:6, 7, 9 (four times), 10 (three times), 11; ἀλήθεια 'truth' in 5:6; and πιστεύω 'believe' in 5:10 (three times).

PROMINENCE AND THEME

The structural prominence of the 5:6–12 paragraph can be observed in a focal CLAIM unit (vv. 11–12) supported by two *justification* units (6–8 and 9–10). The theme statement is derived from all three.

> **EPISTLE CONSTITUENT 5:13–21 (Hortatory Division: Closing of 1:5–5:21)**
> *Theme: Since we are united to both God and his Son, and since he causes his people to live spiritually forever, and since Jesus Christ is the real God, guard yourselves from worshiping unreal gods.*

MACROSTRUCTURE	CONTENTS
closing description	5:13–20 Jesus Christ is the real God, and we are united to both God and his Son, and he causes his people to live spiritually forever.
FINAL APPEAL	5:21 Since Jesus is the real God, guard yourselves from worshiping unreal gods.

INTENT AND MACROSTRUCTURE

In 5:13–21 John makes a *FINAL APPEAL* to the readers' emotions so that all the previous appeals aimed at affecting their behavior will be heeded. In 5:13 he explicitly presents his purpose along with further descriptions of the benefits of living together according to Christ. Then pointedly and succinctly he gives the *FINAL APPEAL* summarizing the letter: avoid anything that is not according to Christ (5:21).

BOUNDARIES AND COHERENCE

The 5:13–21 unit is the close of the Epistle. Its initial boundary has been discussed under 1:5–5:12; its closing boundary, marked by a strong exhortation in 5:21, coincides with the Epistle's end. Coherence is evidenced by the unit's being a summary of the whole letter.

PROMINENCE AND THEME

This unit consists of an expository paragraph summarizing the teachings of the letter and a hortatory paragraph summarizing its exhortations. The theme statement is drawn from the prominent elements of both paragraphs.

DIVISION CONSTITUENT 5:13–20 (Descriptive Paragraph: Closing exposition of 5:13–21)

Theme: Jesus Christ is the real God, and we are united to both God and his Son, and he causes his people to live spiritually forever.

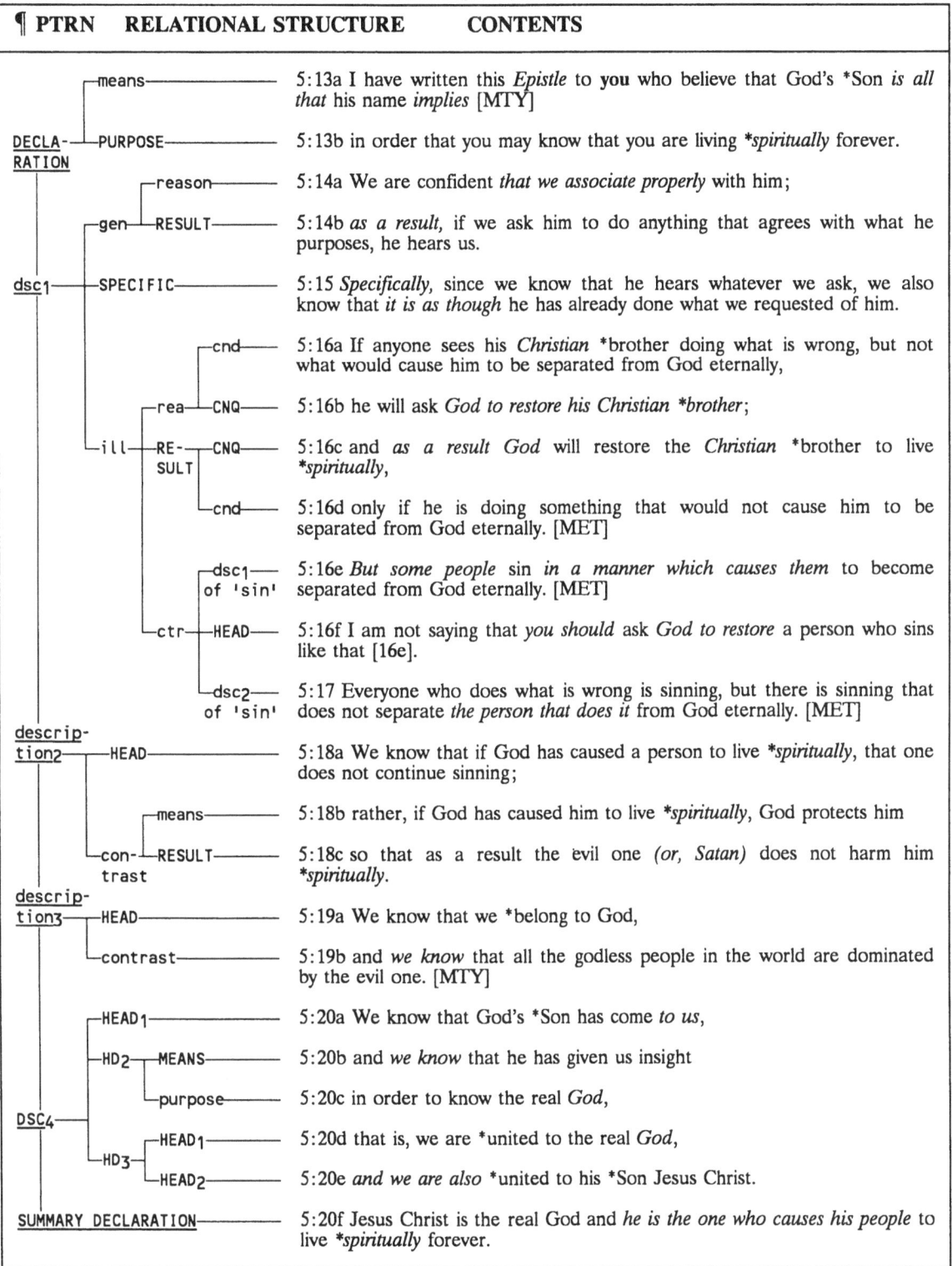

INTENT AND PARAGRAPH PATTERN

One of John's purposes in the 5:13–20 paragraph is to summarize the letter; he describes the benefits of which believers are assured due to their having been caused to live forever. Another of his purposes is to affect the readers' emotions at the closing. (The purpose of a letter's closing, normally, is to affect the readers' emotions in such a way that they will have a good feeling about what was said.) The author's assurance in 5:15 that God answers our prayers is therefore most appropriate here.

This paragraph has six main constituents: 13, 14–17, 18, 19, 20a–e, and 20f. The first and the last of these form an inclusio. Their communication relationship is a generic nuclear unit followed by four specific units, then a closing summary. The paragraph is a volitional descriptive type, with the principal constituents being + *description* + DECLARATION.

NOTES

5:13a I have written this *Epistle* In 1:4 John says 'we are writing to you', but in 5:13 'I have written this to you'. The deictic 'this' is taken to refer to all the author has written in the body of the Epistle between these two mentions of writing.

to you The forefronted pronoun τοῖς 'to those who' makes 'you' in 13a prominent.

is all that **his name** *implies* See the note on 3:23b.

5:14a confident *that we associate properly* **with him** This interpretation and rendering is consistent with 2:28b (see the note there).

5:15 since The author's argument here is not about whether God hears us. That God hears us is a given. Therefore, ἐάν is taken as 'since', rather than 'if'.

whatever we ask The context makes it clear that 'whatever we ask' means 'whatever we ask that agrees with God's purposes' (see 5:14b).

it is as though The text has 'God has already done what we requested', but it is necessary to signal that it has not actually occurred in our perceptual world. Some languages make these distinctions grammatically; in the display it is supplied lexically.

5:16a sees The verb ἴδῃ 'see' implies that the observed sin is an action, not an unobservable internal state. Although 'see' means to observe with the senses, it is not limited to the visual sense.

separated from God eternally Rather than speculate on the difference between mortal and venial sin, we may use John's own words to interpret what he means by sin that causes a person to be eternally separated from God. John speaks of things that are gross sins in 1:8 (deceiving oneself), in 1:10 and 5:10 (making God a liar), and in 2:4 and 4:20 (lying). In 3:10–15 he says of the children of the devil and also of the murderer (a murderer because he hates his brother) that they do not have eternal life. He identifies antichrist and the world spirit with the refusal to confess that Jesus Christ has come in the flesh (2:22; 4:3). Finally he says that the one who does not have a relationship with the Son does not have life (5:12). From these texts and others, we see that the sin that eternally separates a person from God is the deliberate refusal to believe that Jesus is the Christ of God. It is not said that such a one is a brother.

5:16b will ask The verb αἰτήσει 'ask' is in the future tense. While it could be translated as a command, the future tense is more in keeping with the spontaneous love that John has been talking about. It better expresses what the believer will do as a matter of course. This is the understanding of many commentators.

God to restore his Christian brother Because a content of the request is required here, these words based on 16c are supplied.

5:16c *God* **will restore . . . to live** The Greek is 'he shall give him life'. The personal pronoun subject of δώσει 'he will give' is ambiguous. Even if the one who prays is the one who gives life to the one who has sinned, it would be as an indirect agent. But we take the agent to be God, for he alone can give spiritual life. The commentators differ widely depending on their position as to whether the person prayed for is spiritually dead or alive. In the note on 5:16a we took the position that the one observed doing a wrong is a 'brother', a believer, not someone who is spiritually dead and totally separated from God. So, since this verse refers to a person who is already spiritually alive, 'give him life' means either 'restore to associate properly with God' (as in the display) or 'restore to physical health'.

5:16e, 17 separated from God eternally See the note on 16a.

5:18a that one does not continue sinning This is the same construction as in 3:6b, c (see the note there).

5:18b God has caused him to live *spiritually* The Greek is ὁ γεννηθεὶς ἐκ τοῦ θεοῦ 'he who is born from God'. Opinion is divided as to its referent. Is it the believer or Christ? Since 'born from God' nowhere in the Epistle refers unambiguously to Christ, and since all occurrences except this one are in a context that makes it clear that it is the believer who is 'born from God', we take 'the one who is born from God' here to refer to the believer.

God protects him If ὁ 'he who' is taken simply as a relative pronoun introducing a relative clause, the clause refers to the actor of 'keeps/protects'. However, John frequently uses this same construction to reflect a semantic condition ('if one . . . , then . . .'), and in this case 'God' is the actor of 'keeps/protects' and also of 'causes to live' in 18a.

There is a textual problem here. Some texts read ἑαυτόν 'himself' and others have αὐτόν 'him'. We prefer the latter. (Of those who follow the αὐτόν 'him' reading, some take ὁ γεννηθείς to refer to Christ as the one who keeps the believer from sin; the NIV rendering is based on this.) If ἑαυτόν is the correct reading, it must mean that the power of God within the believer by virtue of his spiritual birth makes him able to protect himself.

5:18c so that as a result The conjunction καί 'and' between 18b and c can be taken as simply conjoining. But the relation and the meaning of the conjunction seem more extended here. It could well mean 'furthermore' and the relation be means-RESULT, as in the display.

5:19b Proposition 19b is taken as a contrast to 19a. Alternatively, it could be considered an equally prominent amplification.

all the godless people in the world The Greek is 'the whole world', a metonymy. Here it has the second meaning in the note on 2:2c.

5:20a-b Verse 20 is conjoined to the foregoing by δέ 'but', which could either indicate a new discourse unit (its most frequent function) or a contrast to the previous statement. Here we take it to be a new unit, a fourth description. The MEANS-purpose relation between 20a-b and 20c-e is signaled by ἵνα 'in order that'.

5:20c the real *God* The addition of θεόν 'God' at the end of this clause is judged by UBS and most commentators to be the work of a scribe; therefore we do not accept the word as belonging to the text. However, the identification is obvious.

Between 20c and 20d-e καί 'and' occurs. It signals one of two possible relations to the preceding propositions: (1) that 20d-e continues the list begun at 20a, or (2) that 20d-e is conjoined to 20c and is an equivalent restatement of 'to know the real God'. Here we take 20d-e as continuing the list begun at 20a, as stated in the first alternative.

5:20f Jesus Christ Though some commentators see 'the Father' as the referent of οὗτος, most, both earlier and modern, see it as 'Jesus Christ', which is immediately adjacent. To refer the deictic to the Father would be tautologous. John, in his Gospel, has not hesitated to call Jesus God (John 1:1, 18; 20:28). Moreover, the statement has just been made that eternal life is in God's Son (5:11).

BOUNDARIES AND COHERENCE

The 5:13-20 unit begins the letter's close. The initial boundary here has been discussed as the closing boundary of 1:5-5:12.

At the closing boundary of 5:13-20 no conjunction introduces the next unit, but the vocative in 5:21 certainly suggests a change in focus. Proposition 5:20f forms a structural sandwich with 5:13b in that both mention 'eternal life'. Also, the genre shifts from descriptive to hortatory. Proposition 20f is transitional. It is the culmination of 5:13-20e, but at the same time it functions as the *basis* for the *APPEAL* of v. 21.

An evidence that 5:13-20 is a coherent unit is the prominent motif of being assured about what God has done, seen in the use of οἶδα 'know'. John states in 5:13b that his purpose in writing is that the readers may know, or be assured, that they have eternal life. The verb οἴδαμεν 'we know' occurs in 5:13-20 five times (twice in v. 15, once each in vv. 18, 19, and 20).

Coherence is also shown in the use of ζωὴ αἰώνιος 'eternal life'. It is mentioned at the beginning of the unit (ζωήν 'life' in 5:13) and at the end (in 5:20f).

Semantically, the 5:13-20 unit holds together by its reemphasizing concepts and motifs of the body. Some of these are: belief in the name of God's Son (5:13a; cf. 3:23); assurance of answered prayer (5:15; cf. 3:22); active love for the Christian brother (5:16b; cf. 3:18); protection of God-given life from sinning (5:18a; cf. 3:9); belonging to God (5:19a; cf. 4:6); God's Son's advent (5:20a; cf. 1:2); Jesus Christ as the source of eternal life (5:20f; cf. 5:11).

Cohesion is also seen in the structure of the unit: a DECLARATION of the purpose for writing (that we might experience eternal life) supported by four *descriptions* of the God-given benefits that accompany eternal life, and a SUMMARY DECLARATION.

PROMINENCE AND THEME

Assurance of the possession of eternal life is prominent in this unit. The features that show this prominence occur especially in v. 20, the fourth DESCRIPTION, which is therefore a more prominent unit than the other three:

20a: The Son of God actually came.
20b-c: As a result of his coming we have insight for continuous (present tense) experiential knowledge (γινώσκω) of the real God.
20b-d: The word ἀληθινός 'true/real' occurs three times, making it emphatic.
20d-e: Being united to the Son, we are united to the real God.

The prominence structure of 5:13-20 is an initial DECLARATION (5:13), four specific *descriptions* (5:14-20e), the fourth of which has marked prominence and so is included in the theme, and the SUMMARY DECLARATION (5:20f).

DIVISION CONSTITUENT 5:21 (Hortatory Paragraph: Final appeal of 5:13-21)
Theme: Since Jesus is the real God, guard yourselves from worshiping unreal gods.

¶ PTRN	CONTENTS
basis———————	5:21a *Since Jesus is the real God,*
SUMMARY APPEAL———	5:21b *my *spiritual children, guard yourselves from worshiping unreal gods.*

INTENT AND PARAGRAPH PATTERN

John's intent in 5:21 is to affect the actions of the reader: he commands them not to substitute anything for Jesus Christ. The paragraph consists of a prominent APPEAL and supporting *basis* (20f, but supplied as proposition 21a here). Their communication relationship is one hortatory unit supported by a grounds unit. Thus this is a causal hortatory paragraph, the principal constituents being + *basis* + APPEAL.

BOUNDARIES AND COHERENCE

The opening boundary has been discussed under unit 5:13-20. The closing boundary coincides with the end of the Epistle. Although the relationship between this paragraph and what precedes it is debatable, it is indeed appropriate to end the discourse with this particular exhortation to the believers.

There is structural coherence in that a *basis* unit supports the final strong APPEAL (5:21): Christians must avoid anything which is not truly according to God.

PROMINENCE AND THEME

The theme statement is drawn from the structurally prominent parts of both the *basis* (a summary of 5:20f) and the final SUMMARY APPEAL (5:21).

INTRODUCTION TO THE SEMANTIC AND STRUCTURAL ANALYSIS OF SECOND JOHN

It is of value to the translator to be familiar with the communication situation of a personal letter since it is the communication situation that provides the background against which many exegetical decisions are made. Thus some understanding of the participants and the occasion for writing is vital.

The participants

The question of the authorship of 2 John has already been discussed in the Introduction to 1 John, where our conclusion that the Apostle John is the author of all three Epistles is presented. In 2 John the author refers to himself as "the Elder." Various reasons have been given for this, but for purposes of analysis it seems sufficient to recognize that the recipients knew him by that title and accorded him the honor and authority that the title carried.

Concerning the recipients of the letter, commentators in general agree that there is no sure answer to the question of the identity of ἐκλεκτῇ κυρίᾳ καὶ τοῖς τέκνοις αὐτῆς 'the elect lady and her children'. Smith (1951:162–63) accepts the letter as written to a matron and her children, saying that the "simplicity of the little letter precludes the possibility of so elaborate an allegory [as that of a church congregation and its members], while the tenderness of its tone stamps it as a personal communication." He accepts κυρία as the Greek form of 'Martha'. Plummer (p. 132) also prefers the literal interpretation.

The more generally accepted theory, however, is that this Epistle was addressed to a particular congregation and its members. Westcott (p. 224) points out that the idea of a letter to an individual is unsupported by such personal allusions as might be expected throughout the letter and that "the general tenour . . . favours the opinion that it was sent to a community." Against the theory that ἐκλεκτή 'chosen' was a proper name, it is pointed out that if κυρία referred to an individual, it would be uncommon for her to have a sister by the same name, the one mentioned in v. 13. Stott (p. 201) says, "The unconscious transition from the second person singular to the second person plural . . . seems to betray the fact that the author is thinking of a community rather than an individual." He calls attention to the well-established convention of the use of a female form for such personifications. On this basis, then, the figurative interpretation is assumed in this analysis.

The occasion for writing

The immediate occasion for writing this Epistle was the necessity of warning the recipients against the heresy which was threatening them. According to tradition, the Apostle John wrote this letter to refute the Docetic teachings of Cerinthus (see the discussion about Cerinthus and his Docetic teachings in the Introduction to 1 John); this would indeed account for the emphases found in the letter. The Docetic error was both theological and ethical (Stott, pp. 43–50); both aspects are dealt with in 2 John, but only very briefly, of course, because 2 John is itself so brief (probably the length permitted by a sheet of papyrus).

The need to warn against the itinerant teachers of this heresy may have been brought to the author's attention at a meeting with some members of the group addressed (see 2 John 4). The urgency implied in v. 12 indicates that this warning could not wait for the author's proposed visit. It may be that this Second Epistle is an emergency application to a local situation of the principles presented in the First Epistle.

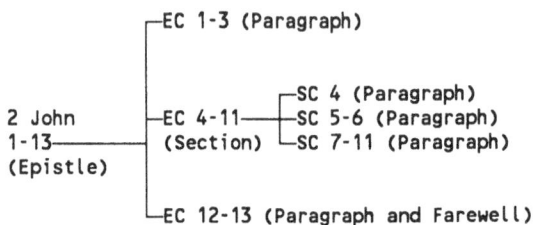

```
                                          EC = Epistle Constituent
                                          SC = Section Constituent
```

The constituent organization of 2 John

OVERVIEW: THEMATIC OUTLINE OF SECOND JOHN

2 John 1–13 (Epistle)
Theme: Continue to live loving each other just as God commanded you to live, and be on your guard so that you receive your reward.

    EPISTLE CONSTITUENT 1–3 (Descriptive Paragraph: Opening of the Epistle)
    Theme: I, the Elder, write to the congregation and to all the members. I love you and know that God the Father and his Son will bless us.

    EPISTLE CONSTITUENT 4–11 (Hortatory Section: Body of the Epistle)
    Theme: Continue to live loving each other just as God commanded you to live, and be on your guard by not welcoming or encouraging any false teachers so that you receive your complete reward of being with God eternally.

        SECTION CONSTITUENT 4 (Descriptive Paragraph: Introduction to the body)
        Theme: I am happy that some of your members are living just as God commanded us to live.

        SECTION CONSTITUENT 5–6 (Hortatory Paragraph: Appeal$_1$ of the body)
        Theme: Continue to live loving each other just as God commanded us to live when we began to believe his true message.

        SECTION CONSTITUENT 7–11 (Hortatory Paragraph: Appeal$_2$ of 4–11)
        Theme: Since many false teachers are going around deceiving people and opposing Christ, be on your guard so that you do receive your complete reward of being with God eternally. Do not welcome or encourage any of these false teachers in any way.

    EPISTLE CONSTITUENT 12–13 (Descriptive Paragraph and Farewell: Closing of the Epistle)
    Theme: Instead of writing more to you, I expect to come and communicate directly with you. The members of your sister congregation greet you.

THE SEMANTIC UNITS OF SECOND JOHN

SECOND JOHN 1-13 (Epistle)
Theme: Continue to live loving each other just as God commanded you to live, and be on your guard so that you receive your reward.

MACROSTRUCTURE	CONTENTS
opening	1-3 I, the Elder, write to the congregation and to all the members. I love you and know that God the Father and his Son will bless us.
BODY	4-11 Continue to live loving each other just as God commanded you to live, and be on your guard by not welcoming or encouraging any false teachers so that you receive your complete reward of being with God eternally.
closing	12-13 Instead of writing more to you, I expect to come and communicate directly with you. The members of your sister congregation greet you.

INTENT AND MACROSTRUCTURE

John's intent in writing this Epistle is to exhort his readers to continue loving fellow believers and to warn them against false teaching. The discourse type is hortatory.

Following the usual epistolary pattern for the New Testament period, John's second letter shows the three characteristic parts of *opening*, *BODY*, and *closing*. The *BODY* has three constituents, which will be described in detail later.

COHERENCE

The letter's coherence derives most clearly from its structure as seen in the above display. Also, first and second person pronouns are frequently used throughout, as expected in a letter.

Adding to the Epistle's coherence is the fact that various concepts appear in the *opening* and are referred to later:

1. The figurative reference in v. 1 to the members of the congregation as τέκνον 'children' is continued in vv. 4 and 13.
2. The word ἀλήθεια 'truth' in v. 2 is repeated in v. 4 and entails both ἐντολή 'command' in vv. 4-6 and διδαχή 'teaching' in v. 9 and v. 10.
3. Truth (2a-b) demands a consistent behavioral pattern: 'walking in truth' (4b) and walking 'according to his commands' (6c).
4. The grace, mercy, and peace conferred upon believers based on love and truth (v. 3) are in contrast to the loss of union with God which would result from not continuing in Christ's teaching (9a-b).
5. The emphatic reference in 3a to the Father and the Son anticipates the same emphasis in 9d.

PROMINENCE AND THEME

From truth (2a) spring love for fellow Christians (1c) and the blessings of grace, mercy, and peace provided by the Father and the Son (3a). Not continuing in the truth concerning the Father and the Son is, therefore, a great danger, which calls forth the exhortation to continue in obedience to the Father's command (6c) and the warning to be on guard so that the future reward not be lost (8b). Then in the closing, joy is anticipated (12d) as a result of meeting each other again.

The theme is drawn from the exhortation and warning of the *BODY*, which are the naturally prominent constituents of the Epistle.

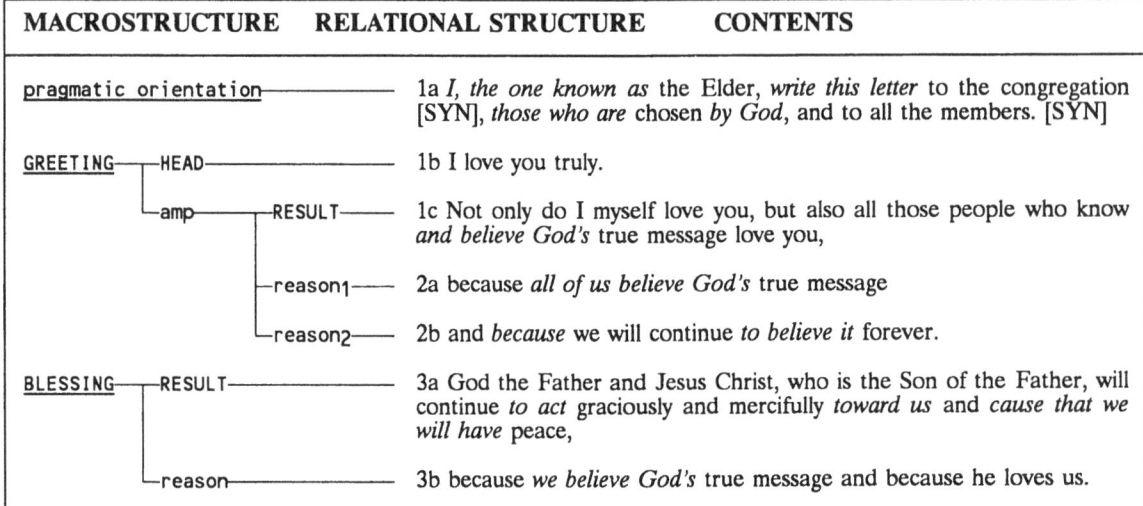

INTENT AND PARAGRAPH PATTERN

John's purpose in vv. 1-3 is primarily to identify himself and establish rapport with the recipients of the letter.

This unit, which is simply to orient the reader to the pragmatic context of the letter, does not fill the requirements of a semantic paragraph pattern. Since the author and reader are removed from each other and not face to face, they must each be identified and rapport established.

The 1-3 unit is composed of three sub-units of equal prominence in accord with the letter-writing convention of the day: identity of the writer and recipients (1a), a greeting (1b-2b), and a blessing (3a-b).

A person normally establishes rapport with his audience by affecting their emotions in such a way that they will be willing to listen to what he has to say. In general, commentators agree that the 1-3 unit is a greeting and introduction combined, intended to affect the emotions. (But translators tend to render it as an expository paragraph, overlooking the fact that the author intended it to have an emotional impact upon the recipients.)

NOTES

1a the Elder This is the author's self-designation. It indicates a high social position in relation to the recipients of the letter. Most probably he was well known to them by this title so that his name was not necessary. As noted in the Introduction, the identity of 'the Elder' is widely accepted as the Apostle John.

write this letter No verb relates the writer to the recipients. The most natural verb to be understood is 'write,' which agrees with the cases used in the Greek, nominative for the writer and dative for the recipients.

the congregation The Greek is κυρία 'lady'. The rendering 'congregation' is based on our interpretation (see the Introduction regarding the participants). If the addressee is taken to be a particular woman, problems arise: Who is the woman? Is her name Cyria? A literal interpretation presents more difficulties than the figurative one.

1b truly The phrase ἐν ἀληθείᾳ 'in truth' is a potential problem. Commentators do not fail to point out that the rendering 'truly' does not convey the full significance here. Rather, 'in truth' represents the framework of truth by which the fellowship of Christians is determined. However, that message is brought out in the BODY of the Epistle and specifically in the admonition of vv. 10 and 11. Therefore, we render it 'truly' following BAGD (p. 36b), Thayer (p. 26b), TEV, and Weymouth.

1c all The use of πᾶς 'all' here may be considered hyperbolic, but most commentators accept the expression as a general reference to the communion of love which embraces all who believe. It points to the solidarity of the universal church.

who know *and believe* The present tense in English retains the present aspect of the Greek perfect participle ἐγνωκότες 'who have known'. The idea of 'believe' is added because of the experiential significance of the verb, which by its perfect tense signifies not only that they know but that they have come to commit themselves to its validity.

God's **true message** The articular use of ἀλήθεια 'truth' here differs somewhat from its use with the preposition ἐν 'in' (1b). The article in this context gives it the meaning of "the content of Christianity as the absolute truth" (BAGD, p. 35*d*.2.b). It is thus all of God's revelation of himself to man, including the incarnation of Christ and his teaching.

2a *believe God's* true message Believing the true message includes the obligation to love each other. It is also the common grounds for loving each other. But 'believe' is not in the text—something of a logical gap; we supply it since in some languages it might be required.

3a–b Verse 3 functions as a formal greeting. Instead of the wish for well-being commonly used in letters of the period, it is elaborated into a confident assertion of God's favor. Paul uses such a greeting without a verb, but John here uses the future indicative in the emphatic position, ἔσται μεθ' ἡμῶν 'will be with us', repeating the phrase from v. 2. Thus it becomes an affirmation of God's blessing.

3a Jesus Christ In some manuscripts κυρίου 'Lord' occurs before Ἰησοῦ 'Jesus'. Metzger considers this an addition since it does not appear in all manuscripts; that a copyist added it is more likely than its having been deleted.

graciously and mercifully ... peace The Greek is χάρις ἔλεος εἰρήνη 'grace mercy peace'. Grace is God's doing for us what we do not deserve, mercy is God's not doing to us what we deserve, and peace is the social well-being between us and God and others that results from grace and mercy. Since these concepts are seldom found to have equivalent single-word terms in other languages, it is necessary to explore ways of making them clear. The phrases that have been used to express these key terms elsewhere may fit here, shortened perhaps as would be appropriate to a greeting.

3b *because we believe God's* true message and because he loves us The Greek is ἐν ἀληθείᾳ καὶ ἀγάπῃ 'in truth and love'. This could be interpreted in many ways: the reason for the blessing, the condition on which the blessing depends, the result expected from it, the means for conveying it, or as an accompaniment. The relationship of reason is the one used in the display. The fact that the two nouns 'truth' and 'love' occur without the article and with one preposition gives them equal force. Dodd comments,

> [John] adds, **in truth and love**, because the grace of God is shown in that revelation of Himself which is the Truth, and in the divine charity expressed in the work of Christ (I John iv.9–10); and takes effect in the true belief and mutual charity of Christians.

Marshall makes a similar comment and says that the phrase prepares the readers for the central theme in vv. 4–11.

BOUNDARIES AND COHERENCE

Verses 1–3 follow the pattern for the beginning of a letter written in John's time: The writer identifies himself and those to whom he is writing and then expresses a formal greeting to them. He gives his name in the nominative case; the recipients are referred to in the dative case. Referring to himself initially with the third person, he changes immediately, as would be expected, to the first person and from then on refers to the addressees with second person pronouns.

The formal opening of 2 John is analyzed as a paragraph consisting of three propositional clusters in the relation of a *description* of the participants followed by two DECLARATIONS. One of them expresses the writer's love for the readers and the other God's blessing upon both the writer and the readers.

The initial boundary of this unit coincides with the opening of the discourse. Its final boundary is marked by the formalized greeting characteristic of the opening of such letters.

The closing boundary of this unit is marked by asyndeton in v. 4, change in tense from present and future to aorist, and change of subject matter from greetings to the exhortations of the BODY of the letter.

The coherence of the unit lies primarily in its function as the letter's opening. Lexical items from the domain of establishing a social communication relationship recur:

1. The writer includes himself in the relationship by the use of the first person plural in vv. 2–3.
2. In the formal greeting (v. 3) the affirmation that God's blessing will remain is expressed in the future indicative.
3. The words ἀγάπη 'love' (vv. 1, 3), χάρις 'grace', ἔλεος 'mercy', and especially εἰρήνη 'peace' (v. 3) refer to social relationship.

PROMINENCE AND THEME

The paragraph is made up of a *description* and two conjoined DECLARATIONS. All three are thematic.

Several features of marked prominence occur within the supporting constituents; these highlight the concepts of love and truth, and thus they are thematic also. The statement of the writer's love for those he addresses is marked by use of the emphatic first person pronoun ἐγώ. The repetition of ἀλήθεια 'truth' marks it as prominent: the paragraph's final words are ἐν ἀληθείᾳ καὶ ἀγάπῃ 'in truth and love'. Both 'truth' and 'love' are prominent, but the fact that 'truth' occurs four times explicitly marks it as having the greater prominence. It is a central motif as borne out by the prominence in the BODY of terms related to 'truth' such as 'command' and 'teaching'. (Attention is called to the relationship of these terms in the discussion of the coherence of the Epistle as a whole.) This emphasis on truth in the *opening* prepares the way for the main exhortations of the letter, and is in harmony with the occasion for writing the Epistle.

EPISTLE CONSTITUENT 4–11 (Hortatory Section: Body of the Epistle)
Theme: Continue to live loving each other just as God commanded you to live, and be on your guard by not welcoming or encouraging any false teachers so that you receive your complete reward of being with God eternally.

MACROSTRUCTURE	CONTENTS
introduction	4 I am happy that some of your members are living just as God commanded us to live.
APPEAL₁	5–6 Continue to live loving each other just as God commanded us to live when we began to believe his true message.
APPEAL₂	7–11 Since many false teachers are going around deceiving people and opposing Christ, be on your guard so that you do receive your complete reward of being with God eternally. Do not welcome or encourage any of these false teachers in any way.

INTENT AND MACROSTRUCTURE

In view of the two *APPEALS*, the 4–11 section is considered hortatory. John's intent here is the same as in the Epistle as a whole. The section consists of three constituents: The v. 4 introductory paragraph is a commendation similar to those frequently found in letters of the Graeco-Roman culture. The two paragraphs that follow, 5–6 and 7–11, comprise three commands, one in 5–6 and two in 7–11.

BOUNDARIES AND COHERENCE

The opening boundary of the 4–11 section (which is the BODY of the Epistle) is marked by the change from the formalized greeting to the main topic of the letter. A tail-head transition serves as a boundary marker: the prominent phrase ἐν ἀληθείᾳ 'in truth' in 3b is repeated in v. 4.

The closing boundary is the final warning that concludes the exhortations. That this is the closing boundary is confirmed by the subsequent remark (v. 12) that the author does not wish to add more in writing.

The unit's coherence derives from its structure: It begins with an expression of rejoicing, and then the immediate occasion for writing is given (4b), which seems to have been a meeting between John and some of the members of the congregation to whom he is writing. Judging from the exhortations of the letter, we conclude that the meeting, whether planned or not, had made John aware of the need for admonition.

The 5–6 command includes wording (in the Greek text it is the last half of v. 6) almost identical to the deictic expression 'this is the commandment' in 1 John 3:23 that introduces the same command there; and since a fuller expression of the Johannine message is given in 1 John, it is assumed that the readers of 2 John were familiar with that message. The emphasis on 'truth' in the *opening* (vv. 1–3) would suggest this, and the repetition of 'truth' in 4b ties the command to love one another to the rest of 2 John. In other words, it is not just an isolated command. The teaching of 1 John is that the love enjoined springs from truth and is experienced by those who have believed the message about God and his Son and have received the Spirit of Truth (1 John 3:23–24; 4:19). The reason the recipients of 2 John are to be on their guard against false teaching is that the truth is being challenged. Verse 7 is a transitional link that specifies the threatening danger. That is, having given in vv. 5–6 a general command basic to Christian experience, John goes on in v. 7 to tell what the danger is. Following this, he specifies the safeguard against that danger in terms of internal and external fortification (vv. 7–11).

The coherence of the BODY is also shown in the semantic relationship of the letter's three commands: (1) the command to continue to love each other as God commanded at the first, in vv. 5–6; (2) the command to be on their guard, in v. 8; and (3) the command to reject false teachers, in v. 10. These three commands stem from ἀλήθεια καὶ ἀγάπη 'truth and love' and follow in logical succession. The first command is fundamental to the Christian belief system: it was ἀπ' ἀρχῆς 'from the beginning' (vv. 5–6), that is, when they first heard the message. They were commanded to love one another (v. 6), love being the action that shows they accept and obey the truth.

However, the deceivers are a threat because they deny the humanity of Christ (v. 7) and thus are in opposition to Christ. Because of this threat, the second command, to be on their guard (v. 8), comes as an internal fortification against loss of the reward for loving obedience. This leads to the third command (see the 7–11 display), which is to completely reject the intrusion of the lie; it is an external fortification against deceivers from outside the community of believers.

There are several contrasts that also lend coherence to the BODY:

1. Those who walk in truth (4a) are contrasted with those who refuse the truth (v. 7) and those who fail to continue in the teaching of Christ.
2. The command is that which was received in the beginning of faith (5c, 6b) in contrast to the teaching of those who have now gone beyond Christ's teaching (9a).
3. Work to be rewarded (v. 8) is contrasted with evil work (v. 11).
4. Those who do not remain in the true teaching are contrasted with those who do (v. 9).
5. Those who refuse to greet a false teacher are contrasted with the (hypothetical) believer who greets him (vv. 10–11).

PROMINENCE AND THEME

The two conjoined *APPEALS* are considered to be of equal prominence. The theme is drawn in a summarized form from both of the *APPEALS*.

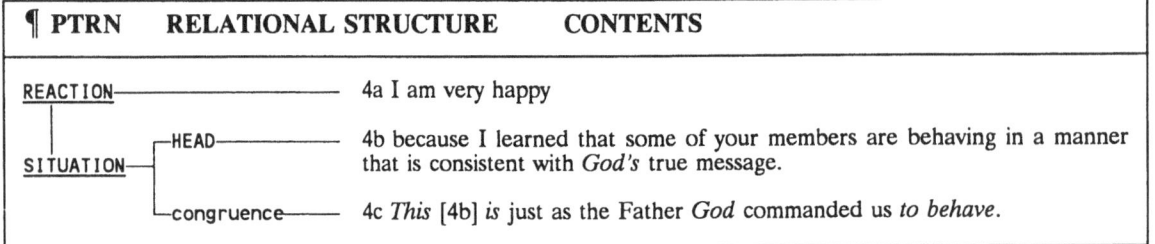

INTENT AND PARAGRAPH PATTERN

In the v. 4 unit the author's intent continues to be to create rapport with the recipients of the letter: here he describes his emotions upon receiving news about them. The paragraph has two main constituents, 4a and 4b-c; the communication relation between them is a result followed by a reason. This paragraph could be considered a causal type, either descriptive or expository. Since the primary intent is to affect the emotions, we take it as a causal descriptive paragraph in which the principal constituents are + SITUATION + REACTION.

NOTES

4a I am very happy The aorist ἐχάρην 'I rejoiced' here is typical of letters of the period: the aorist verb form was favored for use in this part of a letter. In the display it is rendered 'I am very happy' in order to retain the idea of a lasting emotion. The past aspect of the aorist is preserved in 4b.

4b I learned It is assumed by many commentators that prior to writing this letter, John had met some of the members of the congregation, probably as they were traveling. Since we do not have definite information of an actual meeting, and since the interpretation of εὑρίσκω 'learn' is not to be understood as 'finding as the result of searching for', the verb 'learned' is used in the display. In John 11:17 the same construction refers to learning a fact about a person, which tends to corroborate the interpretation here.

some An interpretation by many commentators is that remarking about *some* of the members as faithful would indicate that *others* were not. R. E. Brown is among those who do not agree with this view. He gives three reasons for not accepting it:

1. Theologically, those not walking in truth should not be considered members of the congregation.
2. This verse corresponds to the part of a letter which is used for praise, and other New Testament letters leave negative remarks for later in the discourse.
3. Grammatically ἐκ 'of' does not need to be interpreted in the partitive sense.

However, Brown's position would mean that John is admitting that he knows only some of the members of the congregation. This might be forced; it is not the simple partitive meaning of ἰε 'of'. It is difficult to determine from the context which interpretation to take, so the display is left ambiguous.

behaving in a manner In the Septuagint περιπατέω 'walk', when used figuratively, refers to things religious and moral. In Pauline usage it has moral significance. In Johannine usage it refers to practical conduct and the whole stance of the believer, or to faith itself. The meaning of περιπατέω ἐν ἀληθείᾳ in 2 John 4 would seem to be in line with the Septuagint usage: 'to walk uprightly' (Kittel, vol. 5, 944–45). Thayer (p. 504) notes that when περιπατέω 'walk' is constructed with ἐν 'in' and the dative, it denotes either the state in which one is living or the virtue or vice to which he is given. He also points out the component of progress: a step-by-step progress or movement seems to be implied. Since the expression is regarded as a dead metaphor here, the choice of expression in the receptor language needs to be carefully considered. In Hebrew, Greek, and English the word 'walk' can be used figuratively, but it cannot be taken for granted that it will be accepted as a figure of moral conduct or behavior in all languages.

God's **true message** It will be noted that the interpretation given to ἐν ἀληθείᾳ 'in truth' here in the *BODY* is more specific than in the *opening*. In the *BODY* it could be interpreted as 'sincerely', but the development of the topic seems to call for an interpretation more like that in v. 2, 'God's true message', particularly as the same concept is expressed in vv. 9–10 as 'Christ's teaching'. As such, it is that which we accept by believing and obeying. Thus, περιπατέω 'walk' means very much the same thing whether it occurs with 'truth' or with 'command' (v. 6). In the display 'truth' is rendered as a concrete expression, but the wider implications of the term must be kept in mind. Marshall says,

> For the elder 'truth' signifies what is ultimately real, namely God himself. Hence it can refer to the expression of God in his incarnate Son and in the Christian message. In 2 John 2 it becomes evident that the truth is tantamount to the Spirit of truth who can enter into the believer. The truth stands in contrast to the ultimately unreal and deceptive lies which stem from the devil.

4c just as the Father *God* commanded What follows shows that the command referred to in 4c is to love (see 5d).

BOUNDARIES AND COHERENCE

The opening boundary of the v. 4 unit coincides with that of the *BODY* and is marked by the same tail-head construction that marks the *BODY* (described under the 4–11 display). Verse 4 is considered a separate unit because it forms a descriptive paragraph giving the immediate occasion for writing the letter; it also introduces the topic of the *BODY*, obedience to the true message.

The closing boundary can be seen as the writer, having commented on those whom he has learned are being faithful, turns to address the congregation as a whole under the figure of 'Lady'. The grammatical signal for this is the expression καὶ νῦν 'and now' (v. 5a), often used to draw attention to the main topic of a discourse.

The coherence of the v. 4 paragraph is evident from its single topic, expressed by certain ideas and lexical items that are semantically relevant to it: περιπατοῦντας 'walking' is used to describe behavior, and ἀλήθεια 'truth' is consistent with ἐντολή 'command'. A Christian who accepts the title of Elder would of course rejoice at finding his people obeying the command given by the Father.

The comment on those members whom we presume the writer had met also gives coherence to the unit. Lexical items that describe their behavior (περιπατοῦντας 'walking', ἀλήθεια 'truth', and ἐντολή 'command') would fall in the domain of cause of the Elder's rejoicing. His reaction to what he had learned (as well his previous awareness of certain dangers, not mentioned till v. 7) is the occasion for writing.

PROMINENCE AND THEME

The theme is drawn from both the *REACTION* and the *SITUATION*. The effect of the adverb λίαν 'very' (4a) is to intensify the whole of v. 4.

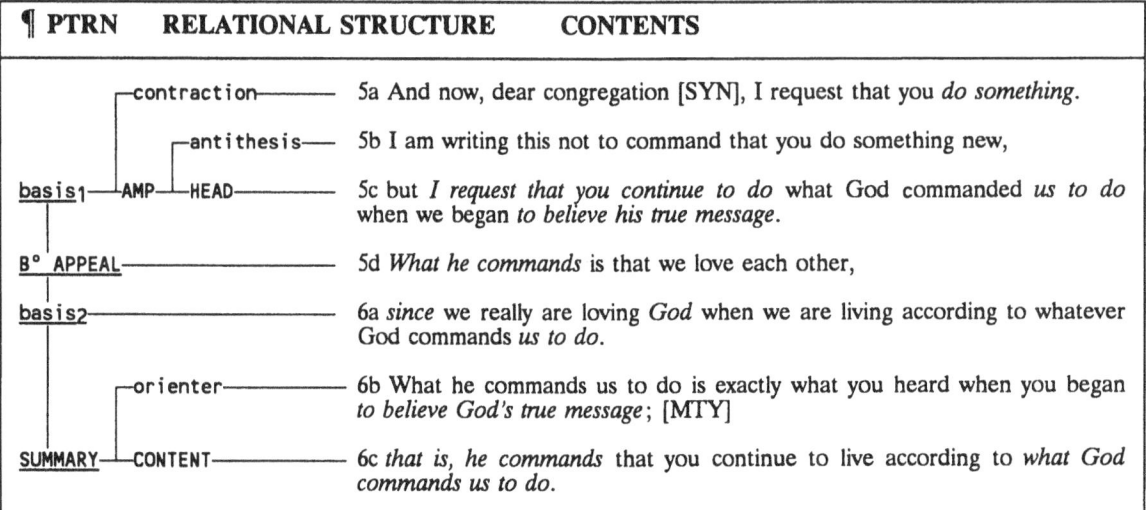

INTENT AND PARAGRAPH PATTERN

In the 5-6 unit, John is getting to the main message of the letter, and his intent here is to affect the actions of the reader by a low-key admonition. He wants to make certain that all the readers will continue behaving correctly. This paragraph comprises four propositional clusters (5a-c, 5d, 6a, and 6b-c). Their communication relationship is a grounds unit followed by its EXHORTATION unit followed by another grounds unit, and the whole matter winds up with a "contraction," a summary unit. The paragraph could be considered either causal hortatory or causal expository; but since the primary intent is to affect behavior, we take it to be causal hortatory, with its principal constituents being + basis + APPEAL.

NOTES

5c when we began to believe The pronoun 'we' is inclusive: God commanded not just the apostles, but all believers.

The phrase ἀπ' ἀρχῆς 'in the beginning' occurs here and also in 6b and in 1 John 2:7. Similar expressions occur in 1 John 2:24 and 3:11. Just *what* began is not specified. Here, since it is used in connection with a command received by the Christian fellowship, we take it to refer to teachings early in their Christian experience of hearing the gospel and accepting it by faith. Thus the phrase can be filled out by supplying a reference to believing God's true message. The 'beginning' is mentioned to enhance the acceptability of the exhortation by referring to the known and accepted values of the Christian message.

6a since The 6a unit is joined to the 5d mitigated appeal by καὶ 'and'. This conjunction means that there is a close semantic relationship with what precedes, but it does not specify what the relationship is. Here the relationship of 6a to what precedes seems to be that of a positive *motivational basis* for the 5d APPEAL. This explanation seems satisfactory enough, since neither the conjoining sense of 'and' nor the contrasting sense of 'but' seems logical here, nor is it an amplification ('we really are loving God' does not amplify 'love each other').

whatever God commands us to do The noun phrase τὰς ἐντολὰς αὐτοῦ 'his commands' is rendered here as an active proposition. Since 'commands' is plural, it conveys an all-inclusive idea. This is expressed in the display as 'whatever'. A command implies that the hearer must do something; hence the words 'us to do' are supplied.

Commentaries and versions, where unambiguous make 'God' the referent of 'his', rather than 'Christ', since 'his commands' is broader than Christ's command to love each other.

6b What he commands ... is The word order in the Greek text indicates that in v. 6 'command' is prominent, hence the cleft construction in 6b. The Greek word for 'command' is followed by ἵνα 'that' making ἐν αὐτῇ 'in it' resumptive, and therefore the clause 'exactly what you heard when you began to believe' must be taken with what follows: 'that you continue to live according to what God commands' (Brooke). It is not to be taken with 6a because 6a is further removed. The antecedent of αὕτη 'it' is 'command'.

BOUNDARIES AND COHERENCE

The unit opens with καὶ νῦν 'and now', which is used both as a connective phrase and to turn attention to the request that follows. Here the phrase introduces a specific way of walking in truth. Another indication of an opening boundary is the tail-head construction: 'command' is repeated in 5a from 4c. Following standard letter forms, the request occurs here with the performative ἐρωτῶ σε 'I request you' and the vocative κυρία 'dear Lady'. The close of the unit is marked by the summary of the request in 6b–c.

Coherence is evident in the presentation and explanation of the request. In presenting the request, it is made clear by the use of ἀπ' ἀρχῆς 'from the beginning' that John is requesting them to adhere to a command of God that is foundational to Christian life, not some new idea that John himself might impose. After expressing this request for mutual love (v. 5), he clarifies its relationship to 'truth' which was so prominently expressed in earlier verses. This he does by linking it with the believer's obligation to behave according to what God has commanded (6a).

Adding to the coherence is a chiasmus:

A command (5b)
  B love (5d)
  B' love (6a)
A' command (6b)

The words 'command' and 'love' are related by definition, contextually given (6a–b). Since the command is 'from the beginning', it is basic to the believer's behavior, and therefore it is reasonable to request obedience to it. These items make the paragraph a close-knit unit.

PROMINENCE AND THEME

The 5d *APPEAL* has natural prominence. But throughout the 5–6 unit marked prominence is evident, signaled by repetition. The word 'command' is prominent because it is repeated and the same is true of 'love' (in 5d and 6a). In 5d 'love' has marked prominence because of its position in the clause. (If accepted as the antecedent of the pronoun αὕτη in 6c, it would have even more prominence.) But the word 'command' is more prominent than 'love' because it is forefronted and is used three times in the unit (in 5b and 6a–b). In 6b the forefronting of 'command' has particular significance in that 'love' (repeated from 5d) is not forefronted in the 6a demonstrative clause whereas in 6b 'command' is put in that position of prominence. Being the "A" of the chiasmus also gives prominence to 'command'. As for the antecedent of αὕτη in 6c, syntax requires it to be 'command' (from the standpoint of nearness).

Another repeated word is περιπατέω 'to walk', which signifies behavior and way of life. The command to love is explained in 6a as living according to whatever God commands. The fact that 'to walk' used in 4b occurs twice in this unit gives it marked prominence. In the display it is expressed in continuative form because it is in the present tense and has behavioral significance. The basic nature of behaving according to God's command is emphasized by the phrase ἀπ' ἀρχῆς 'from the beginning', which occurs twice in connection with the 'command'. This gives the phrase marked prominence and adds prominence to the command itself.

Since all three of the expressions indicated as having marked prominence are included in 6b–c, those two propositions are considered to be a prominent summary.

The theme is drawn from the *APPEAL* in 5d and the 6b–c *SUMMARY*, which summarizes the two *bases*.

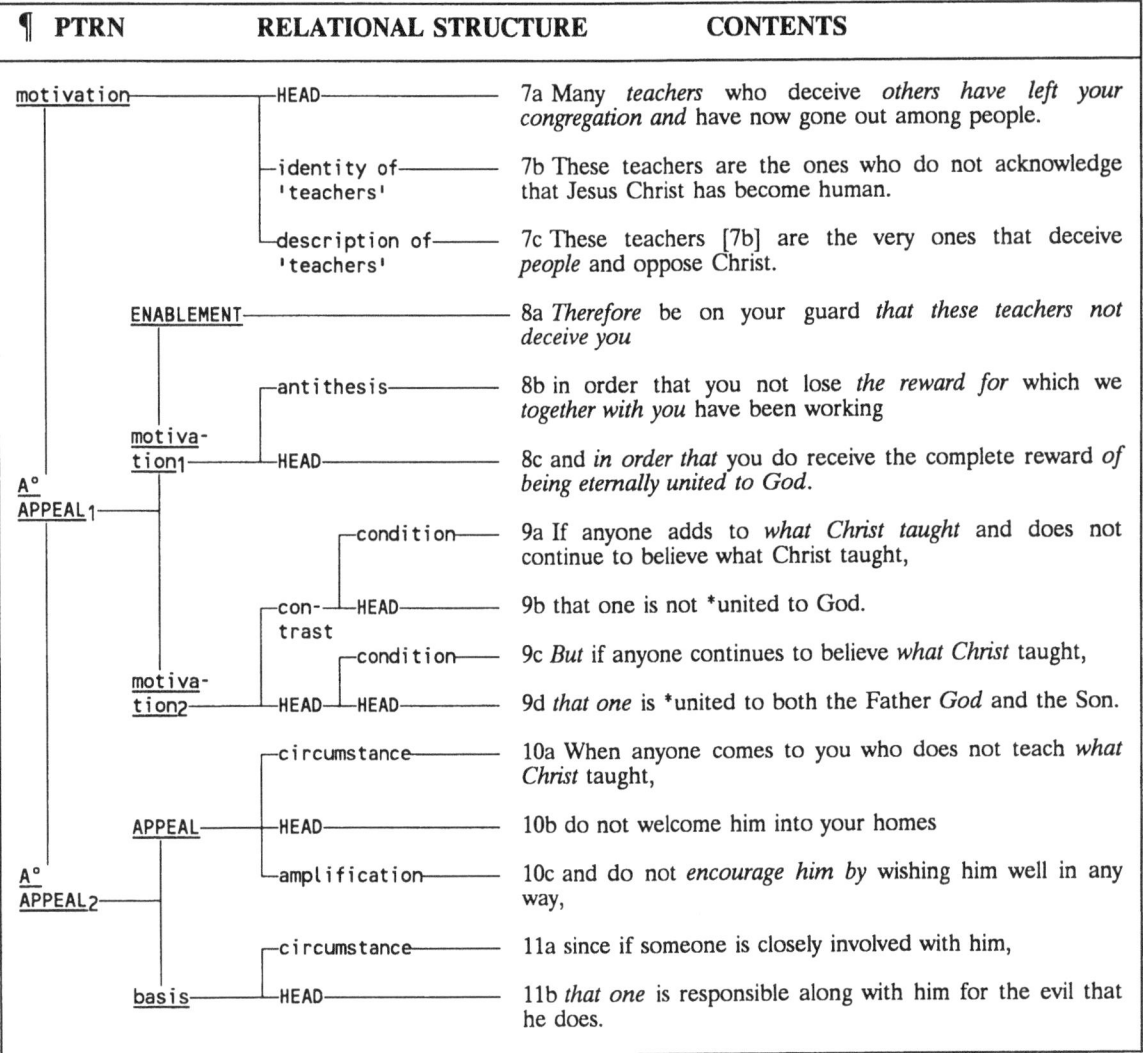

INTENT AND PARAGRAPH PATTERN

As John gets to the second of the letter's two main messages, his intent is to affect the actions of the readers in relation to the false teachers by admonitions to be on guard so as not to lose their eternal reward. They are not to help or encourage false teachers in any way. He wants to make certain that all the readers will continue believing and behaving correctly.

Since this paragraph occurs at the climax of the letter, it presents a rather complex semantic construction. It is made up of three main constituents: a propositional cluster (v. 7), and two conjoined imbedded paragraphs (vv. 8–9 and vv. 10–11). Their communication relationship is a motivational grounds unit followed by two *APPEALS*. Internally, the first of the *APPEALS* consists of an *ENABLEMENT* (8a) and two *motivations* (8b-c and 9a-d), and the second of an *APPEAL* and a *basis*.

Since the 7–11 unit's primary intent, as demonstrated by the imperatives, is to affect behavior, the paragraph is taken to be causal hortatory, with its principal constituents being + *motivation* + *APPEAL*.

NOTES

7a *teachers* who deceive The noun 'deceivers' is rendered 'teachers who deceive' in the display. However, many languages have a regular nominal form similar to 'deceivers' in English, which brings out the habitual implication of the designation. Virtually all of the English versions use some substantive here that means an agent regularly associated with an activity.

have left your congregation and **have now gone out** There is a question about the origin of the deceivers. According to some commentators, ἐξῆλθον 'went out' refers to the exodus mentioned in 1 John 2:19 ('they went out, that it might be plain that they all are not of us'). Westcott, because of the aorist form of the verb, sees it as the result of a crisis. Others (e.g., Wilder and Hoon) give it a broader interpretation, applying it to the emergence of false teachers in general as in 1 John 4:1. Actually, these two views are not necessarily mutually exclusive. In fact, it would seem very probable that though the deceivers were sent forth by Satan, just as Jesus was sent forth from the Father (John 17:18), they could previously have been part of this local congregation as in the case of 1 John 2:19. That they had been in the fellowship and had left would not necessarily mean they were not sent by Satan (so Stott). The Twentieth Century New Testament includes this idea: "have left us to go into the world."

among people The locative expression εἰς τὸν κόσμον 'into the world' is interpreted as 'into the world of people' (the first meaning given for 'world' in the note on 1 John 2:2c). This is the scene of the activity of the deceivers. Because of the warning to faithful believers it may refer more specifically to the people who have been evangelized (Stott). The description of the deceivers as deniers of the incarnation points to their effort to cause believers to leave the true gospel.

7b do not acknowledge that Jesus Christ has become human In identifying these deceivers, the Elder gives new additional information about them. He refers to the "Docetic denial of Christ's humanity and passion, which meant a failure to grasp the full love of the Father and the true basis for our quickening fellowship with the Son" (Wilder and Hoon). Thus the refusal of the deceivers to confess Christ incarnate prepares the readers for the 9b statement that the deceivers are not united to God.

Frequently a question is raised about the verb ἐρχόμενον here, which is a different form of the verb from ἐληλυθότα in 1 John 4:2. In view of the context, we consider the form here in 2 John 7 (ἐρχόμενον ἐν σαρκί 'coming in the flesh') to be another example of the fixed formula referring to the incarnation.

7c the very ones that deceive *people* and oppose Christ Since the author refers to previous information, he is describing these false teachers as a group.

In the previous context the topic, 'false teachers', is plural. At this point the author uses the singular to express who they are, thus indicating that they belong to *a group* characterized as ὁ πλάνος καὶ ὁ ἀντίχριστος 'the deceiver and the antichrist'. "The idea of the 'deceiver' is mainly relative to men: that of 'antichrist' to the Lord" (Westcott). Robertson (1933:253) calls attention to the use of an article with each word, which brings out "sharply each separate phrase, though one individual is referred to."

8a be on your guard The imperative here is βλέπετε 'see to it', which is used by Jesus several times in warning his disciples concerning those by whom they might be deceived (Mark 8:15, 12:38), particularly in eschatological discourses (e.g., Matt. 24:4). The same verb is used in other NT contexts to call attention to danger (e.g., Heb. 3:12).

that these teachers not deceive you These words supply what it is that is to be guarded against. The information is drawn from the topic of the paragraph in 7a.

8b *the reward for* which we *together with you* have been working Among the various MSS the three verbs of v. 8 in the second clause are inflected in different ways. Many commentators and UBS support the variant ἵνα μὴ ἀπολέσητε ἃ εἰργασάμεθα 'that you may not lose what we have worked for', in which 'we' can be interpreted as either 'we(exc)' or as 'we(inc)'. Other commentators (e.g., Wilder and Hoon) prefer the variant εἰργάσασθε 'you worked'. Concerning this use of the second person, Stott concedes that it would indicate an emphasis on a desire for the recipients to receive their full reward rather than a concern that the writer's own work not prove in vain.

This, he says, makes better sense than the use of the first person plural exclusive. However, Metzger considers it highly probable that the change to second person was made by a scribe for the purpose of simplification. Probably for that reason, many commentators (e.g., Smith, Robertson, Westcott) along with UBS and two-thirds of the English versions examined, prefer εἰργασάμεθα 'we (inc/exc) worked'. (Westcott renders it "the manifold results of our labours among you, which were as talents entrusted to your charge for use.") 'We(inc) worked' agrees with the considerable use of the first person plural inclusive in 2 John, expressing a fellowship of the writer with those addressed. The inclusive idea is expressed in the display by the use of 'we' plus the supplied words 'together with you'.

8c *in order that* you do receive the complete reward An alternate interpretation is 'in order that we (the ministers of the gospel) receive the reward', based on a variant reading. But very few commentators and English versions take this position. The interpretation in the display is based on the UBS preferred reading with a {B} rating.

The idea of μισθός 'reward' is to be taken in the nonmaterial sense. According to some commentators, salvation is not involved here, but rather the danger of loosing reward for Christian service. This might fit in with the reading of a few manuscripts, ἀπολέσωμεν 'lest we lose'; based on this reading, the reward would definitely be for ministry. However, most commentators see the reward as eternal fellowship with God. Stott comments, "He who denies Christ thereby forfeits God. He cannot 'have' God, that is, enjoy fellowship with Him." Wilder and Hoon say, "The phrases of v. 9 *have God, ... has both the Father and the Son*, suggest that communion with God constitutes reward in the thought of this Epistle, and the present tense of the verbs implies that it is available now ... [and] in one sense is yet to be won."

These interpretations point to an eternal loss, but it is clear that John anticipates that his warning will be heeded because in his benediction in v. 3 he asserts that the blessing of God will be maintained, the qualification for this being the framework of "truth and love." Brown says that "in Johannine thought correct christological belief is a "work" that opens the recipient to receive eternal life."

9a adds to The verb προάγω 'go before' is used in a figurative sense here and is undoubtedly borrowed from the words used by the Doceticists, who were self-styled advanced thinkers. That it has a negative significance is seen by the parallel clause which follows it. Brooke points out that the article is not repeated before μὴ μένων 'does not continue' of the second clause, thus requiring the two clauses to be interpreted together. He remarks, "All 'progress' is not condemned, but only such progress as does not fulfill the added condition of 'abiding in the teaching'." Stott says, "The Christian's development is not progress beyond Christ's teaching ... but progressive understanding of it." In the display 'goes before' is rendered 'adds to', referring to advance beyond legitimate teaching. Another interpretation takes προάγω to mean setting oneself up as a teacher; Rotherham renders it "Everyone that taketh a lead."

what Christ taught To avoid skewing, τῇ διδαχῇ τοῦ Χριστοῦ 'the teaching of Christ' is rendered 'what Christ taught'.

9b united to God In the construction 'he has God', the verb ἔχει 'has' is used figuratively to mean being in a social relationship of total subjection to the Father and the Son. Thayer (p. 266) defines the meaning of ἔχει in v. 9 as "... to be in living union with the Son (Christ) and the Father by faith, knowledge, profession." We render it 'united to' in both 9b and 9d to indicate 'being in a social relationship with'.

9c continues to believe The concept of μένω 'continue/abide' is in harmony with that of 'walk' in vv. 4 and 6 (cf. 1 John 2:6); both terms are used figuratively. In v. 4 'the children' are commended for 'walking in truth', and here in v. 9 the deceivers are described as going too far and not continuing to believe Christ's teaching. In 2a, where μένω also occurs, the literal rendering of the phrase is 'the truth which abides in us'. According to Kittel (vol. 4, pp. 575–76), the Johannine usage of μένω is a stronger form of the Pauline expression 'in Christ': God abides in believers and believers abide in God. BAGD (p. 504*a*) points out that this expression is a favorite of J[ohn's] used "to denote an inward, enduring personal communion" expressing the relationship between God, Christ, and Christians. Here the expression 'remaining in the teaching of Christ' employs the word μένω and is rendered 'continues to believe'.

9d united to both the Father *God* and the Son
See the note on 9b.

10b do not welcome him into your homes
Some commentators feel that the command to reject these false teachers is inconsistent with the spirit of love, also enjoined. They see the command as an emergency measure required by a certain situation in history, but not applicable in principle to general Christian conduct, since to remain in personal contact with those who differ doctrinally in order to win them back to the fellowship would be a good thing to do.

Other commentators, however, see the command in a different light. They argue that the command is not rejection of a doctrinally confused individual or weaker brother (Rom. 14:1), but of a teacher "systematically disseminating lies," one who is "officially commissioned to teach his error" (Stott). Based on ταύτην τὴν διδαχὴν οὐ φέρει 'does not bring this very teaching', the individuals to be rejected are clearly religious teachers. What is prohibited is an "official" welcome— the command is given to the congregation (going along with the interpretation that the letter is written to a church group, not an individual Christian matron and her children). Although οἰκία 'house' occurs here without the possessive or the article and therefore means a person's home, it could be interpreted as any believer's house; and for this reason, since the verb is plural, it is rendered 'your homes' in the display. (There could be an objection to the interpretation that what is prohibited is an official welcome on the basis of this use of οἰκία 'house/home', but it is nevertheless clear that the purpose here is to prevent the spread of false teaching.) Commentators point out that the heresy calling for this command threatened the central doctrine of the faith, the incarnation of Jesus Christ, not some peripheral doctrine concerning which differing interpretations might be tolerable. At stake was the vital relationship of the believer to God and Christ (cf. 7b-c and 9a-b). The visitor to be rejected was called 'the deceiver and the antichrist' (7c), and his activity 'wicked works' (11b). Although this peril occurred at a particular point in history, the same warning could certainly be considered a Christian principle to be applied in a similar situation at another time and place. As Ellis Deibler (personal communication) says, "Our love for fellow believers (resulting in protecting them from outright heresy) outweighs our love for those who are enemies of Christ." Barclay, likewise, in showing that the command here is not inconsistent with love, comments that the refusal of hospitality under the particular circumstances was the most effective way of stopping the heresy's spread. It would prevent its dissemination in the congregation and indicate to those outside that it was not acceptable. It might even help the heretics see their error. These measures he interprets as true love, adding that the "actual existence of the faith was in peril."

The latter of these views is the one represented in the display. It is consistent with the conservative view of the authority of Scripture and a logical interpretation of the urgency expressed in the Epistle.

Of course, the deceivers would have to be identified before they could be refused hospitality. We know from 2 Cor. 3:1 that some itinerants carried letters of introduction; others might have been known by name. In 2 John it seems clear that they would have been recognized by one means or another. (Some of the rules laid down in the Didache, which was known to be available soon after the accepted date of this Epistle, apply to this situation.)

10c do not *encourage him by* wishing him well
There is some question as to whether χαίρω 'greet' refers to the kind of greeting extended upon meeting another person (the usual NT usage) or upon bidding farewell. In this passage many commentators accept it as the parting greeting. Barclay, however, gives it a broad interpretation: "They are not even to be given a greeting on the street." The thought is of withholding encouragement and sympathy, two of the purposes for greetings, especially the Jewish *shalom* 'peace to you'. For this reason 'wishing him well' rather than 'greet' is used in the display.

Since hospitality was a way of sharing in the work of itinerant preachers in appreciation for their ministry, the prohibition of giving even a greeting was a way of showing the congregation, the world, and the false prophets that they were neither accepted nor endorsed in their propagation of an erroneous "Christian" message. Whether it was a greeting upon meeting or parting is not in focus.

11a closely involved Westcott in referring to John 3:19 and 2 Tim. 4:18 sees the verb κοινωνέω 'to fellowship with' as implying more than participation in the acts of the deceivers: "It suggests fellowship with the character of which they are the outcome" (see 'joined together' in the glossary).

11b evil The adjective πονηρός 'evil' here follows the noun that it modifies (ἔργον 'works'), and an article occurs with both. This construction lends emphasis, showing the climax here; and since 'evil' is in apposition to 'works', it conveys the force of identification (Dana and Mantey, pp. 137, 152). The fact that it is final in the section also lends it emphasis.

BOUNDARIES AND COHERENCE

The 7–11 unit is introduced by ὅτι 'that is', which signals one of three possible relationships to the preceding context:

1. The writer is turning to the main matter he wants to communicate in the letter (so Dodd).
2. The writer specifies his request mentioned in 5a (so Smith 1951).
3. The writer is explaining why he has commanded mutual love and obedience to the original message (so Plummer).

Since 7–11 is the climactic part of the letter, the third possibility does not fit: it would make this a supportive unit rather than the central one. So it seems most reasonable to interpret ὅτι as conveying the first or second relationship, the first being the best because of the function of 7–11 within the whole letter. The initial motivation statement may be viewed as a transitional linkage between the 5–6 paragraph and the positive and negative hortatory statements that make up the central and climactic paragraph of the BODY of the Epistle. These hortatory statements are the alternatives before the readers. Their reward (8c) should motivate their response. In closing, the author warns against the retribution a negative response would bring.

Semantic coherence is established by the instructions given for overcoming the danger described in v. 7. The solution is careful adherence to the teaching already received (9c) and absolute rejection of the false teachers (vv. 10–11).

Lexical coherence is achieved by repetition of the many key words around which the paragraph is built: εἰργασάμεθα 'worked' in 8b and ἔργον 'works' in 11b; μένω 'continue' in 9a and 9c and its near synonym ἔχω 'have' in 9b and 9d; διδαχή 'teaching' in 9a, 9c, and 10a; χαίρω 'greet, wish well' in 10b and 11; πλάνος 'deceiver/ liar' in 7a and 7c; and ἔρχομαι 'go' in 7a, 7b, and 10a.

PROMINENCE AND THEME

The command to guard against false teachers stands out because of the asyndeton here. The word 'teaching' is prominent due to its repetition. To continue in the true teaching is to be eternally united to the Father and the Son (9d). The teaching, the true message given at the beginning of faith, and God's command that governs behavior are three ways of expressing the means of fortification against false teachers. In order to guard against the false teachers it is necessary to continue to believe the teaching of Christ handed down from him in the apostolic message (1 John 1:4). This thought is expanded in 1 John 4:14–16, which specifies the apostolic witness, the confession, and the assurance of reciprocal union with God. The active rejection of the false teachers is the means for meeting the pending danger of their infiltration.

The theme is drawn from the three commands βλέπετε 'watch out, be on guard', μὴ λαμβάνετε 'do not receive', and χαίρειν αὐτῷ μὴ λέγετε 'do not greet him', and also from the motivation for these commands.

> **EPISTLE CONSTITUENT 12-13 (Descriptive Paragraph and Farewell: Closing of the Epistle)**
> *Theme: Instead of writing much more to you, I expect to come and communicate directly with you. The members of your sister congregation greet you.*

¶ PTRN	RELATIONAL STRUCTURE	CONTENTS
situation		12a *Even though* I have much more *that I want* to communicate to you,
	─contrast─	12b I have decided not *to communicate it* by means of a letter.
REACTION─	─HEAD─	12c Rather, I expect to be with you and speak directly with you,
	─purpose─	12d in order that we may be completely happy.
FAREWELL		13 The members of your sister congregation [SYN] *which is* chosen *by God* greet you.

INTENT AND PARAGRAPH PATTERN

The author's intent in the 12-13 unit is primarily to maintain rapport with the readers while finishing the letter in an appropriate manner, affecting the readers' emotions in such a way that they will have a good feeling about what was said and consequently accept it. The unit has two constituents: v. 12, a paragraph; and v. 13, a farewell greeting.

The v. 12 paragraph has, in turn, two main constituents: 12a and 12b-d. The communication relationship is a concession followed by a contraexpectation. The paragraph could be considered either causal descriptive or causal expository; but since the primary intent is to affect the emotions, we take it to be a descriptive causal paragraph, the principal constituents of which are + *situation* + REACTION.

The FAREWELL is not a semantic paragraph: it is a statement appropriate for the pragmatic situation of closing a letter.

NOTES

12a *Even though* The concession is recognized in Goodspeed and Twentieth Century, which have 'though'; NRSV has 'although'.

communicate The verb γράφω 'write' has a secondary meaning of 'communicate'. This is appropriate here and is supported by several commentaries and versions (JB has 'tell you').

12b I have decided The English perfect tense here represents the aorist form of ἐβουλήθην 'wish'. This is an epistolary aorist and indicates that "the writer puts himself in the temporal position of his readers, for whom his act of writing took place in the past" (Marshall).

by means of a letter The Greek is διὰ χάρτου καὶ μέλανος 'by means of paper and ink' in which the instrument for and medium of writing a letter stands for the whole of the letter. This is a metonymy signifying 'by means of a letter' or 'in a letter'.

12c directly The Greek is στόμα πρὸς στόμα 'mouth to mouth', which represents a Hebrew idiom equivalent to the English 'face to face'. Several English versions render it "personally."

12d we There is a textual question in the last clause of v. 12 in that some manuscripts have the second person pronoun rather than first. Metzger says that UBS has chosen the first person pronoun on the basis of its harmony with the author's desire to associate himself with his audience throughout the Epistle and the greater likelihood that the second person form might have resulted from a scribal error. The versions are almost evenly divided, though a slight majority use the first person. We have rendered it as a first person pronoun for the same reasons as Metzger.

13 the members of your sister congregation As stated in the Introduction, we consider ἐκλεκτῇ κυρίᾳ καὶ τοῖς τέκνοις αὐτῆς 'the elect lady and her children' a figure meaning a particular congregation and its members. Consistent with this, we take τὰ τέκνα τῆς ἀδελφῆς σου τῆς ἐκλεκτῆς 'the children of your elect sister' here to be a figure also. Thus, in the display, 'children' is rendered 'members', and 'congregation' has been added after 'sister'. In a language which would not accept the figurative use of 'sister' preceding 'congregation', 'sister' could be dropped entirely. (It should be remembered, though, that commentators are divided on whether the use of 'lady' and 'sister' are in fact figurative or a reference to some individual.)

BOUNDARIES AND COHERENCE

Verses 12 and 13 of this Epistle follow the established pattern for concluding a letter of the period in which 2 John was written. However, instead of the usual benediction (i.e., a wish or prayer for the well-being of the recipients), the writer expresses his plan to visit them with the purpose of completing their mutual happiness.

The initial boundary of the 12–13 unit is indicated by the statement 'I have much to communicate to you', which implies that the writer has presented in this letter only the message that to him is most urgent. The greeting from those present with the writer marks the closing boundary of the unit as well as of the Epistle.

The topic of communication coherence gives the unit coherence. The lexical items from that domain are: γράφω 'write', χάρτου καὶ μέλανος 'paper and ink', στόμα πρὸς στόμα 'mouth to mouth', λαλέω 'speak' (v. 12), and ἀσπάζομαι 'greet' (v. 13). The purpose of the proposed visit fits into this topic because the sharing of complete happiness is shown to depend on communication. Stott (p. 215) says, "The New Testament knows nothing of perfect joy outside of fellowship with each other through fellowship with the Father and the Son."

The closing unit rounds out the Epistle by reference to ideas already presented. Of these anaphora, γράφω 'write' in 12a refers to all that has been written (vv. 1–11), implying that it is only part of what the writer wants to communicate. The affectionate tone and the restraining of further advice (12b) so that it may be given in person (12c) for the completion of their mutual happiness (12d), corresponds to the love expressed in vv. 1 and 4 (and, in fact, throughout the letter). The repetition from v. 8 of the idea of πλήρης 'full/complete' draws together the purpose of the Epistle and corresponds to the μισθὸν πλήρη 'full reward'. The proposed visit, as well as the letter, is intended for the 'complete happiness' of the recipients (12d). The greeting from the constituency (ἀδελφῆς . . . ἐκλεκτῆς 'elect . . . sister' in v. 13) points back to the letter's address (ἐκλεκτῇ κυρίᾳ 'elect lady' in v. 1).

PROMINENCE AND THEME

Natural prominence falls on the REACTION in 12b–d and the FAREWELL in 13. Thus, the theme statement includes these two constituents. The farewell greeting from those with the writer is an expected feature of the letter. The words πολλά 'much' and ὑμῖν 'you(pl)' in 12a are also prominent, marked by forefronting. These have also been included in the theme ('Instead of writing more to you').

INTRODUCTION TO THE SEMANTIC AND STRUCTURAL ANALYSIS OF THIRD JOHN

The value of understanding the communication situation is that it provides the background for many exegetical decisions. It should be noted that the communication situation of 3 John differs somewhat from that of 2 John. Although both are personal letters, 3 John is clearly directed to one person instead of a group of people.

The participants

The writer of 3 John calls himself 'the Elder'. This is John, the beloved apostle, the same one who wrote the First and Second Epistles (see the discussion of authorship in the Introduction to 1 John).

John's Third Epistle is addressed to "Gaius." Two other persons are mentioned by name, "Diotrephes" and "Demetrius." A particular order of "brethren" is also referred to. There is not enough information given in this letter to identify either Gaius or Demetrius with anyone mentioned in the New Testament bearing those names. (These names were very common in the Graeco-Roman culture.) Gaius seems to have been a leader in a local church, well known to the Elder (v. 2) and cooperating fully with him (v. 5). Diotrephes, whose name is uncommon, was also a local leader, but not working in harmony with the Elder (vv. 9, 10). Demetrius is assumed by commentators to have been a member of the "brethren" and probably the bearer of this letter (Marshall 1978:93).

The "brethren," mentioned in vv. 3 and 5-8, are described in such a way that they can be identified with the itinerant teachers or prophets of the time. In 2 John itinerant teachers are denounced for spreading heresy, but those mentioned in 3 John are highly recommended. Apparently it was the apostle himself who would send them out; they would report to him on their return. It was their practice to carry a letter of introduction, perhaps similar to parts of 3 John. Demetrius was probably the leader of such a group of teachers.

The occasion for writing

The problem alluded to in the Third Epistle is different from that of the Second. In the Second it is "intellectual arrogance"; in the Third it is "personal aggrandizement" (David Smith, p. 207), involving a question of authority, church leadership, and perhaps a clash of ministries. Here the great apostle of love lashes out against a lack of Christian humility and love among the brethren.

> Both letters are ... concerned with Christian truth and love and with their relation to hospitality.... the positive instruction of the Third Epistle is complementary to the more negative instruction of the Second. The two letters must be read together if we are to gain a balanced understanding. (Stott, p. 216)

In both letters the author's authority and deep affection are evident. In 3 John the general statement of the spiritual health of his "children" as being the greatest source of his pleasure (v. 4) helps establish his supervisory position as "Elder," the basis on which the exhortations of the letter are made.

Gaius was loved by John and others in the same way that the recipients of the Second Epistle were loved. He was well known to John as one who cooperated in his teaching activities; thus he is addressed with confidence. That John found Gaius's spiritual health a reason for great rejoicing shows the genuineness of the love that he is expressing. This love is particularly emphasized by the repetition of ἀγαπητός 'loved one' in vv. 1, 2, 5, and 11. Gaius is classed among the writer's 'children', which has frequently been interpreted as meaning that he was converted under John's ministry. While this may be true, it seems more likely that the reason John used the term is related to the fact that he was writing a fatherly admonition here, characteristic of the family image established in the Christian community during the apostolic era. (This view harmonizes with John's use of the term 'children' in the First Epistle.) The emphatic ἐγώ 'I' in the expression of love in the address (v. 1) may be taken as showing a contrast in attitude toward some who are *not* trusted or loved because they are not teaching the true message.

This conclusion could well be deduced from the description of Diotrephes in vv. 9-10 and from the general exhortation to Gaius to imitate those who do good and not those who do evil (v. 11). John was aware of Gaius's Christian behavior (v. 2) since he had received assurance of this from the visiting brethren's reports (vv. 3, 6). Diotrephes, on the other hand, had rejected the brethren. It has been suggested that desire for social prestige may have led to his uncharitable attitude.

How closely associated these contrasting participants were can only be conjectured. In trying to reconstruct the background of the letter some have assumed that Gaius and Diotrephes were members of the same church. Others suggest that if that had been so, Gaius would not have needed to be informed of the activities of Diotrephes (v. 10). Perhaps they belonged to adjacent, relatively small local congregations. In any case, it is evident from v. 11 that the Elder felt Gaius was in danger of being influenced by the domineering Diotrephes and needed to be warned.

The itinerant teachers carried on an established ministry under the direction of the Elder. The churches needed their ministry during this time of transition from the apostolic age, and certainly those who carried it on needed the support of the churches they visited. At the same time, another form of leadership was developing which eventually became the monarchical episcopate. It is difficult to judge whether this movement, which strengthened the local leadership, came as a means of dealing with heresy and private ambition or simply as an effort to free the local churches from a supervision formerly provided by apostolic leaders and which later was no longer needed.

In this tension Gaius was probably caught between his loyalty to the Elder and his proximity to local leaders. Diotrephes represents the local leadership. It seems that no doctrinal issue was involved here, though some commentators think Diotrephes may have sided with the Docetic faction. The Elder planned to deal with the situation himself, but needed the continued loyalty of Gaius. Most probably by this letter he was trying to ensure the welcome of Demetrius in his circuit, because the exhortation to Gaius was that he continue receiving the itinerant teachers.

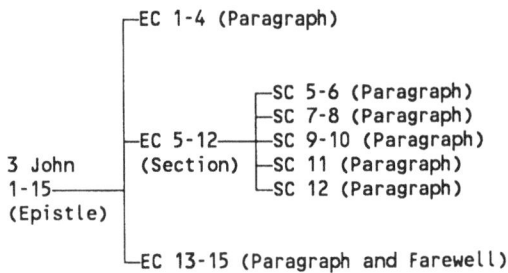

EC = Epistle Constituent
SC = Section Constituent

The constituent organization of 3 John

OVERVIEW: THEMATIC OUTLINE OF THIRD JOHN

3 John 1–15 (Epistle)
Theme: Do not imitate Diotrephes's bad example, but continue to do your good deeds of receiving and supporting the itinerant teachers.

    EPISTLE CONSTITUENT 1–4 (Descriptive Paragraph: Opening of the Epistle)
Theme: I, the Elder, write to you, Gaius, whom I truly love. I ask God that you may do well in all respects just as your soul does well. I am happy because of how you behave.

    EPISTLE CONSTITUENT 5–12 (Hortatory Section: Body of the Epistle)
Theme: Do not imitate Diotrephes's bad example, but continue to do your good deeds of supporting the itinerant teachers.

        SECTION CONSTITUENT 5–6 (Hortatory Paragraph: Appeal$_1$ of 5–12)
Theme: You will do well to continue your faithful work of receiving the visiting Christian brothers as you have been doing.

        SECTION CONSTITUENT 7–8 (Hortatory Paragraph: Appeal$_2$ of 5–12)
Theme: You ought especially to provide for them financially.

        SECTION CONSTITUENT 9–10 (Descriptive Paragraph: Problem of 5–12)
Theme: Because Diotrephes does not recognize our authority, I will publicly expose what he does in opposing us.

        SECTION CONSTITUENT 11 (Hortatory Paragraph: Appeal$_3$ of 5–12)
Theme: Do not imitate a bad example, but continue to imitate a good one.

        SECTION CONSTITUENT 12 (Hortatory Paragraph: Appeal$_4$ of 5–12)
Theme: You will do well to receive Demetrius, who is highly recommended.

    EPISTLE CONSTITUENT 13–15 (Descriptive Paragraph and Farewell: Closing of the Epistle)
Theme: Instead of writing more, I expect to visit you soon, and we will speak directly with one another. Our mutual friends here send their greetings to all of you.

THE SEMANTIC UNITS OF THIRD JOHN

---

3 John 1–15 (Epistle)
Theme: Do not imitate Diotrephes's bad example, but continue to do your good deeds of receiving and supporting the itinerant teachers.

MACROSTRUCTURE	CONTENTS
opening	1–4 I, the Elder, write to you, Gaius, whom I truly love. I ask God that you may do well in all respects just as your soul does well. I am happy because of how you behave.
BODY	5–12 Do not imitate Diotrephes's bad example, but continue to do your good deeds of supporting the itinerant teachers.
closing	13–15 Instead of writing more I expect to visit you soon, and we will speak directly with one another. Our mutual friends here send their greetings to all of you.

INTENT AND MACROSTRUCTURE

Although John's most immediate motivation for writing this Epistle was to secure hospitality for a group of itinerant teachers, his greater concern was that Gaius continue to behave in accord with the Christian message, cooperating with John and supporting the teachers he was sending. This concern arose from Diotrephes's earlier rejection of John and the itinerant teachers. John did not want Gaius to follow his example. So he wrote with the intent of affecting Gaius's behavior so he would continue to live according to true Christian teachings and provide hospitality and support for Demetrius and the teachers with him.

The Epistle has the three parts of a letter characteristic of the apostolic period, namely *opening*, *BODY*, and *closing*. The *BODY* has five constituents (see the organizational chart and the discussion of the 5–12 *BODY*).

The *opening* (vv. 1–4) contains the formal address and an expression of the love and confidence needed to establish rapport with the reader. The *BODY* has a request (v. 6) and the main exhortation (v. 11) (supported by the negative *motivational basis* in vv. 9–10). The *closing* (vv. 13–15) expresses the expectation of communicating in person at a later date as well as the greetings usual in such a letter.

COHERENCE OF THE EPISTLE

As expected in a personal letter, there is a pattern of frequently occurring first and second person pronouns throughout the discourse. Four other features lend further coherence:

1. The structure characteristic of letters of this period: *opening*, *BODY*, and *closing*.
2. Lexical items in the semantic domain of good behavior: ἀλήθεια 'truth' (1, 3, 4, 8, and 12); μαρτυρέω 'report' (3, 6, and 12); περιπατέω 'walk/behave' (3 and 4); ἀγαθός 'good' and κακός 'bad' (11); and ἐργάζομαι, ἔργον, and συνεργέω 'work' (5, 8, and 10).
3. Specific participants (the writer, Gaius, Demetrius, and Diotrephes).
4. Specific problems that are addressed.

PROMINENCE AND THEME

The letter's structure is clear. Following the formal address of the *opening*, the vocative ἀγαπητέ 'dear friend' introduces first the prayer unit (vv. 2–4) and then two additional paragraphs of the *BODY* (vv. 5, 11). The vocative is followed in each case by a direct personal comment. In v. 2 this is a prayer or wish for the welfare of Gaius; in v. 5 a commendation of his work; and in v. 11 personal counsel expressing the letter's theme. The negative *motivational basis* (vv. 9–10) has neither the vocative nor the positive personal comment and is very different in content from the rest, and is thus set off from the *APPEAL* paragraphs of the *BODY*.

Natural prominence falls on the four exhortations of vv. 6, 8, 11, and 12. These are central in the Epistle. Of the four, the third has the greatest prominence. It is an imperative expressed both negatively and positively, while the others are mitigated. Its chiastic structure also gives it prominence (see the discussion under the v. 11 display).

The Epistle's theme is drawn from the constituent that is prominent, that is, the BODY.

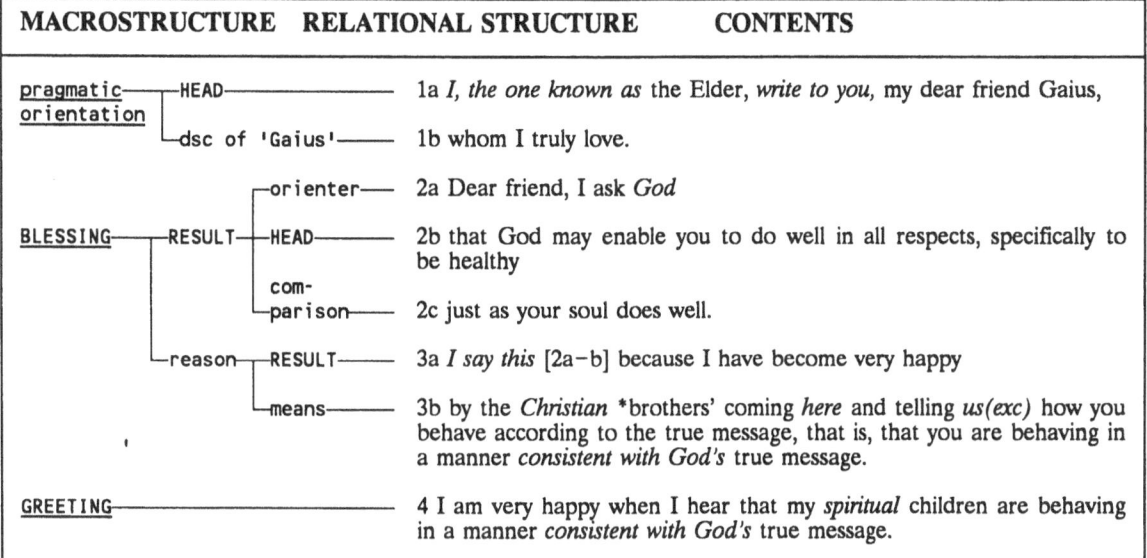

INTENT AND PARAGRAPH PATTERN

The author's intent in the 1–4 unit is to establish rapport with the recipient of the letter and identify himself. The unit does not fill the requirements of a semantic paragraph pattern; it simply orients the reader to the pragmatic context of the letter. Since both the author and the reader are removed from each other and not face to face, the communication is abnormal. That is, the author and reader must be identified, and rapport established. Rapport is normally established with an audience by affecting the emotions in such a way that the audience will be willing to listen.

Following the letter-writing convention of the day, the 1–4 unit comprises three units of equal prominence: identity of the writer and recipient (v. 1), a blessing (vv. 2–3), and a greeting (v. 4).

NOTES

1a *I, the one known as* **the Elder,** *write* . . . See the note on 2 John 1 concerning the identity of 'the Elder' and the address, which is verbless here as it is there.

The verb 'write', which is supplied here, is explicit in the v. 13 closing.

my dear friend In view of the New Testament usage of ἀγαπητός 'dear, beloved', including its use in reference to Christ when God is the speaker, our current English expression 'my dear friend' is perhaps too weak. The translator may be able to find a more suitable rendering in the receptor language.

1b truly The rendering of ἐν ἀληθείᾳ 'truly' is discussed in the note on 2 John 1b.

2b in all respects Commentators generally agree that this expression is to be taken with εὐοδοῦσθαι 'prosper' rather than with εὔχομαι 'pray'. The repetition of the verb εὐοδόομαι concerning the prosperity of the soul indicates that the comparison is made not just between the body and soul (i.e., between 'to be healthy' and 'just as your soul does well'). In fact, as Houlden comments, Jewish thought would not accept a formal and explicit division of man into body and soul. Although 'body' is not mentioned in the text, the verb ὑγιαίνω 'to be healthy' is understood to refer to physical well-being. According to this interpretation, 'health' is taken as specific following the generic 'in all respects'. For this reason some (e.g., Brooke) take the reference to indicate that possibly Gaius was not in robust health, though there is no clear evidence of this. But the Elder does have clear evidence of his spiritual well-being and wishes the external aspects of his life to be as prosperous.

3a because I have become very happy The conjunction γάρ 'because', though not present in some manuscripts, is accepted by UBS and in most of the English versions. It "is adequately supported by a variety of witnesses" (Metzger). As to its meaning, there is a question. Does it mean that this proposition is the reason for knowing that Gaius's soul is well, or that it is the reason for the content of the prayer, or does it stand for an ellipsis that is the reason?

1. Most commentaries say that the news about Gaius brought by some visitors is the reason for knowing that Gaius's soul is well (and possibly that he suffers ill health). This does not seem right, however, since the principle verb of the clause is 'I became happy' and the participial phrases about the news refer to being happy and not the reason for knowing about Gaius's condition. John's being happy is incongruent as a reason for knowing the condition of Gaius's soul.
2. Very few commentaries suggest that this proposition is the reason for the content of John's prayer. Nevertheless, it seems much more coherent than the first interpretation if we take it that John is happy and as a result would pray for Gaius.
3. Although γάρ frequently signals an ellipsis or assumed proposition, no commentaries suggest this. Even so, this might be the true basis of the first interpretation and probably needs to be considered seriously. Some possibilities are: (a) *'I say the previous*, since I have become happy ...'; (b) 'I know your soul is well, because *it has so been reported to me* [implied from the participles], and as a result I have become happy'.

We consider interpretation 3.a the best choice.

The verb ἐχάρην 'I became happy' is in the aorist and is followed by two present participles, which are interpreted as indicating repeated action. Burton points out that the action of the aorist falls within the period covered by the participle. Thus, because the happiness is not a single event, it is rendered with the English perfect tense in the display, implying that the Elder remains happy.

3b behave As in 2 John 4a, περιπατέω 'walk' is interpreted as 'behave' here.

4 very happy There is a textual problem here in that a few manuscripts have χάριν 'favor' instead of χαράν 'joy'. The latter is defended by Metzger as being more typical of Johannine writing and because it is strongly supported by many of the best manuscripts. It is, therefore, our choice also.

hear Hearing is the means by which John knows of Gaius's conduct and character.

my *spiritual* children This could mean either the people under John's supervision or the people who had come to believe in Christ through his ministry.

behaving in a manner *consistent with God's* true message Since 'walk' is a figure that refers to conduct or behavior, the phrase ἐν τῇ ἀληθείᾳ περιπατοῦντα 'walking in the truth' means to behave according to the true standard. The article that precedes ἀληθείᾳ 'truth' is repeated from v. 3, even though it precedes a verb there. It may, therefore, be taken here as referring back to the behavior in v. 3. Some commentators consider the article to indicate a personification in which 'the Truth' signifies Christ.

BOUNDARIES AND COHERENCE

The 1–4 unit is composed of three propositional clusters that follow the standard pattern for the opening of a letter of this period: The writer identifies himself and the person addressed (labeled *pragmatic orientation*) and then continues with a rapport-building prayer (labeled BLESSING) and a commendation (labeled GREETING).

The initial boundary of the unit coincides with the opening of the discourse. The BLESSING begins with a vocative, which serves as an opening boundary marker following the *pragmatic orientation*. The final boundary is the GREETING's conclusion.

That this is a coherent unit is clear from its structure (the structure of a standard opening of a letter). The vocative ἀγαπητέ 'dear friend' immediately after the *pragmatic orientation* (v. 1) is considered to be the main boundary marker between v. 1 and the BLESSING. This boundary is supported by the fact that the three constituents have different purposes: the first one (v. 1) to identify the writer and the addressee, and the other two (vv. 2-4) to establish rapport.

This unit has an emotive intent: it describes the personal relationship of the writer to the one he addresses. He has affection for him (v. 1) and is concerned for his welfare (vv. 2 and 3). He rejoices in the progress he is making in his spiritual life (v. 4).

PROMINENCE AND THEME

The naturally prominent propositions are the BLESSING's HEAD (2b-c) and the GREETING (v. 4). The following add marked prominence: (1) ἀγαπητός 'dear' is prominent because of its repetition throughout the Epistle (in vv. 1, 2, 5, 11); (2) περὶ πάντων 'in all respects' is prominent by virtue of its being forefronted and because it may be a reference to the activity which the author in v. 6 writes to secure (certainly Gaius would need prosperity and health to enable him to continue helping the visiting teachers); (3) ἀλήθεια 'truth' is prominent because it occurs four times in this paragraph (it is a reference to absolute truth according to God's character); (4) περιπατέω 'to walk or behave' is prominent because it occurs linked with the prominent idea ἀλήθεια 'truth' (twice) meaning 'to behave according to the truth'. The scope of these prominent lexical items is limited to the propositions in which they occur, but they give coherence to the paragraph and lead into the main point of the letter. But the structural prominence is even more significant in the 1-4 unit.

The theme statement is drawn from the address (v. 1), the BLESSING (vv. 2-3), and the GREETING (v. 4).

EPISTLE CONSTITUENT 5-12 (Hortatory Section: Body of the Epistle)
Theme: Do not imitate Diotrephes's bad example, but continue to do your good deeds of supporting the itinerant teachers.

MACROSTRUCTURE	CONTENTS
D° APPEAL₁	5-6 You will do well to continue your faithful work of receiving the visiting Christian brothers as you have been doing.
C° APPEAL₂	7-8 You ought especially to provide for them financially.
problem(hort)	9-10 Because Diotrephes does not recognize our authority, I will publicly expose what he does in opposing us.
A° APPEAL₃	11 Do not imitate a bad example, but continue to imitate a good one.
D° APPEAL₄	12 You will do well to receive Demetrius, who is highly recommended.

INTENT AND MACROSTRUCTURE

As John gets into the central part of this letter, he addresses three main problems. The first is that his request that they provide hospitality and financial support for the itinerant teachers he had sent to them had been denied by Diotrephes and others whom he had coerced. The second problem is John's concern that Gaius might be swept away with Diotrephes's evil behavior. The third problem is John's need to secure Gaius's help for the itinerant teachers.

John weaves these three problems into a major chiastic structure covering the BODY of this letter, as follows:

A ἐμαρτύρησάν σου ... καλῶς ποιήσεις προπέμψας 'they report about you ... you will do well to send them' (vv. 5-6)

B ἡμεῖς οὖν ὀφείλομεν ὑπολαμβάνειν 'we ought then to support them' (vv. 7-8)

　C οὐκ ἐπιδέχεται ἡμᾶς ... ὑπομνήσω αὐτοῦ τὰ ἔργα 'he does not receive us ... I will expose his works' (vv. 9-10)

B· μιμοῦ ... τὸ ἀγαθόν 'imitate the good example' (v. 11)

A· Δημητρίῳ μεμαρτύρηται ὑπὸ πάντων 'everyone reports about Demetrius (and you do well to send them on)' (v. 12)

The *APPEAL* in v. 6 ('you will do well to send them on') is greatly mitigated and corresponds to v. 12 where it is totally covert, though supplied in the display. The v. 6 *APPEAL* as well as the covert *APPEAL* in v. 12 (which is set up by John's recommendation of Gaius in v. 6 and of Demetrius in v. 12) addresses the third of the problems mentioned above: securing Gaius's help.

The mitigated *APPEAL* in v. 8 ('we ought to support them'), which corresponds to the outright command in v. 11 ('don't follow Diotrophes's example but a good one'), addresses the second problem: it is aimed at assuring Gaius's kindly behavior.

In v. 10, John in committing himself to deal with Diotrephes personally addresses the first problem, namely Diotrephes's evil behavior. This first problem gives rise to the others and the corresponding appeals which provide the solutions. (Notice how this personal committal functions like an appeal; it affects the speaker's behavior while an appeal affects the hearer's behavior.)

BOUNDARIES AND COHERENCE

The opening boundary of the 5-12 section is clearly marked by the vocative 'dear friend'. The closing boundary is marked by the introduction of a totally different subject matter without any conjunctive particle.

The relational structure of the five paragraphs gives the section its coherence. This, the *BODY* of the letter, has two mitigated hortatory paragraphs (vv. 5-6 and 7-8), which contrast with a negative descriptive paragraph (vv. 9-10), followed by the two main exhortations (v. 11 and v. 12).

PROMINENCE AND THEME

There are four *APPEALS* in this section: 6b, which is highly mitigated ('you will do well'); 8a, somewhat mitigated ('we ought to support'); v. 11, a straightforward imperative ('follow a good example'); and v. 12, the most highly mitigated (see degrees of mitigation on p. 2). The greater prominence is on v. 8 and v. 11. The 9-10 paragraph presents the *problem* to be solved by the exhortations and simultaneously provides a negative motivational basis for the admonition in the v. 11 paragraph by mentioning the evil practices of Diotrephes. As a general statement, it serves to summarize John's purpose for writing the letter.

The theme is drawn from the v. 11 unmitigated appeal and the v. 8 mitigated appeal.

SECTION CONSTITUENT 5-6 (Hortatory Paragraph: Appeal₁ of 5-12)
Theme: You will do well to continue your faithful work of receiving the visiting Christian brothers as you have been doing.

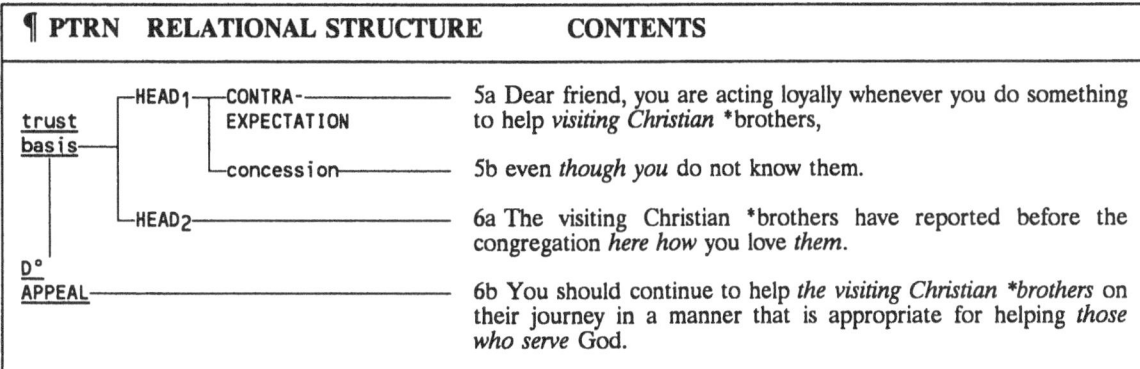

INTENT AND PARAGRAPH PATTERN

As John gets to the main message of the letter, his intent is to affect the actions of the reader by four low-key admonitions. He wants to make certain that Gaius will continue helping the visiting evangelists on their way.

The paragraph has two main constituents (5a-6a and 6b). Their communication relationship is a grounds unit followed by an exhortation. The paragraph could be considered either causal hortatory or causal expository. Since the primary intent is to affect behavior, we take it to be causal hortatory, the principal constituents being + basis + APPEAL.

NOTES

5a *Christian* **brothers** From the context these brothers are specifically understood to be itinerant evangelist-teachers (see Glossary).

acting loyally The phrase πιστὸν ποιεῖς 'you do a faithful thing' has been interpreted to mean more specifically either 'doing what is consistent with what is believed' or 'doing what will assure due reward'. The majority of commentators prefer the former.

whenever Where the focus is on the possibility of the action being carried out several times, as here, ἐάν is appropriately rendered 'whenever' (Louw and Nida 71.8).

5b even *though you* **do not know them** The particle καί 'even' here does not conjoin the two groups of people. It is not 'the itinerant teachers *and* strangers'. Rather, the latter is an included subgroup of the former: '*even* those who are strangers to you'.

6a *Christian brothers* See the note on 5a.

the congregation *here* Commentators agree that this harks back to the believers' report to the congregation in the city from which John was writing.

how **you love** *them* An evaluative statement such as this about the recipient of a letter is commonly used to soften a command.

6b This proposition is a highly mitigated exhortation (see degrees of mitigation on p. 2). The main clause in Greek, 'you will do well', expresses the value of the action in the complementary clause, 'to send them on their way'.

help *the visiting Christian brothers* **on their journey** The further implication of the verb προπέμπω 'to send' is 'to provide the necessary material means for the journey whose purpose is teaching others'.

appropriate for helping *those who serve* **God** The Greek is ἀξίως τοῦ θεοῦ 'worthy of God'. Commentators point out that since the brothers are representing Christ (see 7a) they should be treated as one would treat God (in a way that is fitting for an appointed servant of God) or as God would treat them.

BOUNDARIES AND COHERENCE

The topics of hospitality and the Elder's authority in soliciting the cooperation of Gaius provide the semantic coherence of the 5-6 unit. Lexical items in the domain of hospitality also provide coherence: τοὺς ἀδελφούς 'the (visiting) brothers' (v. 5), ἀγάπη 'love' (v. 6), and προπέμπω 'help in travel' (v. 6).

The opening boundary of 5-6 coincides with that of 5-12 and has already been discussed. The closing boundary of 5-6 is marked by a change in theme from the virtues of Gaius to the necessity of providing financially for the itinerant preachers. There is a connecting particle (γάρ 'since') between this paragraph and the following one.

The question may arise why vv. 7-8 are not joined with 5-6 as one unit, particularly since a close tie to v. 6 seems indicated by γάρ 'since' in v. 7. Some commentators indeed take 5-8 as a unit for this reason. However, we must take into account the antecedent of οὖν 'therefore' in v. 8 together with the forcefulness of the v. 8 exhortation. As do several commentators, we take v. 7 to be the referent of οὖν 'therefore', thus making v. 7 the *basis* for the APPEAL in v. 8. There is a strong lexical tie between v. 7 and v. 8 (λαμβάνω 'receive' and ὑπολαμβάνω 'support'). In fact, no one seems to consider 5-6 the referent of 'therefore'; but if it were, v. 8 would act as a summary. But, from the point of view of semantic theory, the exhortation in v. 8 is more prominent than that of 6b: it cannot be in a supportive role. If γάρ in v. 7 be taken as introducing the reason for 5-6, then v. 8 would be in a supportive role, and this we cannot defend. We conclude, therefore, that γάρ does not function to introduce the reason for 5-6; rather, it functions as a marker of transition to introduce a new but related concept (so Louw and Nida 91.1).

Taking the position that 5-6 is a close-knit unit with all the characteristics of a complete paragraph pattern and that 7-8 has these same characteristics, we conclude that the relation of amplification-contraction between D° APPEAL and C° APPEAL resides at the section level.

PROMINENCE AND THEME

The 6b request (that Gaius continue his good work of providing hospitality to the itinerant teachers), though mitigated, is the central proposition of the 5-6 unit. It is made prominent by the preceding *basis* (that Gaius shows loyalty by doing so) in 5a. This request is an exercise of the Elder's authority. It is further developed in the specific request that follows in 7-8 (that he help the teachers financially). The 6b request is prominent, and it is from this central proposition that the theme statement is derived.

SECTION CONSTITUENT 7-8 (Hortatory Paragraph: Appeal₂ of 5-12)
Theme: You ought especially to provide for them financially.

¶ PTRN	RELATIONAL STRUCTURE	CONTENTS
basis₁	┌circumstance───	7a Also, when they went out *to tell people* about Christ [MTY],
	└HEAD───────	7b *they* received nothing *in return for what they did* from those who do not believe in Christ.
C°APPEAL		8a Therefore, we *who believe in Christ* ought to support such people *financially*
basis₂		8b in order that we can participate with them *as they teach God's* true message.

INTENT AND PARAGRAPH PATTERN

In this second low-key admonition John's intent is to continue affecting the reader's actions. He wants to make certain that Gaius will help the visiting evangelists by "sending them on their way." The unit has three constituents: a grounds unit (7a-b), followed by an exhortation (8a), followed by a purpose (8b). This paragraph could be considered either causal hortatory or causal expository; but since the primary intent is to affect behavior, we consider it causal hortatory, the principal constituents being + *basis* + APPEAL.

NOTES

7a Also For the function of γάρ 'then' see the 5-6 unit's "Boundaries and Coherence."

to tell people The explicit information that they went out 'on behalf of the name' makes it clear that the purpose of this travel was evangelism.

Christ The Greek is simply 'name', a metonymy for Christ. That it is the name of Christ is implicit. To be correctly understood, and for semantic completeness, this is spelled out here.

7b *they* received nothing Elsewhere in the New Testament ἀπό 'from' is used with λαμβάνω 'take' for the exacting of taxes, suggesting that taking something from unbelievers would be in return for ministry.

those who do not believe in Christ The term ἐθνικός 'Gentile' in NT usage almost always means 'non-Jew'. But here where it contrasts with 'we' in 8a, it means 'unbelievers'. Or it could refer to Gentiles who only recently believed through their ministry (Westcott).

8a This proposition is a mitigated exhortation (see p. 2 in the General Introduction).

we *who believe in Christ* This is not 'we Jews' but rather 'we believers in Christ'. The pronoun is forefronted, making a sharp contrast with the previously mentioned 'Gentiles'.

support ... *financially* The word ὑπολαμβάνω 'help' is generic. Some commentators say that it connotes the welcoming of a guest. Here John solicits not only hospitality but financial help for the journey.

8b participate with them An alternate interpretation is 'help propagate the true message', arising from the personification of 'truth'. Most commentators prefer this; but once the figure of speech is spelled out, the meaning is 'they work together with those who propagate the true message'. (This is essentially the same thing.) Most versions have it as in the display.

***God's* true message** The word 'truth' occurs here with the article and is interpreted by some as a personification referring to Christ. Others interpret 'truth' to be the absolutely true gospel message. This phrase also occurs in 2 John 1c (see the note there).

BOUNDARIES AND COHERENCE

The semantic coherence of vv. 7-8 is shown by adherence to the topic of the Elder's authority concerning helping the itinerant preachers as he solicits the cooperation of Gaius. Lexical items in the domain of helping the itinerant preachers add to the unit's coherence: ἐξέρχομαι 'went out' (v. 7) and ὑπολαμβάνω 'support' (v. 8).

The opening boundary of 7-8 coincides with the closing boundary of 5-6 and has already been discussed. The closing boundary of 7-8 is marked by a sharp change in theme, from the virtues of the itinerant teachers to the perverted leadership of Diotrephes. There is no connecting particle between this paragraph and the following one.

PROMINENCE AND THEME

Though mitigated, the 8a request that Gaius provide financially for the itinerant teachers is the central proposition of this unit. It is made prominent by the v. 7 *basis* that the visitors tell people about Christ without receiving support from unbelievers. It is implied that the visitors are worthy of financial help and this is the believers' obligation. The request is an exercise of the Elder's authority. Since it is the prominent element, the theme is derived from it.

> **SECTION CONSTITUENT 9-10 (Descriptive Paragraph: Problem of 5-12)**
> *Theme: Because Diotrephes does not recognize our authority, I will publicly expose what he does in opposing us.*

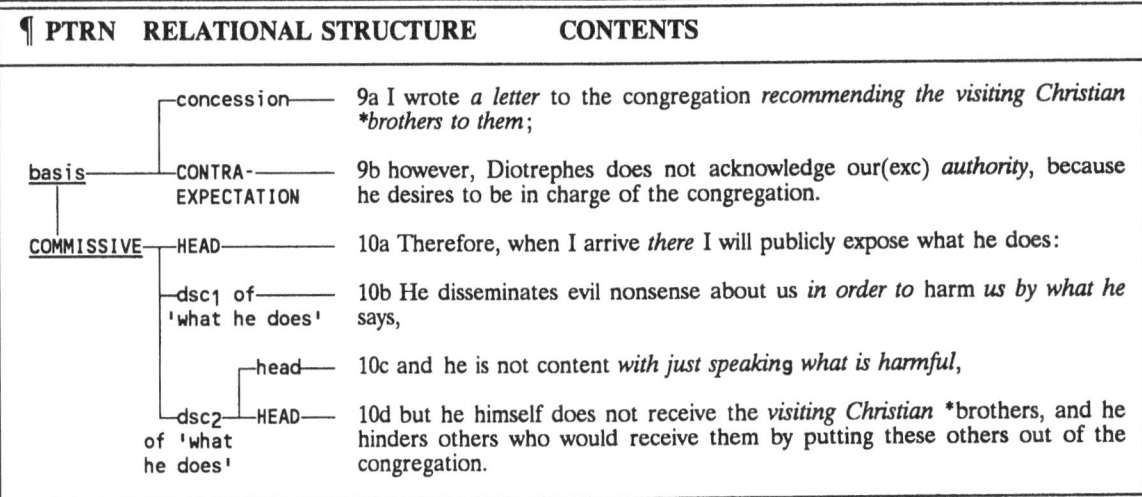

INTENT AND PARAGRAPH PATTERN

In the 9-10 unit John gets to the problem that led him to write to Gaius: Diotrephes's refusal to welcome visiting evangelists. John wants to motivate Gaius so that he not follow Diotrephes's bad example. The paragraph has two constituents, v. 9 and v. 10; their communication relation is a grounds followed by a conclusion. At first glance, the paragraph could be considered causal descriptive, causal expository, or causal hortatory; but since the primary intent is to affect his own actions by committing himself to the action, John is not just informing Gaius what he intends to do. He could well be encouraging Gaius, assuring him that he will resolve the adverse situation. However, because of the clear committal, we take it as causal hortatory, the principal constituents being + *basis* + *COMMISSIVE*. (Since we do not normally talk about appealing to oneself, we use the term COMMISSIVE, meaning that the author affects his own behavior by committing himself to do something.)

NOTES

9a *a letter* The Greek here is τί 'something', but there is a textual question. Some manuscripts have τί, some omit it, and others have ἄν, a particle which would give a conditional meaning to the clause: 'I would have written'. However, commentators generally reject ἄν (as do UBS and most modern versions), accepting τί as the reading that best explains the origin of the other readings. In the display, as in several versions, it is rendered 'a letter', supplying the object.

There is a question as to what particular writing is meant. Is it 2 John or some other letter that met with rejection and which John has now heard about? At best we can only speculate and so have left it ambiguous.

congregation John uses ἐκκλησία 'church' to refer to a group of people who believe in Christ Jesus (cf. 6a). We do not render it 'church' because in contemporary English the primary meaning component of 'church' is a building.

9b **however** The word ἀλλά 'however' introduces Diotrephes's response to the letter. Depending on the identity of the writing referred to in 9a, John might have known Diotrephes's response as reported by the visiting brothers. Or else he does not yet know what Diotrephes's response is, but is writing in the light of what he anticipates it will be.

does not acknowledge our(exc) *authority* The Greek is οὐκ ἐπιδέχεται ἡμᾶς 'does not receive us'. The meaning we give it is supported by several commentators. BAGD is similar: 'does not accept' (p. 292a.2). We take the first person plural pronoun as 'our(exc)' (although it could possibly be considered an epistolary, meaning 'my'). Many versions reduce the plural to singular, but most commentaries support the plural here as referring to a sending group, perhaps including the visitors themselves.

because The relative clause ὁ φιλοπρωτεύων αὐτῶν 'the one loving to be first among them' could be taken either as a reason why 'he does not acknowledge our authority' or as the identity/description of Diotrephes. But neither identity nor description would fit since Gaius most probably had first-hand knowledge of Diotrephes. We take it as reason, which is very appropriate to the context.

desires to be in charge The Greek is φιλοπρωτεύω 'desires to be first'. Commentators see in this the ambition for leadership, giving orders to others, which was condemned by Christ in Matt. 20:27.

10a when I arrive Marshall interprets the conditional ἐάν 'if' here as a condition not necessarily in doubt (see Marshall on 1 John 2:28 also). This is better expressed in English as 'when' (as several modern versions do).

I will publicly expose The verb ὑπομνήσω may be translated 'I will remember', but Brooke interprets it as "I will recall and show in the right light." Strong words of denunciation accompany ὑπομνήσω in this passage, so it is important to avoid too weak an interpretation. At the least a public exposure was in view (cf. 2 Tim. 2:14). Barclay has "remind the congregation."

10b us We take the pronoun here to be inclusive: all who support the group of preachers. (Or it could be considered an epistolary 'us' meaning 'me': the leader of the preachers and of the congregations in the area.)

10d The verbs in 10d that refer to Diotrephes's actions (not receiving, hindering, putting out) seem to indicate his policy, his usual course of action. As for expelling people from the church, we do not have information as to how much power he had in influencing the church to do this. Brooke thinks expelling a person would require the concurrence of the church.

putting these others out of the congregation Alternatively, this could be interpreted as 'putting the visiting brothers out of the congregation', but support for this is weak.

BOUNDARIES AND COHERENCE

The opening boundary of this unit coincides with the closing boundary of the 7-8 paragraph (see the discussion there). The closing boundary is marked by John's characteristic vocative, ἀγαπητέ 'dear friend', introducing the next exhortation, and it is also marked by asyndeton. There is a clear change from a hortatory paragraph (John committing himself to act against Diotrephes's evil deeds) to the following hortatory paragraph (urging Gaius not to follow the evil example).

PROMINENCE AND THEME

The topic of the 9-10 unit is Diotrephes's rejection of the Elder's ecclesiastical authority. The deictic phrase in v. 10, διὰ τοῦτο 'because of this', refers to this rejection; the words τὰ ἔργα ἃ ποιεῖ 'what he does' also point to it. The action of the Elder in exercising his authority is the COMMISSIVE in 10a: ὑπομνήσω αὐτοῦ 'I will expose what he does'. Thus 10a is the naturally prominent central proposition of the paragraph. Verse 9 serves to set the stage for 10a by indicating the *basis* that demands the COMMISSIVE. The remaining propositions (10b, c, d) give the specific charges against Diotrephes—the actions that demonstrate his rejection of the Elder.

In addition to its natural prominence, the central proposition also has marked prominence, marked by the deictic 'because of this' and heightened even more by its being in contrast to the Elder's exercise of authority in 6b where he presents his request of Gaius.

The theme is drawn from the nuclear propositions of the *basis* and the COMMISSIVE.

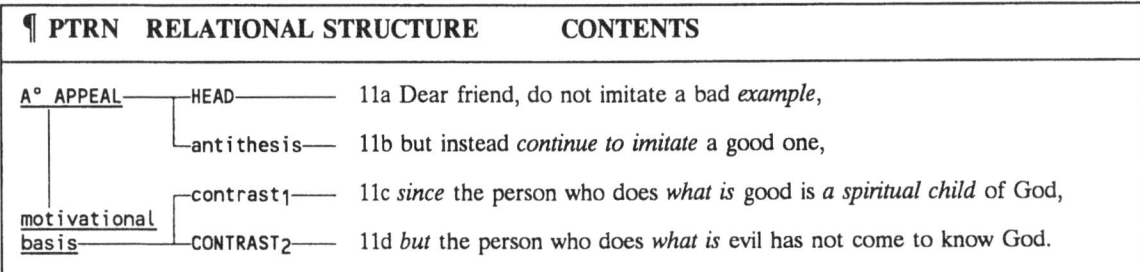

SECTION CONSTITUENT 11 (Hortatory Paragraph: Appeal₃ of 5-12)
Theme: Do not imitate a bad example, but continue to imitate a good one.

INTENT AND PARAGRAPH PATTERN

In v. 11 John comes to the climax of the letter's main message. His intent is to affect the actions of the reader by two direct commands, 11a and 11b. He wants to make certain that Gaius will not follow Diotrephes's bad example.

The paragraph has two constituents, 11a-b and 11c-d. Their communication relation is an exhortation and its grounds. Because of this structure and because the primary intent is to affect behavior, we consider this a causal hortatory paragraph, the principal constituents being + *basis* + APPEAL.

NOTES

11a do not imitate The force of the present tense prohibition μὴ μιμοῦ is that the prohibited action has still not taken place and must not be begun and that the positive action is to be continued. This would indicate that the Elder was aware of the domineering attitude of Diotrephes and intended this letter to prevent the influence that he might exert over Gaius.

11c since No lexical or grammatical particle joins 11a-b to 11c-d, but it is assumed that the 11c-d statement is a *motivational basis* for the exhortation since 11c-d expresses a positive desired value (essentially, the communication relation is exhortation + grounds). The chiastic form of v. 11 (see "Prominence and Theme" below) demonstrates the close relationship of 11a-b and 11c-d, bolstering the validity of what we propose as their relationship.

11d come to know The verb ὁράω 'to see' is rendered as 'come to know' since this is seeing with the mind rather than with the eyes.

BOUNDARIES AND COHERENCE

The v. 11 paragraph begins with the vocative ἀγαπητέ 'dear friend', which as we have seen is a boundary marker in this Epistle. It also returns to personally addressing Gaius. The closing boundary lacks any conjoining particle, but the next paragraph takes up a different topic: recommending Demetrius.

The imperative verb form in 11a is naturally prominent. In addition there is marked prominence in v. 11 in that there are references pointing back to the evil practices of Diotrephes (vv. 9-10) and the good deeds of Gaius (vv. 5-6). The chiastic structure of v. 11 (see "Prominence and Theme" below) gives it even more marked prominence.

At the higher level, the 9-10 paragraph functions not only as the *difficulty* addressed by the various APPEALS of 5-12, but also as the *basis* for the v. 11 APPEAL. However, the relationship between v. 11 and v. 12 has been assessed by commentators in different ways. Some indicate no connection of thought between them, leaving the relationship ambiguous as it is in the Greek text. Some of the modern versions even make a paragraph division after v. 11. On the other hand, some commentators see 11-12 as connected, taking Demetrius to be the good example of 11b. He is certainly to be classified as doing good, but there are *two* examples here, one good and one bad, and it may well be that this exhortation is not aimed at pointing out a specific good example (Brooke). If this is the case, the connection between 11 and 12 is not so apparent.

However, if the following is a correct reconstruction of it, the communication situation itself can be seen to give coherence to v. 11 and v. 12 as the final two paragraphs of the

BODY and also to the BODY itself: As commentators agree, Demetrius was one of the visiting teachers, probably a leader. Many suggest that he was the bearer of this letter. (Such a letter was the usual credential of an itinerant missionary.) If this was indeed his role, and if one of the purposes of the letter was to recommend him for hospitality, the exhortation of v. 11 finds its application in his being received hospitably. Thus it is probable that the exhortation was not intended to point out to Gaius a specific good example (Gaius has already been presented as exemplary in his activities and loyalty). More likely, it was a caution against Gaius's coming under the influence of Diotrephes to the neglect of his ministry. This would make it all the more important to encourage Gaius to accept Demetrius. The polite request of 6b, which is an encouragement to Gaius to continue his hospitality, is in v. 12 applied to a specific instance.

PROMINENCE AND THEME

The vocative ἀγαπητέ 'dear friend' gives additional marked prominence to the exhortation. Contrast and repetition (τὸ κακόν 'evil' and τὸ ἀγαθόν 'good' in v. 11) also give it prominence. The exhortation is presented as a chiasm, adding to the prominence of the exhortation as a whole:

A κακός 'evil' (11a)
  B ἀγαθός 'good' (11b)
  B' ἀγαθοποιέω 'one who does good' (11c)
A' κακοποιέω 'one who does evil' (11c)

Since the "A" of a chiasm is prominent, it is the evil that the Elder wishes Gaius to avoid that is given emphasis. This reinforces his concern lest the evil influence of Diotrephes draw Gaius away from his present commendable practice. The theme statement includes only the APPEAL (11a-b).

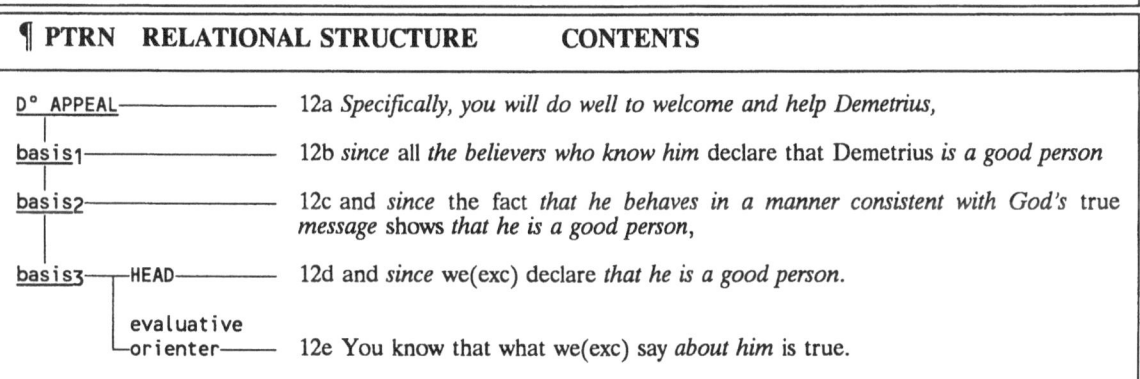

INTENT AND PARAGRAPH PATTERN

In v. 12 John comes to the resolution of the letter's main message. His intent is to affect the actions of the reader using a low-key admonition. He wants to make certain that Gaius will help the visiting evangelist, Demetrius.

The v. 12 paragraph has four semantic constituents: 12a, b, c, and d-e. A difficult analytical and interpretive problem exists in that the surface structure seems to present no more than a simple declaration: "Incidentally, Demetrius is a good person." But since this statement immediately follows the 11b command to continue doing good, which would include providing for visiting evangelists, the function of v. 12 must be seen as a specific of the command. John, in his typical way, makes his point with an exhortation so mitigated as to be totally covert (hence the supplied proposition 12a). This extreme mismatching between the lexicogrammatical form and the total meaning within the context is appropriate to the resolution and the relationship between John and Gaius.

The communication relation here is an exhortation followed by grounds. Because of this structure, and because the primary intent is to affect behavior, we take this to be a causal hortatory paragraph, the principal constituents being + *basis* + APPEAL.

NOTES

12a *Specifically, you will do well to welcome and help Demetrius* An ellipsis of the phrase used in 6a (καλῶς ποιήσεις 'you will do well') is assumed here because of the chiastic structure of the BODY of the letter (see the discussion under the 5-12 display). Thus, this is a request that Demetrius be received and given hospitality.

12b all *the believers who know him* The word πᾶς 'all' may include more than the Christian community, but for both the Elder and Gaius the commendation of that group would be significant.

declare that Demetrius *is a good person* Three witnesses to the character of Demetrius are cited. This is in harmony with both Old and New Testament custom. Note that the same three witnesses aver the good character of Gaius: the Elder's witness to Gaius's spiritual well-being is in v. 1 and to his faithfulness in v. 5; the brethren's witness is in v. 3 and v. 6; the witness of Gaius's own conduct is in v. 4.

12c the fact *that he behaves in a manner consistent with God's* **true message** Commentators discuss at length 'the witness of the truth itself' here. It is generally agreed that the phrase αὐτῆς τῆς ἀληθείας 'the truth itself' does not refer to the Holy Spirit, though one writer suggests the internal witness mentioned in 1 John 5:10. To take the phrase as a personification referring to Christ does not supply an available witness in this instance. Therefore, in the display ἀλήθεια is rendered 'the fact that' and Demetrius's behavior is considered to be what is implicit. Hardly any English version expands upon 'the truth itself', even though the literal translation has little meaning.

12d-e we(exc) Several commentators consider the plural pronoun here to be an editorial 'we' meaning 'I'. Others say it refers to the Elder and his close associates.

12d and since Here δέ 'and' can be interpreted either as introducing the weightiest evidence or, assuming that Gaius already knows Demetrius, as adding to Gaius's confidence in him.

BOUNDARIES AND COHERENCE

The v. 12 paragraph begins with asyndeton and a marked shift from a direct command to recommending Demetrius. The closing boundary coincides with that of the Epistle's BODY.

The coherence of the paragraph is evident. The role of Demetrius as one who is to be warmly received and given hospitality is an application of the v. 11 exhortation and is in keeping with John's endorsement in v. 12.

The relationship between v. 11 and v. 12 has been discussed under the v. 11 paragraph. Verse 12 is the final paragraph of the BODY.

PROMINENCE AND THEME

The v. 12 paragraph is prominent due to its being a specific application of the 6b request. The threefold witness to the good character of Demetrius harks back to 5-6 where John commends Gaius for his hospitality. The previous reference to Diotrephes's bad example helps set up the implied request to provide hospitality to Demetrius.

The theme statement for v. 12 includes the implicit APPEAL to Gaius to give hospitality to Demetrius and a summary of the explicit endorsements of Demetrius.

EPISTLE CONSTITUENT 13-15 (Descriptive Paragraph and Farewell: Closing of the Epistle)
Theme: Instead of writing more, I expect to visit you soon, and we will speak directly with one another. Our mutual friends here send their greetings to all of you.

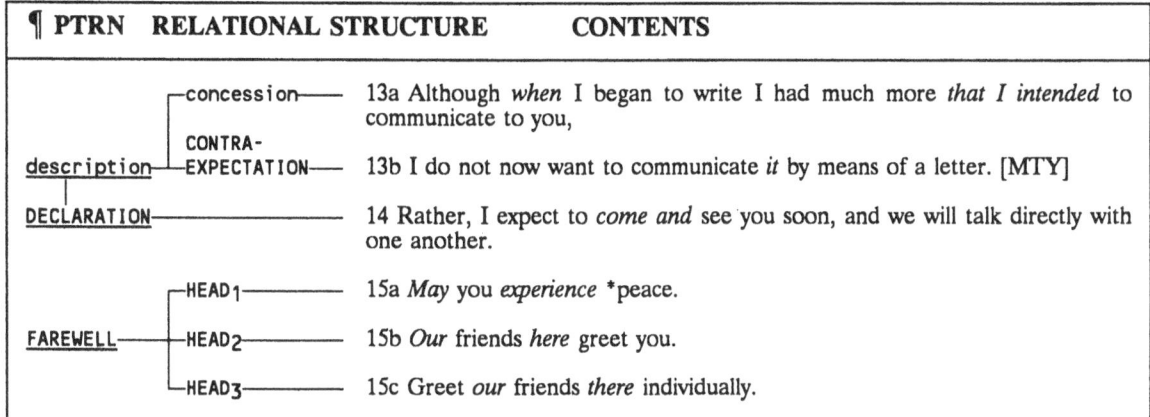

INTENT AND PARAGRAPH PATTERN

John's intent in the 13-15 paragraph is primarily to maintain rapport with Gaius while he closes the letter in an appropriate manner. This is in keeping with how letters are usually ended, affecting the audience's emotions in such a way as to produce a good feeling about what was said.

The unit is composed of two constituents: a paragraph (v. 13-14) and a farewell greeting (v. 15).

The paragraph, in turn, has two main constituents: v. 13 and v. 14, whose communication relation is a contrasting negative statement followed by a positive statement. Since the primary intent in this paragraph is to affect the emotions, it is taken as a volitional descriptive paragraph, the principal constituents being + *description* + DECLARATION.

The FAREWELL, though it is not a semantic paragraph, is a statement appropriate for the pragmatic situation of closing a letter in that day.

NOTES

13a when I began to write I had much more *that I intended* to communicate The infinitive γράψαι 'to write' is classified by Robertson (1933) as an ingressive aorist infinitive. The main verb, εἶχον 'I had', which is in the imperfect tense, is interpreted by many as referring to the moment of the Elder's beginning to write.

13b by means of a letter The Greek is διὰ μέλανος καὶ καλάμου 'by means of ink and pen' in which the instrument for writing a letter stands for the whole of the letter. This is a metonymy signifying 'by means of a letter' or 'in a letter'.

14 to *come and* see you The reference in 2 John 12 to the Elder's proposed visit makes γίνομαι 'to be present' explicit. In 3 John it is explicitly mentioned in 10a, and for that reason it is only implicit here. Since languages vary greatly as to the reference point of verbs of action, some languages might require 'go and see you' here.

talk directly To talk 'mouth to mouth' (στόμα πρὸς στόμα) is based on a Hebrew idiom and is equivalent to the English expression *face to face*. Several English versions express this in more contemporary speech as "personally."

15b *Our* friends The Greek is οἱ φίλοι 'the friends' (also in 15c), a word that indicates a social relationship to someone. Hence 'our' is supplied. These are mutual friends of both the writer and the addressee. People would not send a greeting to people with whom they were unacquainted.

15c individually The greeting was to be given distributively by name, to every one of them, not in a general way as a letter does perforce.

BOUNDARIES AND COHERENCE

The 13-15 paragraph begins with a change of subject. John turns from the problem discussed in the BODY of the letter to the act of communication. The paragraph ends coterminously with the Epistle in the expected style for letters of the period following the pattern of the close of 2 John.

Coherence is seen in the Elder's concern for the individuals involved: Gaius and their mutual friends. He refers to the abundance of what he has to tell Gaius and expresses his desire to communicate it personally, mentioning his intention of visiting him. In v. 14 he uses the first person plural, λαλήσομεν 'we will talk'. We take it as inclusive, indicating John's intention of conversing rather than giving a one-sided discourse. In v. 15 he prays for Gaius's welfare, sends him greetings from his own like-minded associates, and greets those involved with Gaius. The use of φίλοι 'friends' in both greetings marks the letter as an affectionate personal letter.

PROMINENCE AND THEME

In the Greek what is central in the first sentence (vv. 13-14) is the final clause, στόμα πρὸς στόμα λαλήσομεν 'we will talk together'. It is introduced by the declaration ἐλπίζω ... σε ἰδεῖν 'I hope to see you'. The concession (13a) and contraexpectation (13b) provide orientation for this communication. The desire for the communication is emphasized by εὐθέως 'soon', which indicates the urgency of the desire and gives marked prominence to the DECLARATION.

The FAREWELL consists of the usual benediction (15a) and greetings (15b and 15c). To emphasize his farewell greeting to the church where Gaius is, John requests that the members be greeted individually.

The theme statement is drawn from the central proposition concerning the subject of communication (v. 14), with its contrasting element (v. 13b) included for perspective. Also included is a summary of the benediction and greetings.

GLOSSARY

anyone Reflects the definite article plus the present participle. (Admittedly, such a gloss favors the grammatical structure rather than the semantic relation underlying the construction.) When the participial phrase is followed by a main clause, it is in a condition-CONSEQUENCE relationship. It should be noted that this construction is not always rendered with an explicit 'anyone'.

Some languages (e.g., many Indo-European languages) can use this same construction to show a conditional relationship. In many other languages, however, an entirely different sort of construction must be used.

There are some occurrences of two coordinate present participles in a conditional relationship with the main clause. The relationship between the two participles in such a construction is that of coordinate simultaneous actions (as in 1 John 2:4, 9).

Aorist or perfect participles may likewise signify a condition (as in 3:9 and 5:4, 18); but they also often signify identity, comparison, content of some events, or modification.

belong Renders the expression εἶναι ἐκ 'to be of', which carries the idea of source, origin, nature, or belonging. Brooke (1957:115) indicates that the meaning may go beyond belonging to include dependence upon. Brown (1982:313) says, "The phrase covers both origin and appurtenance, i.e., not only coming from but also belonging to. In the second aspect of its meaning it describes the very being of that to which it is applied ... We catch the double meaning of einai ek in John 3:31 where the phrase is repeated: The one who is from the earth [origin] is from the earth [appurtenance]." Bultmann (pp. 36, 64, 103) also comments on this range of meaning: "It is characteristically Johannine to designate the nature of something by reference to its origin." BAGD (p. 225a:III.3) gives a good treatment of 'belong', especially regarding origin.

brother A figure of speech meaning a mutual member of a social group. The term is used in 1 John 3:12 to express blood relationship, but usually in the Johannine Epistles it is used as a figure to express the spiritual relationship of members of the family of God. This extended usage is common not only in the New Testament, but also in Hebrew culture. It is also, of course, found outside the Jewish and Christian cultures of antiquity and in many present-day cultures. In the displays 'Christian brother' is used when the term refers to this spiritual relationship.

Father The word πατήρ 'father' is used frequently in the NT to describe the relationship between God and Jesus, and between God and his people. When the relationship is specifically between God and Jesus, it signifies that they are equal and of the same character (see 1 John 2:22–24 and 4:14). When the relationship is between God and human beings, it signifies that God is our source, creator, behavioral model, and authority (see 1 John 1:2, 3; 2:1, 14–16; and 3:1).

In many languages 'father' is never used with an extended or figurative meaning, the meaning being limited to male biological progenitor, connoting family tie, high status, and all social privileges and responsibilities of the family head. A word-for-word translation would not be meaningful in such languages. See *Son of God*.

joined together Renders the word κοινωνία, used by John to mean being joined together by a common ground. It is variously translated ('share', 'participate', 'fellowship', etc.), but is recognized by commentators as having a special usage in 1 John, where it occurs in the first chapter with the basic idea of 'have something in common with'.

Since the purpose of 1 John is to promote commonality with God and other believers, it is important to have a clear understanding of the term's significance. Lexicons and commentators interpret this word as (1) 'to share, partake, participate' or (2) as a social interaction. The latter is rendered in different ways: social interaction, association, communion, fellowship, close relationship, bond of Christian communion, mutual relationship, reckoning ourselves among Christ's friends, communion with God, etc. Barnes (p. 281, in his note on 1 John 1:3) takes the first of the two views: John "partook, in some respects, of the feelings, the views, the aims, the joy which God has." Vine (1966:430) renders it similarly (in connection with 1 John 1:3): "having in common . . . a) the share which one has in anything, a . . . fellowship recognized and enjoyed."

According to Louw and Nida, κοινωνία and κοινωνέω (from which κοινωνία is derived) have four main areas of meaning:

1. 'associate': "an association involving close mutual relations and involvement" (sec. 34.5)—1 John 1:3 is used as an illustration.
2. 'give': "to share one's possessions, with the implication of some kind of joint participation and mutual interest—'to share' " (sec. 57.98).
3. 'do, perform': "to join with others in some activity" (sec. 42.16).
4. 'human beings': "κοινωνέω αἵματος καὶ σαρκός: (an idiom . . .) to have the characteristics and nature of a human being" (sec. 9.15).

Although the fourth meaning is an extended or special use of κοινωνέω, it does give insight into John's usage. This is very much in line with other NT usages (2 Pet. 1:4 says that believers are θείας κοινωνοὶ φύσεως 'partakers of the divine nature').

In 2 John 11 κοινωνέω is used in a negative sense to refer to participation in evil activity. (It is used similarly in 1 Tim. 5:22.)

The uses of κοινωνέω mentioned by Louw and Nida have the common element of joining together. Thus the word could be defined as 'people joined together in a close association, in an activity, in sharing possessions, or partaking in characteristics'.

Being joined together by a common ground is a central concept for 1 John even though the word κοινωνία is used only in 1:3, 6, and 7. The same idea continues on in 1 John but in different words. In 1:5–7 a new expression is introduced by John's special use of ἐν 'in'. Verse 7 is notable: 'if we conduct ourselves *in the light*, just as God is *in the light*, we *are joined together among ourselves (by a common ground)*, and the blood of Jesus, his Son, purifies us from all sin'.

In 1 John ἐν 'in' has four main meanings:

1. 'to possess a characteristic or act according to a characteristic', as in 1:5, 6, 7 (twice), 8, 10; 2:6, 8 (twice), 9 (twice), 10 (twice), 11 (twice), 15, 16, 24 (twice), 27; 3:5, 6, 9, 14, 15, 17, 18; 4:2, 12, 16, 18 (twice); 5:6 (three times), 11, 19, 20.
2. 'to be in union with God or a person', with the focus on possessing mutual characteristics, as in 2:5, 14, 24, 27, 28; 3:6, 24 (three times); 4:4 (twice), 9, 12, 13 (twice), 15 (twice), 16 (twice); 5:20.
3. deictic, pointing toward the following linguistic context (the specific form ἐν τούτῳ 'by this' is used), as in 2:3, 5 (twice); 3:10, 16, 19, 24; 4:2, 9, 10, 13, 17; 5:2.
4. an adverbial phrase of time or location as in 2:28; 4:3, 17.

peace The primary meaning of εἰρήνη 'peace' is the absence of war; but in the NT it also expresses the Hebrew *shalom*, which in the OT carries the idea of wholeness and material well-being, a gift of God. In the Prophets, *shalom* is associated with righteousness and salvation. The word εἰρήνη is often used by the NT writers to signify the new relationship with God which has been secured for those who believe through the atoning work of Jesus Christ. In 2 John 3 'peace', coming from the Father and his Son, is linked with 'grace' and 'mercy' to signify reconciliation and the wholeness of life in union with God. Both εἰρήνη and *shalom* were also used as greetings.

Son of God Used frequently in the NT to describe the relationship between Jesus and God, signifying that they are equal and of the same character. The meaning of υἱός 'son' in the phrase 'Son of God' is the same as 'son' linked with other genitive nouns, its main components being close relationship, equal authority, same character, unity of purpose, and same nature.

In many languages 'son' is never used with an extended or figurative meaning. Rather, the meaning is limited to male biological progeny, connoting family tie, lower status, and some social privileges and responsibilities. A word-for-word translation of this phrase would not be meaningful in such languages.

Since John's letter was speaking out against false teaching concerning the Person of Christ (see p. 6, "occasion for writing"), his use of the term 'Son of God' is an important term in the Epistle, addressing as it does the central problem.

spiritual The words *spiritual* and *spiritually* qualify certain terms in the displays, showing that they are being used figuratively. In the New Testament, that which is spiritual is transcendent and divine in origin. When John addresses his 'children' (1 John 2:1), clearly they are not his natural offspring; but he considers their progress in their new life from God as his responsibility, as a father is concerned for his biological children's well-being. He has nurtured them from the start; they are his "spiritual" children. To "live spiritually" (1 John 2:29) is to associate properly with God and others of God's family. One who is born into the family of God is God's "spiritual child" (1 John 3:1). A person who has not been born into God's family and is not living united to God is "spiritually dead" (3:14-15).

united Signifies a close social relationship based on sharing the same characteristics. In the Johannine Epistles this relationship of the believer to God is expressed by the following phrases: κοινωνία 'partake in characteristics (with the Father and the Son)' (1 John 1:3); εἶναι ἐν 'to be in (God)' (1 John 2:5); ἐν αὐτῷ μένειν 'to remain in (God)' (1 John 2:6); ἐν αὐτῷ μένει καὶ αὐτὸς ἐν αὐτῷ 'to remain in (God) and (God) in (the believer)' (1 John 3:24); τὸν πατέρα καὶ τὸν υἱὸν ἔχει 'to have the Father and the Son' (2 John 9 [cf. 1 John 5:12]); ζωὴ αἰώνιος 'eternal life' (1 John 5:11, 20). All of these terms have reference to a spiritual relationship with God. Basic to this union is the believer's partaking of divine moral characteristics. Just as birth involves a new permanent relationship, so, even more profoundly, entrance into the family of God involves a new permanent relationship and way of life. And just as life in the physical realm progresses towards maturity, so the divine life involves growth. (Hence μένω 'remain' must not be interpreted as simply a state of being. The emphasis must be more on living than on any static factor.)

The proposed theme of the first section of 1 John (1:5-2:27) is "Continue to live united to Christ." Near the close of the second section (1 John 2:28-4:6) the double relationship in which God and believers are united to each other is specified, to be verified by the presence of the Holy Spirit (3:24). In this double relationship there is a semantic complement rather than a parallel between the divine and the human natures, for the double relationship (the believer in God and God in the believer) is different from anything in purely human experience. The human relationship to God involves dependence on God since human nature is limited and subject to him. God, on the other hand, who is unlimited, independent, and sovereign, relates to the believer by giving spiritual life through the Holy Spirit. He sustains the life he has given, guiding and controlling it. At the end of the third section (1 John 4:7-5:12) are the words "the one who has the Son has life." Finally, at the close, John expresses his purpose, that the readers may be assured of the possession of eternal life (5:13). In 5:20 he reiterates "we are in him who is true—even in his Son Jesus Christ. He is the true God and eternal life." It is against this background that the union between God and regenerated man is frequently referred to in the displays.

world spirit One of the meanings of κόσμος 'world' is a spiritual power in opposition to God. In 1 John 2:15-17 this word refers to the way godless people live in the world. In 4:1-6 where the opposing force is identified as the source of error, John is warning against the danger of being deceived by teachers speaking for false spirits, and he draws a picture of an organized system antagonistic to God with Satan at its head. An antichrist who refuses to recognize Jesus as the Christ is also identified (4:3). Just as in 2:14 the believer has overcome the 'evil one', so in 5:4-5 the one who is born of God and acknowledges Jesus as the Son of God is enabled to overcome the "world spirit." In 5:19 the people of the world spirit are said to be dominated by the evil one.

From these passages the concept of κόσμος 'world' emerges as something distinct from the created material world but not identified with the world's inhabitants either. It is an organized system in rebellion against God, its focus being on self-gratification and self-sufficiency (2:16). Human self-sufficiency perversely refuses to do the will of God (2:17). It is this system in rebellion against God that is called the 'world spirit', a dominating force which influences those who refuse to believe the true message of the revelation of Jesus Christ (4:5-6). As an ordered segment of human society it can be called an entity. The evil one, Satan, is the recognized source (3:12), and the antichrist is its personification (4:3).

The area of meaning of πνεῦμα 'spirit' is different from that of κόσμος 'world spirit'. For example, in 4:1–3 'the spirit' is portrayed as an active power that controls the false prophets as they speak. In this passage it is generally taken to be the human spirit which can be activated by a supernatural power distinct from the individual. Hoon (p. 272) calls it "a supernatural, diabolic power that attacks man on the deeper, non-rational levels of his being, and that can control his existence and determine his fate unless broken by an equally superhuman agency of good."

BIBLIOGRAPHY

Reference Works, Commentaries, and Articles

Abbott-Smith, G. [1937] 1954. *A manual Greek lexicon of the New Testament.* Reprint. Edinburgh: T. & T. Clark.

Alexander, Neil. 1962. *The Epistles of John.* Torch Bible Commentaries. New York: Macmillan.

Alford, Henry. [1861] 1958. *The Greek Testament,* vol. 4. Reprint. Chicago: Moody.

Alsop, John, ed. 1966. *An index to the Arndt and Gingrich Greek lexicon.* Santa Ana, Calif.: Wycliffe Bible Translators.

Arndt, William F., and F. W. Gingrich. 1979. *A Greek-English lexicon of the New Testament and other early Christian literature.* A translation and adaptation of Walter Bauer's *Griechisch-Deutsches Wörterbuch zu den Schriften des Neuen Testaments und der übrigen urchristlichen Literatur.* 2d ed., augmented from Bauer's 5th ed. Chicago: Univ. of Chicago Press.

Barclay, William. 1976. *The letters of John and Jude.* Philadelphia: Westminster.

Barnes, Albert. [1861] 1962. *Notes on the New Testament.* Reprint. Grand Rapids: Kregel.

Beekman, John, and John Callow. 1974. *Translating the Word of God.* Grand Rapids: Zondervan.

Beekman, John, John Callow, and Michael F. Kopesec. 1981. *The semantic structure of written communication.* Prepublication draft, 5th revision. Dallas: SIL.

Blass, F., and A. Debrunner. 1961. *A Greek grammar of the New Testament and other early Christian literature.* Tr. and rev. Robert W. Funk. Chicago: Univ. of Chicago.

Blight, Richard. 1977. *A literary-semantic analysis of Paul's first discourse to Timothy.* Prepublication draft. Dallas: SIL.

Bloomfield, S. T. 1844. *The Greek New Testament,* vol. 2. 5th American from the 2d London edition. Philadelphia: Perkins & Purves.

Brooke, Alan E. [1912] 1957. *A critical and exegetical commentary on the Johannine Epistles.* International Critical Commentary. Reprint. Edinburgh: T. & T. Clark.

Brown, C., ed. 1975–1986. *The new international dictionary of New Testament theology.* 4 vols. Exeter, England: Paternoster; Grand Rapids: Zondervan.

Brown, Raymond E. 1966. *The Gospel according to John.* The Anchor Bible. Garden City, N.Y.: Doubleday.

———. 1982. *The Epistles of John.* The Anchor Bible. New York: Doubleday.

Brown, Raymond E., Joseph A. Fitzmyer, and Roland E. Murphy. 1969. *The Jerome biblical commentary.* Englewood Cliffs, N.J.: Prentice-Hall.

Bruce, F. F. 1979. *The Epistles of John.* Grand Rapids: Wm. B. Eerdmans.

Bullinger, E. W. [1898] 1968. *Figures of speech used in the Bible.* Grand Rapids: Baker Book House.

Bultmann, Rudolf Karl. 1978. *The Johannine Epistles.* Tr. R. Philip O'Hara, Lane C. McGaughy, and Robert Funk. Philadelphia: Fortress.

Burton, Ernest De Witt. 1896. *Syntax of the moods and tenses in New Testament Greek.* 2d ed. Chicago: Univ. of Chicago.

Callow, John. 1982. *A semantic-structure analysis of Second Thessalonians.* Dallas: SIL.

———. 1983a. Does the (English) Bible have a future. *Notes on Translation* 96:36–48.

———. 1983b. Word order in New Testament Greek, part 1. *Selected Technical Articles Related to Translation* 7:3–50. (Dallas: SIL.)

———. 1983c. Word order in New Testament Greek, part 2 and 3. *Selected Technical Articles Related to Translation* 8:3–32. (Dallas: SIL.)

Callow, Kathleen. 1974. *Discourse considerations in translating the Word of God.* Grand Rapids: Zondervan.

———. 1989. *Meaning and the Analysis of Texts.* Prepublication draft. Dallas: SIL.

Dana, H. E., and Julius R. Mantey. 1927. *A manual grammar of the Greek New Testament.* New York: Macmillan.

Dodd, Charles H. 1946. *The Johannine Epistles.* Moffatt New Testament Commentary. London: Hodder and Stoughton; New York: Harper and Row.

du Rand, J. A. 1979. A discourse analysis of 1 John. *Neotestamentica* 13:1–42.

Duthrie, Alan. 1983. Semantic structure and translation. *Notes on Translation* 96:25–36.

Friberg, Barbara, and Timothy Friberg. 1981. *Analytical Greek New Testament.* Grand Rapids: Baker.

Haas, C., M. De Jonge, and J. L. Swellengrebel. 1972. *A translator's handbook on the letters of John.* New York: UBS.

Harm, Harry. 1983. Word order in Jude. *Selected Technical Articles Related to Translation* 8:32–39. (Dallas: SIL.)

Hoon. See Wilder and Hoon.

Houlden, James Leslie. 1973. *The Johannine Epistles.* New York: Harper & Row.

Kistemaker, Simon J. 1986. *Exposition of the Epistle of James and the Epistles of John.* New Testament Commentary. Grand Rapids: Baker.

Kittel, G., and G. Friedrich, eds.. 1964–76. *Theological dictionary of the New Testament.* Tr. Geoffrey W. Bromiley. 10 vols. Grand Rapids: Wm. B. Eerdmans.

Kopesec, Michael F. 1980. *A literary-semantic analysis of Titus.* Preliminary edition. Dallas: SIL.

Lenski, R. C. H. 1945. *The interpretation of the Epistles of St. Peter, St. John, and St. Jude.* Columbus, Ohio: Wartburg.

Longacre, Robert E. 1983. Exhortation and mitigation in First John. *Selected Technical Articles Related To Translation* 9:3–44. (Dallas: SIL.)

Louw, Johannes P., and Eugene A. Nida, eds. 1988. *Greek-English lexicon of the New Testament based on semantic domains*, vol. 1. New York: UBS.

Marshall, I. H. 1978. *The Epistles of John.* New International Commentary on the New Testament. Grand Rapids: Wm. B. Eerdmans.

Marshall, I. H., and W. W. Gasque, eds. 1979. *New international Greek Testament commentary.* Exeter, England: Paternoster; Grand Rapids: Eerdmans.

Metzger, Bruce M. 1975. *A textual commentary on the Greek New Testament.* Stuttgart: UBS.

Miehle, Helen. 1980. *The semantic structure analysis of First John.* Prepublication draft. Dallas: SIL.

Plummer, A. 1906. *The Epistles of St. John.* Cambridge Bible for Schools and Colleges. Cambridge: Cambridge Univ.

Richardson, Alan, ed. 1950. *A theological word book of the Bible.* New York: Macmillan.

Robertson, A. T. 1931. *A short grammar of the Greek Testament*. New York: Harper.

———. 1933. The General Epistles and the Apocalypse. In *Word pictures in the New Testament*, vol. 4. New York: Harper.

Schnackenburg, Rudolf. 1975 [1992]. *The Johannnine Epistles*. New York: Crossroad.

Smith, David. [1910] 1951. *The Epistles of John*. Vol. 5 of *The expositor's Greek Testament*. Reprint. Grand Rapids: Wm. B. Eerdmans.

Smith, Robert E., and John Beekman. 1981. *A literary-semantic analysis of Second Timothy*. Dallas: SIL.

Stedman, Ray C. 1980. *Expository studies in 1 John*. Waco, Texas: Word Books.

Stott, John R. W. 1969. *The Epistles of John*. Tyndale New Testament Commentaries. Grand Rapids: Wm. B. Eerdmans.

Thayer, Joseph Henry. [1901] 1953. *A Greek-English lexicon of the New Testament*. Corrected edition. 4th ed. Reprint. Edinburgh: T. & T. Clark.

Tuggy, John C. 1992. Semantic paragraph patterns: A foundational communication concept and Interpretative tool. In *Linguistics and New Testament interpretation*, ed. D. A Black, 45–67. Nashville: Broadman.

Turner, Nigel. 1963. *Syntax*. Vol. 3, *A grammar of New Testament Greek*. Edinburgh: T. & T. Clark.

———. 1965. *Grammatical insights into the New Testament*. Edinburgh: T. & T. Clark.

Vincent, Marvin R. 1946. *Word studies in the New Testament*, vol. 2. Chicago: Moody.

Vine, William E. 1965. *John: His record of Christ*. Grand Rapids: Zondervan.

———. 1966. *An expository dictionary of New Testament words with their precise meanings for English readers*. Old Tappan, N.J.: Revell.

Webster's eighth new collegiate dictionary. 1980. Springfield, Mass.: G. & C. Merriam.

Westcott, Brooke Foss. [1883] 1966. *The Epistles of St. John*. Reprint. Grand Rapids: Wm. B. Eerdmans.

Wilder, Amos N., and Paul W. Hoon. 1957. The First, Second, and Third Epistles of John. In *The interpreter's Bible*, vol. 12, 209–313. Nashville: Abingdon.

Texts and Versions

Aland, K., et al. *The Greek New Testament*. 1975. 3d ed. New York: American Bible Society.

Amplified New Testament. 1958. La Habra, Calif.: Lockman Foundation.

Barclay, William. 1969. *The New Testament, a new translation*, vol. 2. London: Collins.

Good News Bible: The Bible in today's English version. 1976. New York: American Bible Society.

Goodspeed, Edgar J. [1923] 1965. *The New Testament: An American translation*. Chicago: Univ. of Chicago.

The Holy Bible, authorized (or King James) version. 1611.

The Holy Bible: New international version. 1984. Grand Rapids: Zondervan.

The Jerusalem Bible. 1966. Garden City, N.Y.: Doubleday.

Knox, Ronald A. 1945. *The New Testament*. New York: Sheed and Ward.

Marshall, A., ed. 1980. *The NIV interlinear Greek-English New Testament*. Grand Rapids: Zondervan.

The modern language Bible: The new Berkeley version. 1971. Grand Rapids: Zondervan.

Nestle, Eberhard, and Erwin Nestle. 1953. *Novum Testamentum Graece.* Stuttgart: Wurttemberg Bibelanstalt.

New American standard Bible. 1975. Philadelphia: A. J. Holman.

The New Testament: Revised standard version. 1971. New York: Amercan Bible Society.

Phillips, J. B. 1962. *The New Testament in modern English.* New York: Macmillan.

Rotherham, Joseph Bryant. 1923. *The emphasised New Testament.* London: Sampson Low, Marston.

The twentieth century New Testament. 1904. Chatham: W. & J. MacKay.

Wescott, Brooke Foss, and Fenton J. A. Hort. 1928. *The New Testament in the original Greek.* New York: Macmillan.

Weymouth, Richard Francis. 1930. *The New Testament in modern speech.* 5th ed., revised by J. A. Robertson. London: James Clark.

Williams, Charles Kingsley. 1963. *A new translation in plain English.* Grand Rapids: Wm. B. Eerdmans.

www.ingramcontent.com/pod-product-compliance
Lightning Source LLC
Chambersburg PA
CBHW081421230426
43668CB00016B/2313